UNDERWORL

GW00671539

With the first book of its kind to provide a detailed analysis of the history of the unconscious from the underworlds of Greek and Egyptian mythology to psychoanalysis and metaphysics, Jon Mills presents here a unique study of differing philosophies of the unconscious.

Mills examines how three major philosophical systems on the nature of the unconscious emerge after modern philosophy, finding their most celebrated elaborations in Freud, Lacan and Jung. These three psychoanalytic traditions, quite separate from one another in terms of their emphasis and philosophical presuppositions, are scrutinized alongside contemporaneous movements in existential phenomenology, semiotics, epistemology, transcendental psychology and Western metaphysics in the texts of Hegel, Heidegger, Sartre and Whitehead. *Underworlds* provides a scholarly exegesis and critique of the main philosophies of the unconscious to have transpired in the history of ideas.

Exploring the unconscious from its philosophical beginnings in antiquity to its systematic articulation brought about by the rise of psychoanalysis, *Underworlds* is ideal for practising psychoanalysts, academics of Freud, Jung and Lacan, and scholars of psychology, philosophy and the humanities.

Jon Mills, Psy.D., Ph.D., ABPP, is a philosopher, psychoanalyst and psychologist in private practice and Professor of Psychology and Psychoanalysis at the Adler Graduate Professional School, Toronto. He is the author of many works in psychoanalysis, philosophy and psychology, including *Conundrums: A Critique of Contemporary Psychoanalysis* (Routledge, 2012), for which he won the Goethe Award for best book in 2013. Mills was also the recipient of a 2013 Gradiva Award from the National Association for the Advancement of Psychoanalysis in New York City for his television series *The Talking Cure*.

UNDERWORLDS

Philosophies of the unconscious from psychoanalysis to metaphysics

Jon Mills

Routledge
Taylor & Francis Group

LONDON AND NEW YORK

First published 2014
by Routledge

27 Church Road, Hove, East Sussex, BN3 2FA
and by Routledge
711 Third Avenue, New York, NY 10017

*Routledge is an imprint of the Taylor & Francis Group,
an informa business*

British Library Cataloguing-in-Publication Data
A catalogue record for this book is available from the British Library

Library of Congress Cataloging-in-Publication Data

Mills, Jon, 1964–
Underworlds : philosophies of the unconscious from psychoanalysis to metaphysics / Jon Mills.
    pages cm
    Includes index.
    1. Subconsciousness—History. I. Title.
    BF315.M553 2014
    154.2—dc23   2013038894

ISBN: 978-0-415-66052-5 (hbk)
ISBN: 978-0-415-74989-3 (pbk)
ISBN: 978-1-315-79594-2 (ebk)

Typeset in Times
by Apex CoVantage, LLC

CONTENTS

ABOUT THE AUTHOR

Jon Mills, Psy.D., Ph.D., ABPP, is a philosopher, psychoanalyst, and psychologist in private practice and runs a mental health corporation in Ontario, Canada. He is a Diplomate in Psychoanalysis and Clinical Psychology with the American Board of Professional Psychology, Fellow of the American Academy of Clinical Psychology, Fellow of the Academy of Psychoanalysis, and is Past-President and Fellow of the Section on Psychoanalytic and Psychodynamic Psychology of the Canadian Psychological Association. He received his Ph.D. in philosophy from Vanderbilt University, his Psy.D. in clinical psychology from the Illinois School of Professional Psychology, Chicago, and was a Fulbright scholar at the University of Toronto and York University. He is Professor of Psychology and Psychoanalysis at the Adler Graduate Professional School in Toronto, is editor of two book series, and is on the editorial board of *Psychoanalytic Psychology*. He is the author of many works in psychoanalysis, philosophy, and psychology including twelve books, among which are *Conundrums: A Critique of Contemporary Psychoanalysis*; *Origins: On the Genesis of Psychic Reality* (which was translated into French); *Treating Attachment Pathology*; *The Unconscious Abyss: Hegel's Anticipation of Psychoanalysis*; and an existential novel, *When God Wept*. He won the Goethe Award in 2013 for his book *Conundrums*, has won a Gradiva Award three times from the National Association for the Advancement of Psychoanalysis in New York City for his scholarship, and in 2008 was given a Significant Contribution to Canadian Psychology Award by the Section on Psychoanalytic and Psychodynamic Psychology of the Canadian Psychological Association.

ABOUT THE TEXTS

From the *Encyclopaedia of the Philosophical Sciences*, M.J. Petry, ed., outlines Hegel's *Philosophy of Spirit* in *Hegel's Philosophy of Subjective Spirit*, vol. 1: *Introductions*; vol. 2: *Anthropology*; and vol. 3: *Phenomenology and Psychology* (Dordrecht, The Netherlands: D. Reidel Publishing Company, 1978). Petry's edition provides a photographic reproduction of Hegel's original text published in the 1830 revision, along with the *Zusätze*, or *Additions*, supplied by Boumann when the material was republished in 1845. Petry's edition also indicates variations between the 1827 and 1830 editions of the *Encyclopaedia*. His edition has several decisive advantages over A.V. Miller's edition of the *Philosophie des Geistes*, which was translated as the *Philosophy of Mind*. In addition to having the original German text and his notations of the variations between the 1827 and 1830 editions, Petry also provides notes from the *Griesheim* and *Kehler* manuscripts. Further, he accurately translates the word *bewußtlos* as 'unconscious', whereas Miller translates it as 'subconscious'. For these reasons, Petry's edition is a superior text to the Miller translation. For comparison, I have also examined Hegel's 1827–28 lectures on the Philosophy of Spirit: *Vorlesungen über die Philosophie des Geistes* (Hamburg: Felix Meiner, 1994). I have mainly relied on Petry's translation but provide my own in places that warrant changes. Hereafter, references to the *Philosophy of Spirit* (*Die Philosophie des Geistes*), which is the third part of Hegel's *Enzyklopädie*, will customarily be referred to as *EG* followed by the section number. References to the *Zusätze* are identified as such.

All references to Freud's texts refer to the original German monographs compiled in his *Gesammelte Werke, Chronologisch Geordnet*, 18 vols, edited by Anna Freud, Edward Bibring, Willi Hoffer, Ernst Kris and Otto Isakower, in collaboration with Marie Bonaparte (London: Imago Publishing, 1968 [1940–52]). Most translations are mine. Because most English-speaking psychoanalysts neither own nor readily have access to these original texts, I have cited *The Standard Edition of the Complete Psychological Works of Sigmund Freud*, 24 vols (1886–1940), translator and general editor James Strachey, in collaboration with Anna Freud, assisted by Alix Strachey and Alan Tyson (London: Hogarth Press, 1966–95 [1886–1940]). References to quotations are designated by *SE* followed by the appropriate volume and page numbers.

For the same reasons regarding the likely lack of familiarity with original texts, I have cited the English translations of Heidegger's *Sein und Zeit*, Sartre's *L'Être et le Néant*, Lacan's *Écrits* and *Séminaires,* and Jung's *Gesammelte Werke* (published in Switzerland) but compiled and translated in the Bollingen Series as his *Collected Works*, which were almost exclusively written in German. All references to Fragments of the pre-Socratic philosophers are culled from the Wheelwright and the Kirk, Raven and Schofield compilations, and are designated as *Fr.* followed by the appropriate number. All references to Plato are from *The Collected Dialogues of Plato*, and to Aristotle from *The Complete Works of Aristotle*, which are generally considered by scholars to be the best English translations in circulation.

Attempts have been made to use gender-neutral referents. Most references cited in the text refer to the following abbreviations followed by their volume, section, and/or page numbers. For complete details, see the Bibliography.

AI	*Adventures of Ideas*
BN	*Being and Nothingness*
BT	*Being and Time*
CN	*The Concept of Nature*
CP	*Collected Papers of Charles Sanders Peirce,* 6 vols
CPR	*Critique of Pure Reason*
CW	*The Collected Works of C.G. Jung*
E	*Écrits: A Selection*
EG	*Philosophie des Geistes,* trans. *The Philosophy of Spirit,* part 3 of the *Encyclopaedia of the Philosophical Sciences*
EL	*Encyclopaedia Logic,* vol. 1 of the *Encyclopaedia of the Philosophical Sciences*
FC	*The Four Fundamental Concepts of Psycho-Analysis*
FR	*The Function of Reason*
GW	*Gesammelte Werke, Chronologisch Geordnet,* 18 vols
IS	*The Interpretation of Science*
MT	*Modes of Thought*
PN	*Philosophy of Nature,* vol. 2 of the *Encyclopaedia of the Philosophical Sciences*
PR	*Process and Reality*
PS	*Phenomenology of Spirit*
RH	*Reason in History,* the Introduction to the *Lectures on the Philosophy of History*
RM	*Religion in the Making*
S	*Symbolism: Its Meaning and Effect*
SE	*Standard Edition of the Complete Psychological Works of Sigmund Freud,* 24 vols
SL	*Science of Logic*
SMW	*Science and the Modern World*
STI	*System of Transcendental Idealism*
W	*Wissenschaftslehre,* trans. *The Science of Knowledge*

In reality we know nothing, for truth lies in the abyss.
Democritus

INTRODUCTION

Underworlds and the ancient soul

The Papyrus of Ani, a massive folio detailing a funerary account of the afterlife, is one of the most famous and earliest accounts of the legend of the underworld in recorded history. It continues to fascinate the public due to its hieroglyphic and colourful blending of text, scene and symbolism in Egyptian art, polytheistic culture and cosmology, and its focus on a chthonic netherworld. This artefact of occult philosophy is known as *The Egyptian Book of the Dead*.[1] Many ancient cultures were preoccupied with life after death, concerns which have conditioned contemporary religious beliefs and social customs to this day, but few have imagined a more convoluted and horrific afterlife than the ancient Egyptians. Death marked the beginning of a treacherous journey through the underworld, where kings and mortals alike battled a series of creatures, dead ghosts and dark forces for the resurrection of their souls. Their principal guide was a collection of magic spells, prayers, hymns and mortuary knowledge outlined in the *Book of the Dead*.

The ancient belief in an afterlife was literal and real, not merely folklore or conceived of metaphorically. All royals were mummified so their souls could recognize them in the underworld, and pharaohs were often buried with hundreds of ancillary servants (who were routinely murdered) to assist the King-God in the afterlife. This battle for resurrection transpired in an Egyptian version of hell, a nightmarish netherworld envisioned circa 2,400 years before the birth of Christ and nearly 3,700 years before Dante's *Inferno*.

The Egyptian underworld is an apt starting place for our exploration of the philosophy of the unconscious, for it is the anthropological correlate to an ancient obsession with the questions of being and nothingness, order and disorder, terrestrial and celestial domains, and a phantasmal account of the topography of the afterlife. The wisdom and mortuary literature reflective of Egyptian religion was designed to teach moral virtue and prepare the individual for the netherworld, much like the *Bardo Thödol*, or Tibetan *Book of the Dead*, which is a guidebook or funerary version of the art of dying as a metaphysical preparation for rebirth. Here the most important question facing the ancients, which was the central focus of communal consciousness, was the destiny (*telos*) of the human soul. The underworld can be interpreted as both a cultural symbolic for the unconscious and a metaphor for the ineffable, unknown and tempestuous forces that populate inner

1

life, what Freud (1933) famously referred to as 'the dark, inaccessible part of our personality . . . chaos, a cauldron full of seething excitations' (*SE* 22:73). This 'cauldron', itself a spatial analogy for the It (*Es*), mirrors the primordial waters of Nun dispersed throughout the underworld, the subterranean counterpart to the sky-heavens or light of consciousness. The ancient soul aspired toward resurrection and immortality in an afterworld free of suffering, the emergence and emancipation from our *pathos*. It is no coincidence that much of the world today pines for such an afterlife.

Before the field of psychology came into being as a distinct discipline in the nineteenth century, all reflections on human disposition, motivation and action were attributed to mental faculties and qualities belonging to the soul. For the Egyptians, the soul (*ba* or *ka*) took on many spiritual forms, such as a state of nobility and blessedness (*akh*) or a shadow (*shut*) in the next world (Faulkner and Goelet, 1972/1994, p. 150). The Greeks referred to soul as the *psuchê* (ψυχή), what we customarily think of as mind and/or personality as a whole. Although all human experience is ultimately mediated by mind, in antiquity they did not have a concept for the unconscious. This was represented by myth, allegory, ritual, religion and anthropomorphic cosmogony, what was deemed to belong to a netherworld that was believed to lie beneath the material world of telluric appearances, and was thought to be the host to the most sacred of all human hopes and desires for an immortal afterlife. The human quest for eternal life, purity, peace and satisfaction (through the avoidance of persecution, damnation, torture and punishment) was thought to be due to the soul's ability to transmute itself in the next world in negotiation with events and environs it encountered. These potential transformative states of being depended upon how successfully one was able to navigate the perils of the underworld, what may not be inappropriately compared to the psychoanalytic notion of surviving the throes of our own unconscious conflicts and enactments informing the quality of our experiential lifeworld (*Lebenswelt*).

Although underworld mythologies may be observed in aboriginal, Graeco-Roman, Oriental, Indian, Indo-European, Middle Eastern, Norse, Native American and Mesoamerican cultures, just to name a few, Egyptian fantasy life canonized the way we have come to transculturally envision another psychic reality juxtaposed to consciousness. In this primordial dreamscape, we are judged for our character and past deeds by an omnipotent ruler, where souls reside in equivalent forms of heaven and hell espoused today by Judeo-Christian and Islamic monotheism, and where we must face our most ghastly fears in order to transcend death through embracing our destinies, namely, the psychological dispositions and deposits of our own unconscious experience.

Entering the *Duat*

The *Duat* or underworld is conceived in terms of dynamic intricate spacings and dialectical complementarities, much like the topographical features of the psychoanalytic unconscious where vast spatial regions, locality, depth and foreign or alien activities transpire, both horrific and sublime. The underworld is sometimes referred to as an 'Abyss', as in Faulkner's original translation of Nun in the Ani Papyrus, the primordial waters that permeate the bottomless infinity of the nether-world. Nun also contains both positive and negative dualities, at once the origins of chaos and the baptismal bath essential for rebirth that cleansed and rejuvenated the aged sun (Re) as it entered the underworld at night only to re-emerge the next morning as Khepri, the newborn sun (Faulkner and Goelet, 1972/1994).

In Egyptian cosmology, Osiris is the Lord of Eternity, King of the Underworld. Emerging from a state of nonexistence, he presided over death and became the supernatural superego that judged the purity of a soul by weighing a man's heart in relation to a feather. Only after passing through a series of gates, caverns and mounds in the netherworld, and running a gauntlet of serpents, demons, hybrid monsters, and deadly challenges such as fires of damnation, was a journeyman to face Osiris on the Day of Judgment. If the heart was pure (i.e. free of sin and evil), the *ba*-spirit was allowed to pass into eternity and experience a favourable immortality in the blessed Field of Reeds. If not, the guilty party's heart was devoured by a beast (part-lion/crocodile/hippopotamus) and condemned to the cauldron of dead souls that populated the netherworld.

Although Osiris governed over his underworld kingdom, he was not alone. There were several Duat-gods and supernatural beings that occupied the netherworld, and these dark forces were as menacing to Osiris as they were to the deceased. Even when the sun-god Re made his nocturnal journey within the night sky underneath the earth's firmament, the Egyptians feared that the sun would not emerge from the evil potencies that inhabited the abyss unless they engaged in a daily encircling (*pekher*) ritual or prayer, a cultural practice similar to that of the Pueblos of the American Southwest.

The Osiris legend is obscure and makes its first appearance by the Fifth Dynasty in the *Pyramid Texts*, which is the oldest religious record discovered to date. Osiris was heralded to be a living ruler during the dawn of Egyptian civilization but was believed to be murdered, dismembered and tossed into the Nile by his jealous brother Seth who wished to rule as king over Egypt in his place. Osiris's wife (and sister) is said to have gathered his body parts and reassembled them with magical powers, after which he came back to life and presided over the Duat. Here we may observe uncanny themes of fratricide and incest that later appear in various versions of Greek mythology from Oedipus to Antigone. Resurrected in the underworld, but mainly appearing in half-mummified forms, Osiris has his reign and revenge, because he is now the God of Judgment over the dead. Here the fate of souls is subjected to his critical scrutiny, either to be redeemed, punished or damned to nonexistence or torture.

The wishful fantasy constellations these ancients adopted in their polytheist worldview contended that the soul was subject to transmogrifications in form and substance in the next world, to the degree that the denial of death was an entrenched fixture of the Egyptian psyche or cultural unconscious. There may be said to be an isomorphism between the fantasy of an afterlife resurrection and the transformative paths the soul could assume in the underworld, itself a projection of the human need for transcendence, divinity and immortality that prefigured and conditioned the foundations of monotheism. The soul or spirit in early Egyptian philosophy is envisioned as acquiring different forms that are contingent upon the context of the deceased's entry into the netherworld, from more base or degraded facsimiles such as a ghost-image or amorphous silhouette, where the individual's personality is embodied within an incorporeal death-shadow (*shut*), to a blessed state of existence. The *akh*, for example, is the form of a spirit that has attained a state of exaltation or celestial incorporeal existence, something akin to a solar or divine being. Generally, the *ba* is depicted as a bird-like entity (such as a Jabairu stork) with a human head that flies over the coffin of the deceased, itself symbolic of transcendence. It further personifies the notion of freedom and being unencumbered by worldly restrictions, such as a transference or flight from one life to the next. The *ba*-form appears at death and signifies the soul in an afterlife plain, which could be reunited with the earthly (material) body of the departed. This imagery also suggests that the soul is the substance of what lives on beyond the grave and can recognize its previous terrestrial form as human mummification, itself a qualitative function of self-consciousness that is attributed to the transcendent powers of the soul.

What is most interesting in Egyptian eschatology is the *ka*. The *ka* is a form the human personality can adopt at death, but it is also an alteration of the soul that can transpire in the living. Unlike the *ba* or *akh*, the *ka* could assume a double image or identical form independent of the physical body of the person who is still alive. This may be compared to a person's *Doppelgänger* or double self that is often depicted in tomb iconography as a protector standing behind the king, a sort of guardian angel. Here we may say the soul is like a self-state or alter-ego/agent that is the spiritual embodiment of the person's physical body. I would suggest this is more of the essence of an individual's psyche that can transmute the sensible world through immaterial instantiations, something more akin to an apparition or what a human becomes upon death of the physical body. Yet it is in the living being all along, awaiting to enter another medium or psychic spacing. We may equate the *ka* with the spiritual sustenance, vital energy, or life force that animates the soul, its truth and essence.

Not only are the ancient Egyptians credited for introducing the psychomythology of the soul, they may also be recognized for introducing the postmodern reification of language, for the deceased could only pass to safety through the various gates and mounds of the netherworld by naming the creatures and deities that inhabited them. The Egyptian word 'spell' is literally translated as 'utterance', as is the common expression *djed medu* – 'words to be spoken' (Taylor, 2010, pp. 29–30). For example, various spells, mortuary texts and hieroglyphic inscriptions were placed all over burial tombs including the walls, sarcophagi and coffins themselves, and engraved shabtis (magical funerary statuettes) along with other purposeful objects were placed in burial chambers to aid in servitude. Even bandages used to wrap the flesh of mummies had writings from the *Book of the*

Dead to help protect and guide them in the afterworld. Speaking these spells aloud was an act of creation: prescribing words accompanied funerary rites as these formulas were thought to be used to gain safe passage through the obstacles and lethal hazards in the netherworld. Hence the spoken and written word was itself a fundamental source of determinate power. Here the word – the agency of the letter – was literally thought to transform the course of being.

One of the most salient notions of the Egyptian afterlife is its mystery, secrecy and uncertainty. At once the underworld remains hidden, yet it conditions the earthly social structures that guide human engagement and cultural (domestic and religious) practices, as well as the solar forces that govern the cosmos. Here the underworld becomes the bedrock of earth and sky, of flesh and spirit, what might not be inappropriately analogous to the human psyche in its struggle with bodily desires, social relations, irrationality and the pursuit of value. An interesting note is that there is an inherent democracy to the underworld, for the judgment of the heart was initiated by Ma'at, the goddess of truth and justice, where it was weighed in the balance of a feather (the symbol of truth) and recorded by Thoth, the god of wisdom, before offering the verdict to Osiris. The fate of an individual's soul was ultimately based on the determination of one's moral character.

Aspiring to be worthy, to be recognized by Authority (Father as Lord) – the ultimate Deemer of good and bad – the underworld mythos interweaves at least four major interdependent elements that constitute human unconscious dynamics: (1) a domain and dominion of obscurity, negation, death, and unknown forces that condition the soul, waking consciousness and cultural phenomena; (2) the omnipresence of turmoil and suffering is permeable and capable of being tamed by agentic forces that intervene to create stability and concord; (3) an antithetical yet orderly co-existence of opposites between danger and safety (good and evil) mediated by emotion and reason; and (4) a moral tribunal where competing desires and conflicts are adjudicated by basic principles of truth and justice. It is no accident that the ancient Egyptian underworld myth was the object of identification by the Greeks, who subsequently developed their own underworld mythology; but more importantly, the values and dreamscape of Egyptian culture set the stage for the Hellenic and Hellenistic emphasis placed on reason or intelligence (*nous*), wisdom (*sophia*), and virtue or moral character (*aretē*). Here we may say that the birth of the conception of the unconscious was unconsciously configured within the dynamic complexities of the Egyptian psyche informing these early occult philosophies preoccupied with the telos of the soul.

Hades

'Souls smell in Hades.' This is a standard translation of Heraclitus's Fragment B 98: αἱ ψυχαὶ ὀσμῶνται καθ᾽ ῞Αιδην. This pithy comment implies the foul decay of rotting flesh, the soul reduced in death to the underworld, a place of degeneration. A less literal interpretation is not the offensiveness of stench, but the vulgarity of the living embodied psyche being degraded in worth by impersonal death

5

itself, a stripping away of a person's vitality, which is now a former image of what one used to be, but nevertheless still existing. Yet Burnet's (1957, p. 136) translation is misleading. Freeman (1956) is less ambiguous: 'Souls have the sense of smell in Hades' (p. 31). And for Wheelwright (1966), 'In Hades souls perceive by smelling' (p. 73). This fragment is handed down by Plutarch in the second century ACE, whose depiction Sallis (1995) favours in its emphasis on an active purpose: 'Souls employ the sense of smell in Hades' (p. 186). Souls smell, have the sense of smell, employ this sense, and perceive. The notion that dead souls have a sense – that they suspect something – speaks to the uncanny. This is its context.

For the early Greeks, the soul was equated with breath, as is the Latin *spiritus*, derived from Byzantine Greek orthography, to breathe. Soul or spirit signifies life, which requires air, and only by breathing through the nose can we inhale and discern smell. Therefore souls in Hades are divested of their other senses, but retain the basic earthly functions of smell that belong to their bodiless yet sentient existence.[2] Beyond the discrepancies in translation and the contexts of interpretation, not to mention how the historical fragment itself survived, was acquired, and attributed to Heraclitus himself, the questions of what was and is *lost* remains. Souls lose sense, just as intelligibility is lost in translation. Mythos aside, this Heraclitusean fragment remains sensible only on the condition that we interpret it from the standpoint of what was common Greek opinion (*doxa*) on the nature and qualities of the soul, something that was originally conceived by Thales as causing movement. Noted ancient scholar Jonathan Barnes (1979) tells us that the word *psuchê* is popularly translated as 'soul', what he prefers to call 'animator' due to its lack of theological undertones implicated with the word soul. To have soul is to be animate (*empsuchos*) or living, what Aristotle says 'by which primarily we live, perceive, and think' (*De Anima*, 414a13). Hence, to have soul is to be alive, even in death.

Hades ("Αιδης) means hidden or 'unseen'. Here Hades symbolizes the unconscious, both figuratively as well as a spacing, itself present yet obscured, cryptic, veiled. Although it is designated as a place, an invisible location, in classical Greek literature it is associated with a god.[3] In the *Iliad*, Homer tells us of when and how the world was divided into three parts; three brothers cast their lots and each was assigned to a domain: Zeus was granted the sky, Poseidon the sea, and Hades the dark underworld (15:187ff). The underworld is withdrawn from the light of the sun, antithetical to the sky, hence consciousness, a place of concealment as delimitation (Sallis, 1995). For Homer, Hades is the unseen god who is not only withdrawn from the world into a nether region or nocturnal abyss, but like Osiris, he is also the monarch of the dead. Here is where souls travel and reside in an afterlife where they are reduced to shadows, what is described in the *Odyssey* as phantoms (εἴδωλα) or images of dead men (11:475f). This is their abode, where they reside in opacity yet remain hidden from the light of awareness, hence suppressed, buried. Souls comport themselves to Hades *as* and *within* radical concealment.

Hades the god is equated with his underworld domain, destined to embody and fulfil the meaning of his name, that which was portended. He/It is the unseen, that which is concealed, where souls abide, ruled by unconsciousness itself. Dead souls are vestiges of life, merely shadows or images, hence appearances, within a vast interior netherworld that is fathomless. They have lost consciousness in their psychic retreat into a ghostly cavern of metaphysical proportions. They are no longer conscious, but sense. Heraclitus goes on in Fragment 27 to foreshadow the unanticipatory nature of the soul in death: 'There await men after they are dead such things they neither expect nor have any conception of.' We do not know what goes on in the abyss, for we have no conception or opinion of it whatsoever, only a sense, a sense of smell.

It is no coincidence that the underworld is the dialectical inversion of 'disclosedness', what the ancients called truth or *aletheia* (ἀλήθεια), the hidden side of appearances. For the pre-Socratics, truth was the manifest; yet whatever appeared or disclosed itself always transpired within a backdrop of a covering-over or concealment. Truth as *aletheia* is 'unconcealment' or disclosure, but only on the condition that whatever appears emerges from the veil of hiddenness. And for Heraclitus, 'Nature loves to hide' (*Fr.* 123). The hidden abyss of the underworld is tantamount to a collective unconsciousness, whether this be a world soul (*anima mundi*) or the archaic deposit of human experience organized on primordial levels of internalized representations (*représentations collectives*), desire and conflict as cultural identifications that fuel the *mythos* of collective peoples.

The notion of the spectral soul living on in death in a morbid state of abeyance, clouded in mystery and phantasmal imagery, echoes the uncanny or 'unhomely' (*unheimlich*) resonance of the unconscious. For the Greeks, the underworld was strange, foreign (ξένος), unfamiliar. Yet for Freud (1919), 'the uncanny is that class of the frightening which leads back to what is known of old and long familiar' (*SE* 17:220). The quality of feeling is one of familiar unfamiliarity, a sense of discomfort amongst a sense of recognition, the diaspora of the soul within its new home, that which is unidentified but vaguely known.

From the Duat to Hades' lair, souls linger, or more precisely, aspects of the disembodied psyche reorganize within their uncanny domain, one that is foreclosed in concealment, not unlike repressed content from consciousness slumbering away in a dreamscape of irrealism. Like Hades, the unconscious is not seen; it is in fact unseeable, the Kantian *Ding an sich*, that which reveals itself from its hiddenness but can never be known in-itself. Here we may observe the double character of *aletheia* as a revealing that simultaneously conceals, just as consciousness is the counterpart to unconscious process, each the extension of the other, ontologically conjoined yet differentiated by their appearances. And as Anaxagoras reminds us, 'Appearances are a glimpse of the unseen' (*Fr.* 21a).

Lethe is the river of forgetfulness in Greek mythology. *A-letheia* is its reversal; hence, an unforgetting of what was previously hidden. But unless one enters the underworld, it can never be experienced directly, only known through its spacings or modes of manifestation. And with every disclosure there is also simultaneously a closing, a covering-over, for truth may only be shown in its passing over from concealment. This process of uncovering in the presence of covering is its double truth. Here this discourse fits nicely in a psychoanalytic paradigm because we are principally interested in: (1) the *act* of 'uncovering' the unconscious elements of subjectivity, and (2) the *specific* 'uncoverings' of what is disclosed, namely, the contents and details of mental objects, memories, fantasies, linkages to past representations, and so on. The notion of truth as unhiddenness also points to a process of how unconscious phenomena unfold and divulge themselves to the subject and analyst. Truth can only exist if it is revealed, but as we will later see in Heidegger, what is disclosed or shines forth is something that was already present but hidden. Here we have the making of a fine discourse on unconscious phenomenology.

The Homeric psyche is imbued with a primordial conflict saturated in *pathos* (πάθος), namely suffering. This is one reason why Heraclitus emphasized universal strife as part of the human condition. He characterized human relations in particular as a primal strife, even a state of war (πόλεμος); what he says in his famous Fragment 53 is the father and king of all. This 'compulsion of strife' (*Fr.* 80) is analogous to the ontological conflict that fuels the unconscious, what Hegel identifies as the general (universal) structural invariances that propel the movement of the dialectic, first having its edifice in the nocturnal, feeling soul. Not only do souls sense, they also feel.

The Hellenic soul

The Greek conception of the psyche or soul (ψυχή) may be said to be ultimately concerned with the essence of the human being, and various dispositions, composites, or *natures* have been attributed to its organization. By today's standards, what we typically refer to as Mind as a totality, including the unique features that comprise individual personality and subjectivity, the Greeks tended to emphasize its multimodal features as universal dimensions of the human condition. Because the notion of consciousness is a modern (not an ancient) concept, early cultures did not have a word for the 'unconscious' in the way it is commonly used today; therefore, the nature of the soul was not examined in this light. But the unconscious depths of the soul were not entirely neglected, as many pre-Socratic philosophers attempted to delineate. Testimonia from Aristotle notes that it was Thales who attributed a 'motive force' to the notion of the soul (*De Anima*, 405a20), hence a purpose or telos that animates mind as a life-principle. For Anaximenes, our souls 'hold us together' (*Fr.* 2), what Democritus equates with thought (*De Anima*, 405a9) as well as a 'lust for pleasure' (*Fr.* 159). Perhaps it is in Heraclitus where we first get some glimpse of unconscious process when he points out that the soul follows an inner law of growth (*Fr.* 115) that has no limit, 'such is the depth of its meaning' (*Fr.* 45), yet one that is corrupted by 'impulsive desire', for 'whatever it wants it will buy at the cost of the soul' (*Fr.* 85).

The desirous or lustful features of the soul were often separated from its more rational faculties attributed to the intellect, reason, or mind (*nous*), the 'bright jewel' of which is wisdom (Gorgias, *Fr.* 11). For the Pythagorean school, like the Egyptians, the soul was immortal: life on earth was a sojourn and preparation (through purification, self-discipline and self-harmonization) for entering the afterlife, the destiny of which was to prepare for eternity. And for Philolaus, a contemporary of Socrates, the immortal *harmonia* of the soul becomes 'incorporeal' as it separates from the body upon death (*Fr.* 22). Because the ancients believed in reincarnation, metempsychosis, and the transmigration of the soul, they believed that they had lived before and that learning or education was a matter of recollection (*anamnesis*). Philip Wheelwright (1966) explains:

> The fundamental truths are already known to us, in the depths of our unconscious selves, and the purpose of education should therefore be to stir these hidden parts of us into activity, rather than to impose truths upon them from outside sources.
>
> (pp. 209–210)

Here we can appreciate how the Socratic method of dialectic was designed to question truth claims imposed by others and elicit knowledge that was previously forgotten, such as was demonstrated in Plato's famous dialogue, *Meno*.

Plato's treatment of the psyche in his *Dialogues* is vast and varied, but he takes up the Pythagorean concept of the soul as comprising three parts: intelligence, reason and passion. In the *Republic*, he discusses the desirous or appetitive soul as pursuing pleasure and avoiding pain, and that the 'lawless', base, 'beastly and savage part' concerned with gratifying 'its own instincts' (9:571c) is found in everyone. Plato not only anticipates the Freudian unconscious, he also stipulates how desire can override reason and a sense of shame belonging to our ethical compass. It is here that we may see how Plato was the first psyche-analyst when he articulates the intimate relationship between desire, reason and morality, how the soul possesses a natural constitution that is instinctually driven, develops habits in relating to others and the environment, and that our true characters awaken during sleep when the soul is at rest, whether this be the 'rational, gentle and dominate part' (9:571c) or disquieted passion, unruliness, and anger (9:572). In fact, Plato accounts for good and evil within the soul, or a 'better part and a worse part', which is subject to 'control' and 'self-mastery' (4:431a). When the soul is able to attain a sense of 'self-consciousness' (9:571d), the more primitive forms of our nature are 'tamed', which 'settles down in a compromise' between our competing tendencies (9:572d), only to find a middle ground or synthetic function where unbridled desires are transformed into lawful order and democratic inclinations. Here are the seeds of Freud's tripartite theory of the mind.

Although stemming from Sophocles, following these remarkable passages in Book IX, Plato may be even credited with elaborating upon Oedipal rivalry and competition when he compares a son's insolence, outrage and autocracy toward others as a reaction formation to a thrifty and niggardly father who personifies self-restraint, renunciation of pleasure, and inner discipline. Here Plato succeeds in showing how the ruling passions of the unconscious are under the influence of that 'tyrant Eros' (9:573d) responsible for every 'erotic' *and* 'evil' impulse, including the 'atrocity of murder' that lives 'in utmost anarchy and lawlessness'

9

(9:575) in our sleeping souls, which is based in part on habit and nature (9:573c; 575) in reaction to and defiance of 'the control of his father and the laws' (9:574d). This could read straight out of Freud. It is no accident that he referred to psychology as his 'tyrant'.

The division of the psyche is further described by Plato as a dialectical structure composed of opposites (*Phaedo*, 70e), 'in fact, of all contraries' (*Laws*, 10:896d), where psychological dispositions such as thought, feeling, sensation, perception, memory and judgment transpire in order to 'write words in our souls' (*Philebus*, 39a). It is also the harbinger of moral qualities, such as excellence, ends and virtues (*Republic*, 1:353d), aesthetics, and the 'pursuit of knowledge' (*Cratylus*, 420b). The soul is also the house of creativity (*Symposium*, 209), truth and reality (*Republic*, 9:585d), beauty (*Republic*, 3:402d), and wisdom (*Epinomis*, 974c). Furthermore, the soul is not only 'the cause of good and evil', 'right and wrong', but a 'universal cause' (*Laws*, 10:896d) of all mental activity, which affects a person's overall character (*Laws*, 10:904c). Being both rational and irrational (*Republic*, 4:439d), of pleasure and pain, the psyche is the essence of man.

Although Plato states that the psyche possesses temperament and physical constituents that belong to our embodiment (*Phaedo*, 86d), hence showing the interdependence of the mind and body, following the pre-Socratics, he ultimately believed that the soul was immortal (*Phaedo*, 71e–73; 105e). I will not critique this notion here, given the long contentious debate in the history of philosophy and theology; however, we can metaphysically infer a type of unconscious infinity that we may by analogy apply to the soul, what Freud (1933) refers to as a timeless, boundless immediacy that is 'virtually immortal' (*SE* 22:74).

While Plato provides a rich backdrop to the question, nature, and discourse on the quandaries of the soul, it was Aristotle's treatise on *De Anima* that continued to dominate our conception of mind until modern day psychology was established as a distinct discipline. For Aristotle, the object of psychology is to discover the 'essence' of soul and its attributes or properties (402a8). In Book I of his treatment *On the Soul*, he lays out the mind–body problem by asking whether the soul is divisible into parts, and if so, whether they are distinct from the body. Here he contextualizes the notion of parts as a plurality of functions with discernible properties as distinct from the whole, as well as the problematic of separating out affections such as sensation, appetite, passion, perception, emotion, and so forth from our experiential embodiment including thinking (403a5). Aristotle concludes that in order to act or be acted upon, soul has to possess a body as a prerequisite of its existence. Therefore, any study of the soul falls within the 'science of nature' (403a29) as a composite of embodied events. This is the making of modern psychological science.

It is in Book II where Aristotle gives an answer to the question, What is soul? Here he provides his famous distinction of *matter* (as potentiality) from *form* or essence (as actuality) and concludes that soul is a compound of the two as *life* (412a5–15). Here psyche and soma form a unit or union as a living being. Soul is not only a living thing with degrees of actuality and potentiality, it is an enactment of actualized potential as a *capacity* (412a27). Aristotle continues to delineate various functions, characteristics, or 'psychic powers' (414a30) of the soul that belong to organized natural (living) bodies such as self-nutrition, growth, decay, and so forth, with hierarchical degrees of enhancement in animals such as sensation and perception, and for humans, intellect or thought. For Aristotle, the capacity to sense, perceive and desire is common to all animal species, but what differentiates the human being from animals is the outgrowth or 'derivative properties' (415a15) of cognition. Here there are three advanced faculties humans possess: (a) *imagination*, which in turn relies on (b) *memory*, and (c) *reason*, which is unique to man (415a11).

Aristotle viewed imagination (φαντασία) as a derivative of sensation whereby the manifold sense objects and after-images appear to the soul as distinct psychical phenomena, even while dreaming (427b27–429a9). The distinguished Aristotelian scholar (Sir) David Ross (1923) notes that the acts of imagination involve 'not a conscious state of mind but an unconscious modification of the mind' (p. 148) due to the fact that mental processes are operative before recollection takes place, which is dependent on memory. Until mind recollects the deposits of sense perception recorded within the tableau of the unconscious, they persist in a state of potentiality before they are made actual by the imaginative faculty. In extending Aristotle's views, we may also say that potentiality *as such* is an unconscious presence that is always there, the task of which is to make it actual through recollection.[4] Here Aristotle anticipates Hegel's psychology, which we will examine shortly, where there is a sort of unconscious intelligence that mediates images and stored objects within the abyss of the mind. Originally laid down and retained as sensations, after-images can take on a life of their own, as we may observe in fantasy, and are reproduced by the faculty of imagination as re-presentations that are unconsciously derived. This is why Aristotle states: 'Thinking is different from perceiving and is held to be in part imagination, in part judgment' (427b28–29). Notice that imagination and thought intermingle. Here we may appreciate why Hegel (1830) claims that 'phantasy is reason' (*EG* § 457).[5] In other words, unconscious valences intervene during any act of thinking, especially fantasy.

It is important to emphasize that these advanced forms of cognition are epigenetic achievements: they develop from primordial organic processes such as biological instincts and gain a synthetic organizational ability or endowment responsible for reflective thought and behaviour. This is why the soul is *determinative*; it executes a causal impetus over the life activities of a living thing through animate action as *agency*. For Aristotle, the soul is the psychic facility that allows us to live as sentient and thinking beings (414a13), but with this single caveat: it cannot exist without a body. The standard (Ross) translation reads: 'the soul cannot be without a body, while it cannot *be* a body; it is not a body but something relative to a body' (414a18–20). In comparison, the Creed (1965) translation is similar: 'neither can the soul exist without the body nor is it a body; it is not a body, but has something to do with a body, and for this reason it is present in body' (p. 250). On the one hand, soul possesses a body, but on the other, it is not

11

a body. In other words, the soul is embodied but it cannot be reduced to matter or a material substance. This is Aristotle's language for what today we may refer to as non-reductive materialism.

If mind is embodied (as inhering within mass extended in space), where the 'affections of the soul are enmattered accounts' (403a25), then what becomes of the question of immateriality generally attributed to the soul? Keep in mind, this question is prefaced on the historical Christianization of the word 'soul', which typically signifies an immaterial, incorporeal, or supernatural independent existence that the so-called immortal psyche assumes over the physical cessation of the body at death, where in other languages, such as in German, soul (*Seele*) is devoid of these theological connotations, as is mind or spirit (*Geist*). Unlike Plato, for Aristotle the soul is not an independently existing substance, nor is it incorporeal. It is neither a material object, nor is it separated from the body. In other words, soul is not *separable* from the body, nor is it conceived as a body. Herein lies the paradox of inseparability of soul from body: while the psyche is not a body, it is not immaterial, yet it remains embodied. Psyche and soma are not different substances; rather, they are differentiated elements of the same substance, hence conjoined within a monistic structure. Yet Aristotle may be said to introduce a contradiction here, and even waffles on the notion of form and matter being independent of one another.[6] While they may be categorically separable, hence thought of as distinct through the act of abstraction, ontologically they are not. Furthermore, mind and body are not ontologically identical, hence they are not the same and cannot be collapsed into one another (contrary to the 'identification thesis' advanced by modern materialism); nor are they merely categorical distinctions, because the soul qua form transcends its biological counterpart in terms of its capacities, functions, organizational complexity and self-defining agency, which by definition gives it greater powers and valuing properties matter itself does not intrinsically possess, although sentience, desire and perception are necessarily embodied and cannot exist independently of soul.

By today's standards, Aristotle has set the stage for a discourse on the irreconcilability of the dialectic between psyche and substance, what we often see in contemporary cognitive neuroscience as a duality or polarity between mind and brain. The tendency today among the biological sciences to boil down mind to brain states, or neurochemical–physical systemic substances, vitiates the philosophical need to preserve the integrity of soul as a vitalizing, self-directing, regulatory process of generative, valuative self-creative agency that transpires within the embodied parameters of its natural 'givenness' or 'thrownness'. Aristotle's views on the soul preserve both the natural scientific attitude of explaining the physical world as an empirical object of investigation, as well as valuing the transcendental properties of mind that resist reductionist strategies hell-bent on displacing its determinative freedom through the mendacity and simple-minded devolution of materialism.

Although soul is an actuality, it is in its self-capacity to actualize itself as the coming into being of potentiality that signals its agentic potency. It is in the prowess of agency that soul achieves its pinnacle as thought. This is one reason why we do not phenomenally equate our minds with our bodies, for our reflective experience of our internal experiences is a higher-order accomplishment of self-consciousness, or, in Hegelianese, a sublation (*Aufhebung*) of mind. We do not relate to our Self as brain, but rather as a transcendent organizational being with a qualitative mediatory purpose (as self-imposed pursuit and meaning) that determines the course of how we wish to act over our body, despite the fact that our bodies (including brain dependence as supervenience) have functional and organic constraints over how we choose to think and behave.[7] What is extraordinary about Aristotle's arguments is that he both venerates the naturalized notion that mind cannot exist independent from our embodiment, what contemporary science would reiterate is simply an empirical fact, while at the same time refusing to reduce mind to matter or material substance, which admonishes scientific prejudices favouring reductionism by allowing mind to enjoy concurrent degrees of freedom in causal efficacy, form, qualia and self-definition. Here the existential capacity to think, reflect, choose and deliberately act qualitatively differentiates the human soul from its simple biological (causal) constitution.

For Aristotle, the crux of what it is to be a psychic entity or possess mind ultimately subordinates individuality and personal experience to a general collective essence, for soul is *universal form* that applies to all. This is why soul entails a metaphysical factor, for it epitomizes a universality within a concrete particularity. We participate of a general, impersonal psychic essence that may be said to apply to all people regardless of historicity, gender, race, location, or time, an *anima mundi* so to speak. From Aristotle to Hegel and Whitehead, we may see why Logic (as the essence of pure thought thinking about itself and its operations) may be attributed to a supraordinate process animating the universe. And what is most peculiar to this universal form is that it obeys an unconscious logic, a logic of the interior, something concealed yet manifest.

Setting aside for the moment the ancient tendency to import an immaterial, incorporeal and immortal dimension to the soul that carries with it naïve, incredulous supernatural properties, the Greeks were the first to give serious thought to the essence of the psyche as a complex psychological composition and governance responsible for interceding in all human experience, including the quest for the spiritual and the equiprimordiality of desire pining for satisfaction. To this day, the ancients' meditations on psychic reality remain an unequivocal bedrock for understanding human phenomena, including the psychodynamics of motivation, cognition and reason; individual and social psychology; mental well-being and suffering; communal relations; political and economic unconscious structures; ethical, aesthetic and cultural cultivation; and the convoluted process of civilization forged on power, aggression, violence, love and compassion, social negotiation and democracy. From tragedy to thanatology, the struggle over bodily passions, affective impulses, rational choice, and ethical comportment, including reconciling the good with the bad, pleasure and pain, creativity amongst destruction, truth over opinion, and folly from wisdom – all transpiring within a dialectical underworld vacillating between sex and death – is the hallmark of modern consciousness. It is rather remarkable that in all of the philosophies of the unconscious we will examine, from the summit of German idealism to psychoanalysis, existentialism and process metaphysics, we may rightfully appreciate what Whitehead (1929) means when he says that all of Western European philosophy is merely a 'series of footnotes to Plato' (p. 39). The notion of depth psychology, with its topography of the soul, including the interdependence of drive, desire and *pathos* instrumental in the ascendance of reason, aesthetics and ethical self-consciousness, may be viewed as an ancient discovery; but like Hades and the notion of *aletheia*, one that remained hidden in those times, concealed yet always present. Just as the Delphic maxim inscribed in the pronaos at the Temple of Apollo cautioned all visitors to 'Know Thyself', the psychoanalytic attitude upholds the value of insight and self-knowledge over the shrouded interior of the life within.

From antiquity to the rise of psychoanalysis

Psychoanalysis has entered a new phase in its evolution and identity by adopting various philosophical paradigms in theory and in its methods of inquiry. Since the philosophical turn, there has been more rigorous attention paid to the fundamental underlying assumptions governing theoretical and clinical models that lie outside the purview of mainstream behavioural science. The most basic of these philosophical postulates is the predication of an unconscious ontology. This book examines the major philosophical systems on the nature of the unconscious that emerge after the modern turn in philosophy, which find their most celebrated elaborations in Freud, Lacan and Jung. These systems are examined as a philosophical project and not merely presented as a psychological or scientific programme, as is common in most commentaries. These three psychoanalytic traditions, quite separate from one another in terms of their emphasis and philosophical presuppositions, are explored alongside contemporaneous movements in existentialism and Western metaphysics all taking place within continental Europe during the same era in the history of ideas. What also differentiates this work from other expositions is that I further attempt an integration and critique of each theoretical system.

The way we have come to understand the human soul, from its inception in ancient times to how it has been reconceived since the rise of modern science and the advent of psychoanalysis, offers competing (although in my estimate complementary) perspectives that gain their full recognition as a stratified theory of human nature. What differentiates the ancient soul from contemporary mind is the discovery and elucidation of an unconscious nucleus only prefaced in days of old, an anticipation we may nevertheless say was an unconscious intuition of its unconscious origin.

Although derived from antiquity, our analysis of the psyche will be principally concerned with an exegesis of the main metaphysical paragons that inform a systematic account of the philosophy of the unconscious over the past 200 years beginning with the stamp of German idealism, then formally schematized by psychoanalysis, and further instantiated within existentialism and process philosophy. Because the cognizance and study of the unconscious is a relatively new phenomenon in the history of the humanities and social sciences, the most vigorous theories of the soul lie within the comprehensive frameworks outlined by the great thinkers of the nineteenth and twentieth centuries, namely, Hegel, Freud, Heidegger, Jung, Lacan and Whitehead. It is here that we may observe the most sophisticated theoretical systems that directly offer a philosophical treatise on the ontology of the unconscious. Prior to this timeframe in human history, the unconscious was merely tacit, speculated, or inferred. Unlike Lancelot Law Whyte's (1960) survey of the history of the concept of the unconscious in *The Unconscious Before Freud*, which lacks any systematic attempt to delineate a robust theory of the unconscious, but rather traces a historical progression of how this psychological idea was developed in post-medieval Europe from approximately 1700 to 1900, I wish to provide a philosophical overview and critique of the main metaphysical systems of the unconscious since it was properly introduced in the history of ideas. This way the reader is afforded an opportunity to compare and contrast various schools of thought that are more coherently organized, rather than reiterate the terse and inchoate scatterings of allusions or references to unconscious processes by poets, philosophers, mystics, theologians, literary authors, scientists and the like who never fully conceived of nor developed their ideas in works preceding the nineteenth century.

Prior to the formation of psychology as a distinct discipline, theories of the unconscious were foreseen by modern philosophers such as Leibniz and Kant and refined by German idealists, most notably Schelling and Hegel. Although glimmerings of the unconscious may be observed in romantic and transcendental philosophies of the will, from Rousseau to Emerson, as well as the more methodological works of Schopenhauer and von Hartmann, not to mention the anti-systematic psychologism of Nietzsche, it was not until Freud that the unconscious was elevated in scope and parity with consciousness. Despite the fact that Schelling had offered a transcendental philosophy of nature (*Naturphilosophie*) and philosophy of identity (*Identitätsphilosophie*), where an unconscious mind may be said to permeate everything, and that Schopenhauer delineated an unconscious will underlying world consciousness, a theme further developed by von Hartmann, we will begin with Hegel because he provides the first systematic metaphysics in the history of philosophy that begins with an account of spirit or mind (*Geist*) that makes the unconscious a central feature of the human soul.

Once Hegel's system of unconscious spirit is presented, Freud's unconscious ontology will be explored from his early topographical and economic writings to his mature turn with the introduction of his tripartite process theory. Simultaneous with the rise of psychoanalysis was the explosion of phenomenology and existentialism in French and German philosophy. These movements often opposed psychoanalytic thought due to their negation of the unconscious for a privileging of consciousness. I explore how the works of Heidegger and Sartre complement a theory of psychopathology based on unconscious self-deception. Also occurring during this period was the growing interest in structuralism and semiology. Lacan's post-structural semiotics and mature tripartite theory of the imaginary, symbolic and real is further explored in relation to his epistemology that hinges on the thesis of paranoiac knowledge. After this, a meticulous examination of Jung's metaphysics, with a close analysis of his doctrine of archetypes, the collective unconscious and transpersonal phenomena, will be critiqued. We will end our journey with an examination of Whitehead's cosmology, which rests on a fundamental unconscious ontology.

What emerges from our exploration is several discrete forms of unconsciousness that may be loosely grouped into four distinct (yet interdependent) conditions: (1) psychological naturalism, (2) environmental determinism, (3) transpersonal supervenience, and (4) cosmic emanationism. In *psychological naturalism*, we may observe the emphasis on natural desire, instinct, and the embodied organizations of the psyche that are inherent in many theoretical systems, particularly in Freud, where biologism informs the higher-order epigenesis of cognition. *Environmental determinism* may be attributed to anything outside the subject that is given or superimposed, such as in the Heideggerian notion of historicity or our thrownness over world conditions that precede the birth of the agent, but it could also be deemed to be part of one's biological constitution and social facticity. When a matter of emphasis is placed on the causal factors attributed to linguistic construction, symbolic and political structures imposed by culture and otherness that determine the constitution of the subject, this may be said to dominate a particular theoretical position. We observe this mainly in Lacan. *Transpersonal supervenience* is primarily attributed to Jung's project, which posits a collective unconscious agency that supervenes on a set of psychological properties belonging to distinct individuals and their unique phenomenal organizations of the world, although Hegel may be accused of this as well with his notion of objective or absolute spirit; while *cosmic emanationism* finds its fullest expression in Whitehead, who envisions a valuing and emotive universe that may be properly said to be an unconscious life force permeating the cosmos. Although I do not wish to pigeon-hole any theorist into one category, and to be fair, many of the philosophical systems examined here share in overlap and mutual inner relations between these conditions, it is a matter of emphasis that differentiates the nuances of each theoretical treatise. I hope the reader will be able to appreciate the subtleties that distinguish each system, as well as the immense conundrums with which these great thinkers grappled in their attempt to offer a coherent explanation of human nature despite the unremitting complexifications and tedious fine-tuning problems we are left to resolve.

Notes

1 Here I rely on Faulkner's 1972 translation and Goelet's 1994 further translations and commentary on *The Egyptian Book of the Dead: The Book of Going Forth by Day* (Faulkner and Goelet, 1972/1994) which is the complete *Papyrus of Ani* with integrated

text and full-coloured images that was written circa 1250 BCE by royal scribes and un-known artists. This is generally considered by Egyptologists to be the most respected presentation and translation of the Ani Papyrus. I further rely on Taylor's (2010) broad compilation of several ancient books of the dead recovered from pyramid and funerary sources detailing the various narratives and hieroglyphic artistry characteristic of the ancient Egyptian journey through the afterlife.

2 An interesting side note is that the immediacy of smell is more refined at birth over sight, which is part of the newborn's initiation into consciousness.

3 Homer himself introduces this ambiguity between Hades as a location versus a god when he refers to Tartaros as the lowest part of the underworld, 'far beneath Hades as sky is from earth' (*Iliad*, 8:13), what Xenophanes proclaims 'continues indefinitely' (*Fr.* 28).

4 See Section 2 in Aristotle's essay, 'On Memory', where he discusses recollection at length.

5 Because reason is a developmental feat, it is grounded upon our natural embodied consti-tution that acquires advanced forms of cognition through human maturation. Therefore, reason is the epigenetic evolution of its prior shapes that transform yet derive from our natural corporeality as desire, sentience, affect, and the life of imagination.

6 Despite the problematics Aristotle introduces in Book III.5 of *De Anima* when he sug-gests that active reason, the highest element of the human soul, can exist independently of the body, where thought is 'separable' and 'disengaged from matter' (430a9–25; cf. 413a4–7), hence compounding his obscurity by failing to show the connection between reason and the other faculties of the soul, he nevertheless favours the view that the soul cannot exist as disembodied.

7 Here we may say there is a reciprocal determinism between our natural embodiment as constitutionally given and our free consciousness that maintains an executive function over its mediatory relations with endogenous forces exerting pressures over our embod-ied experiences.

1

HEGEL ON UNCONSCIOUS SPIRIT

In all his works, Hegel makes very few references to the unconscious. In fact, the account is limited to only a few passages in his *Encyclopaedia of the Philosophical Sciences*, and these do not explicitly develop a formal theory of the unconscious. Yet Hegel does not completely ignore the issue. In the *Encyclopaedia*, as outlined in Petry's presentation of *Hegel's Philosophy of Subjective Spirit*, Hegel describes the unconscious processes of intelligence as a 'nightlike abyss'. It is important to understand what Hegel means by this nocturnal 'abyss' and what role it plays in mental functioning. Despite a few noteworthy exceptions, which largely focus on Hegel's theory of mental illness,[1] Hegel's treatment of the unconscious has been largely overlooked. It will be the overall focus of this chapter to introduce Hegel's contributions to our understanding of unconscious processes and, through extrapolation, show how he in many remarkable ways anticipates key notions formally investigated by psychoanalysis a century later. As an arch-rationalist, Hegel provides one of the first attempts in the history of Western metaphysics to show how unconscious psychic forces precede reason, and how the abyss is an indispensable aspect of his entire philosophy. Before we examine the structural processes and specific functions the unconscious assumes in Hegel's system, it may prove useful for readers unfamiliar with Hegelian studies to have an overview of his philosophical project.

Hegel's dialectical method

Geist is customarily translated as 'spirit' or 'mind', both of which have entirely different meanings in English. There is no appropriate German equivalent for the word 'mind', which, in English, is often associated with brain dependence and its emergent mental processes, the field of cognitive neuroscience, and consciousness studies, while 'spirit' often evokes religious sentiments, theology, mysticism, or supernatural ideology. Neither is the case in German; therefore, making any translational meaning of *Geist* is difficult at best. In general, psychoanalysis would possibly contend that the dialectical modes of *Geist* are themselves differentiated and modified forms of the mind as psychical agencies, registers, self-states, or projected part-objects maintained by unconscious motivations or through ego manoeuvres of intentionality, dissociation, or defence,[2] yet this does not fully capture Hegel's project.

Geist intimates a complex integration of an individual's personality as a whole, including one's intellect, character, ethical or moral sensibilities, and personal maturity, as well as the refinement of one's more basic desires or passions. Therefore, *Geist* assumes a developmental ascendance and transcendental quality that embodies an ideal value, human striving, or pursuit. To refer to a person's *Geist* is to import a measure of respect for its superiority because it implies a cultivated degree of self-awareness through laborious developmental achievement. *Geist* is also a term used for God – *Der Heilige Geist* (the Holy Ghost) – thus, it commands a degree of exaltation. Of course, this process is not the same for all people. While all human beings are primarily equal with regard to their soul (*Seele*), in German a term devoid of any religious connotations whatsoever, people are vastly different when it comes to their *Geist*. This is why, when we refer to spirit, we signify the coming into being of a privileged form of subjective transcendent awareness, hence, the coming to presence of pure self-consciousness. Hegel wants to extend this notion of the individual mind to the collective element of humankind realized through our historical cultural practices, which define the process and progress of civilization. Therefore, spirit is the unification of nature within mind, hence, body and soul instantiated throughout history and objective social life as the sophistication and sublimation of human subjectivity. In psychoanalytic language, *Geist* is the amalgamation of Freud's tripartite division of the psyche within the process of actualizing its rational, aesthetic and ethical potential, hence, a triumph of the human spirit.[3]

Although Hegel is one of the most prodigious and influential thinkers in the history of philosophy, his dialectical method remains one of his least well understood philosophical contributions. While philosophers have made scores of commentaries and interpretations of Hegel's dialectic (Beiser, 1993; Burbidge, 1981; Hibben, 1984; McTaggart, 1964), some interpreters have gone so far as to deny Hegel's method (see Solomon 1983) or to render it opaque, simplistic and imprecise (Forster 1993). Hegel's dialectical method governs all three dimensions of his overall philosophical system, namely, the *Logic*; the *Philosophy of Spirit*, including the *Phenomenology*; and the *Philosophy of Nature*. The dialectic serves as the quintessential method not only for explicating the fundamental operations of mind but also for expounding the nature of reality.

Hegel's philosophy of mind or spirit rests on a proper understanding of the ontology of the dialectic. Hegel refers to the unrest of *Aufhebung* – customarily translated as 'sublation' – a continuous dialectical process entering into opposition within its own determinations and thus raising this opposition to a higher unity, which remains at once annulled, preserved and transmuted. Hegel's use of *Aufhebung*, a term he borrowed from Schiller but also an ordinary German word, is to be distinguished from its purely negative function, whereby there is a complete cancelling or drowning of the lower relation in the higher, to also encompass a preservative aspect. Therefore, the term *aufheben* has a threefold meaning: (1) to suspend or cancel, (2) to surpass or transcend, and (3) to pre-serve. In the *Encyclopaedia Logic*, Hegel makes this clear: 'On the one hand, we understand it to mean "clear away" or "cancel", and in that sense we say that a law or regulation is canceled (*aufgehoben*). But the word also means "to preserve" ' (*EL* § 96, *Zusatz*).

Hegel's dialectical logic has been grossly misunderstood by the humanities and social sciences largely due to historical misinterpretations dating back to Heinrich Moritz Chalybäus, an earlier Hegel expositor, and unfortunately perpetuated by current mythology surrounding Hegel's system. As a result, Hegel's dialectic is inaccurately conceived of as a three-step movement involving the generation of a proposition, or 'thesis', followed by an 'antithesis', then resulting in a 'synthe-sis' of the prior movements, thus giving rise to the popularized and bastardized phrase: thesis – antithesis – synthesis. This is not Hegel's dialectic; rather, it is Fichte's (1794) depiction of the transcendental acts of consciousness, which he describes as the fundamental principles (*Grundsätzen*) of thought and judgment.[4] Yet this phrase is a crude and mechanical rendition of Fichte's logic and does not properly convey even his project. Unlike the meaning that Fichte assigns to the verb *aufheben*, which he defines as to eliminate, annihilate, abolish, or destroy, Hegel's meaning signifies a threefold activity by which mental operations at once cancel or annul opposition, preserve or retain it, and surpass or elevate its previous shape to a higher structure.

Fichte's dialectic is a response to Kant's (1781) *Critique of Pure Reason*, in which Kant outlines the nature of consciousness and addresses irreconcilable con-tradictions that are generated in the mind due to inconsistencies in reasoning.[5] For both Kant and Fichte, their respective dialectics have firm boundaries that may not be bridged. Hegel, on the other hand, shows how contradiction and opposition are annulled but preserved, unified and elevated within a progressive evolutionary process. This process of the dialectic underlies all operations of mind and is seen as the thrust behind world history and culture. It may be said that the dialectic is the *essence* of psychic life for, if it were to be removed, consciousness and uncon-scious structure would evaporate.

The process by which mediation collapses into a new immediate provides us with the logical model for understanding the dynamics of the mind. An architec-tonic process, *Geist* invigorates itself and breathes its own life as a self-determining generative activity that builds upon its successive phases and layers, which form its appearances. Mind educates itself as it passes through its various dialectical configurations, ascending towards higher shapes of self-conscious awareness. What spirit takes to be truth in its earlier forms is realized to be merely a moment. It is not until the stage of pure self-consciousness, what Hegel calls Absolute Knowing as lucid conceiving or conceptual understanding,[6] that spirit finally inte-grates its previous movements into a synthetic unity as a dynamic self-articulated complex whole.

In common language, spirit is a developmental process of self-actualization realized individually and collectively through reflective, contemplative thought and action. The notion of spirit encompasses a principle of complex holism whereby higher stages of development are attained through dynamic, laborious dialectical mediation. At its apex, subject and object, mind and matter, the particular and the universal, the finite and the infinite, are mutually implicative yet subsumed within the Absolute or Whole process under consideration. This is what Hegel refers to as the 'Concept' (*Begriff*), or what we may more appropriately translate as 'comprehension'. *Begriff* is the noun to the verb *begreifen*, literally, 'to grasp with one's hands'. *Begreifen* implies a depth of understanding, an ability to comprehend fully all aspects of a subject matter or thing under question. Therefore, *Begriff* is a concise one-word description that captures the essence of something, namely Spirit, what we aim to comprehend.

Hegel's account of the concrete actuality of the Concept (or Notion) as individual personality may be said to present a theory of human psychology with unconscious elements always prefiguring intrapsychic and logical operations of thought. In fact, the unconscious makes thought possible. Yet, for Hegel, individuality is ultimately explained within the larger context of a collective historical anthropology that informs human relations and the coming to presence of pure self-consciousness. In this sense, we may say that the unconscious is not only non-self-consciousness, which is much of world history until spirit returns to itself and comes to understand its process, but is furthermore the competing and antithetical organizations of 'impulses' (*Triebe*) that are 'instinctively active', whose 'basis is the soul [*Seele*] itself' (*SL*, p. 37), which informs spirit's burgeoning process. In articulating both the *subjective* (i.e. personal individuality, particularity) and *objective* (universal, generalizable) elements of spirit, Hegel illuminates both a personal and collective unconscious as a precursor to Freud and Jung.

Philosophy of mind

Hegel's theory of mind is comprehensively outlined in the *Philosophy of Spirit* (*Philosophie des Geistes*), which is the third part of the *Encyclopaedia of the Philosophical Sciences*. Unbeknownst to psychoanalysis, Hegel provides one of the first theories of the unconscious. He gives most of his attention to the unconscious within the stage of presentation (*Vorstellung*) in the context of his psychology, thus belonging to the development of theoretical spirit or intelligence, what we today refer to as cognition. Here Hegel refers to a 'nocturnal mine (*Schact*) within which a world of infinitely numerous images and presentations is preserved without being in consciousness' (*EG* § 453). Hegel explains that the night-like pit – what I have translated as the *abyss* – is a necessary presupposition for imagination and for higher forms of intelligence (cf. Hegel, 1830, 3:405nn). While these more complex forms of the psychological would not be possible without the preservation of images within the unconscious mind, the unconscious is given developmental priority in his anthropological treatment of the soul (*Seele*).

For Hegel, the unconscious soul is the birth of spirit that developmentally proceeds from its archaic structure to the higher-order activities of consciousness and self-conscious rational life. Like Freud, who tells us that the ego is a differenti-ated portion of the It (*Es*), the conscious ego is the modification and expression of unconscious activity. For Hegel, the soul is not an immaterial entity (*EG* § 389) but, rather, the embodiment of its original corporeality, the locus of natural desire (*Begierde*) or drive (*Trieb*).[7] As the general object of anthropology, Hegel traces the dialectical emergence of the feeling soul from the abyss of its indetermina-tions. At first unseparated from its immediate universal simplicity, it then divides and rouses itself from its mere inward implicitness to explicit determinate being-for-self. Through a series of internal divisions, external projections, and reinter-nalizations, the soul gradually emerges from its immediate physical sentience (*EG* § 391) to the life of feeling (*EG* § 403) to the actual ego of consciousness (*EG* § 411), which becomes further refined and sophisticated through perceptual cognition, conceptual understanding, ethical self-consciousness and rational judg-ment, the proper subject matter of the *Phenomenology*.

It is beyond the scope of this immediate synopsis to give a comprehensive over-view of Hegel's philosophy of mind, a subject I have already attended to with precision (see Mills, 2002a); rather, I provide a terse introduction that is germane to the discussion at hand. Hegel's philosophy of *Geist* is presented in the third division of the *Encyclopaedia*, which is further subdivided into three sections: namely, 'Anthropology', 'Phenomenology', and 'Psychology'. Each subdivision is concerned with explicating a specific feature and function of the mind. Because Hegel's dialectical method is suffused throughout every aspect of his philosophy – the dialectic being the force and substance of spirit – each domain of psychic life may only be properly understood in relation to the whole. For our purposes, how-ever, it becomes important to see how the epigenesis of the mind proceeds from its most primordial unconscious configurations to the higher-order functions of rational self-conscious understanding. In many remarkable ways, Hegel's treatise on mind parallels the psychoanalytic account of psychic development, a topic that will preoccupy us shortly.

Anthropology

As the general object of anthropology, that is, what is common to us all regardless of culture, race or gender, Hegel is first concerned with the universal significance of the soul (*Seele*). Here the role of the unconscious in Hegel's conceptualization of the mind is an integral aspect of his philosophy. In fact, the higher forms of mental life emanate from an unconscious ontology and are the phenomenological development of an original unconscious ground. For Hegel, as too for psycho-analysis, the unconscious is the foundation of the soul, which, in turn, is the foun-dation of consciousness and self-conscious *Geist*. In the 'Anthropology' section of the *Encyclopaedia* Hegel painstakingly delineates how the soul dialectically evolves from an original unconscious unity. Through a series of internally medi-ated dynamics beginning as natural soul (*EG* § 391), spirit 'awakens' as a sentient feeling subject (*EG* § 403), which further becomes actual (*EG* § 411) as the ego of consciousness, the initial subject matter of the *Phenomenology of Spirit*. The unconscious soul undergoes development through its own dialectical divisions, projections and reconstitutions as the mediated process of sublation, entering into opposition with its natural corporeality and elevating its unconscious structure to the form of ego. Thus, ego development is constituted through unconscious process.

It is in his anthropological treatment of the soul that Hegel first refers to the unconscious as a nocturnal abyss (*Abgrund*). The unconscious abyss is integral to spirit's constitution, which remains a central aspect in the normative psychological operations of conscious intelligence or cognition. But the abyss is also responsible for the primal activity behind *all* appearances of spirit, which Hegel affirms is always 'unconsciously busy' (*SL* 36). Thus the unconscious becomes the indispensable psychic foundation of mind. While the unconscious soul is sublated as ego, it nevertheless remains a repository for lost, alienated or conflicted shapes of spirit. Therefore, the soul becomes the locus in both mental health and psychopathology.

Phenomenology

The Greek term *phainomenon* (φαινόμενον), derived from the verb *phainein*, means 'to appear' or 'to show itself'. Although the dialectical activity of the soul may be considered the pre-phenomena of the unconscious mind, the ego of consciousness is that which appears. The 'Phenomenology' section of the *Encyclopaedia* presents Hegel's mature theory of consciousness. For Hegel, consciousness (*Bewußtsein*) is distinct from the soul (*Seele*) and the unconscious (*Unbewußte*), yet it is an outgrowth of the unconscious soul and is hence the soul's appearance as ego (*EG* § 413). As self-certainty, the ego is an immediate being or subject that must confront its otherness, namely, its object (i.e. external reality). Before the ego encounters the sensuous world, the ego's object is the natural soul itself, what the ego was but no longer is in its presently evolved shape. By confronting the natural soul and denying its suffocating restriction to the corporeal, the ego attains its own independence, no longer belonging to the soul but to itself. Because the ego thinks in a form that is now proper to it, its determinations are no longer of the soul but of consciousness.

Hegel states that the goal of spirit as consciousness is to raise its self-certainty to truth, that is, to pure self-consciousness (*EG* § 416), the culmination of absolute reason. Like the soul's progressive dialectical unfolding, this requires spirit to advance through a series of mediated shapes beginning with (1) *consciousness* as such, where sense, perception and understanding have a general external object; then (2) *self-consciousness*, where desire, self-recognition and universal self-consciousness as ethical revelation have the ego as its general object; culminating in (3) *reason* as the unity of consciousness and self-consciousness determined in and for itself – the Concept (*Begriff*) of spirit as pure conceiving or absolute understanding (*EG* § 417).

Like the natural soul's initial apprehension of its immediacy as feeling, Hegel (1807) consistently views the initiation of consciousness as the manifestation of 'the sheer *being* of [a] thing' (*PS* § 91) to a subject that only knows its simple and immediate sense certainty. Consciousness as such is sensuous consciousness of a sensory presentation or impression with spatial and temporal singularity, simply the '*here* and *now*', what Freud would call a 'thing-presentation'. But, as Hegel continues to describe this process: 'Strictly speaking this belongs to intuition' (*EG* § 418). Here we may see the inextricable interrelatedness between consciousness and the psychological operations of cognition and intelligence that preoccupies Hegel's later psychological analysis of the ego. The ego senses that something is external to it by reflecting into itself, thus separating the material from itself and thereby giving it the determination of being.

The initial divisions of the *Phenomenology* may be viewed by contemporary standards as a treatise on the unfolding operations of cognition. Here Hegel sees three primary stages of consciousness: (1) sensuous, (2) perceptive, and (3) understanding, with consciousness itself being the first of three developmental stages of the phenomenological unfolding of spirit resulting in self-consciousness and reason, respectively. In immediate sensuousness – the empty or abstract recognition of being – consciousness then proceeds to grasp the essence of the object, which it accomplishes through perception. The essence becomes the general object of perceptive consciousness, where singularity is referred to universality. There is, in fact, a multiplicity of relations, reflectional-determinations, and range of objects with their many properties that perceptive consciousness apprehends, discerns and brings into acuity (*EG* § 419). Having mediated the immediacy of sense-certainty, sensuous thought-determinations are brought into relation with concrete connections to universals. This constitutes 'knowledge' (*EG* § 420). The linking of singulars to universals is what Hegel calls a 'mixture' that contains their mutual contradictions (*EG* § 421). Because singularity at this juncture is fused with universality, contradictions are superseded in understanding consciousness. Understanding consciousness is the unity of the singular and the universal in which the general object is now raised to the appearance of being for the ego. In the next stage, self-consciousness arises where the ego takes itself as its own object, and the process continues until spirit wins its truth in pure reason.

Hegel's exposition of consciousness is essentially an exposition of the functions of the ego that Freud (1933a), although conceived differently, also finds as the object of science (*SE* 22:58). Both Hegel and Freud were preoccupied with the science of subjectivity and articulating the universal processes that govern mental functioning. It is for these reasons that psychology becomes an essential ingredient in our appreciation of the abyss and why Hegel needed to address the psychological processes of cognition within his *Philosophy of Spirit*.

Psychology

In the 'Psychology' section of the *Encyclopaedia*, Hegel gives greater consideration to the cognitive processes of attention, perception, imagination, fantasy, memory, thought and understanding. For Hegel, psychology is primarily restricted to the domain of intelligence under the direction of reason, but this does not impede the psychological significance of the soul and the phenomenology of consciousness. Intelligence is what Hegel calls a 'spiritual faculty' (*EG* § 445), not as a fixed or ossified agglomeration but, rather, as a malleable and determining process of cognition. Intelligence finds itself as naturally determined, insofar as it cannot will itself not to think, and is concerned with the empty form of finding reason. Cognition is therefore the concrete dialectical activity of mediating and unifying objects with concepts.

Hegel describes the unfolding of cognition as an intelligent process that progresses from (1) intuition (*EG* § 446), or apprehending objects of sense impression, to (2) presentation (*EG* § 451), as perception of images, to (3) thought (*EG* § 465), which is the formal activities of comprehension and reason.

Although Hegel isolates the contingent events of each intellectual manoeuvre, he stresses the point that each operation of intuiting, representing, and so forth is merely a moment of the totality of cognizing itself, which underscores the necessity of rational thought (*EG* § 445). Throughout the various substages of each operation, he shows the mutual relations between contingency and necessity and how one dialectically prepares the path for the other.[8] First, intelligence has an immediate object; second, material is recollected; and third, it is rendered objective.

In Hegel's anthropological, phenomenological and psychological treatment of spirit, the dialectic becomes the underlying dynamic force behind all activities of mind. Hegel cogently shows how the mind undergoes a formal and logical process of development, starting from the most primitive features of unconscious activity that subsequently sublate into higher cognitive organizations. Because the dialectic informs every aspect of mental life, from the normative to the pathological, Hegel underscores the notion that psychic reality is a process of becoming. The primacy of process becomes an essential component of psychodynamic thought. Because the dialectic remains the rudimentary force behind the appearances of mind, Hegel's process philosophy bears a direct relation to psychoanalytic psychology.

Historical origins of the abyss

Hegel himself did not originate the notion of the unconscious abyss, rather he took it over in large measure from Schelling, Boehme and neo-Platonism. Schelling was among the very first philosophers to underscore the importance of the unconscious and the role of irrationality in human experience (Beach, 1994). However, it was two arch-rationalists, Leibniz and Kant, who first paved the way for this development. In his *New Essays on Human Understanding*, Leibniz (1981) propounded a theory of unconscious *petits perceptions* while Kant discussed 'obscure representations' (*dunkele Vorstellungen*) that remain just below the level of conscious awareness in his *Anthropology*. Schelling's revision of Kant's and Fichte's transcendental idealism, as well as his philosophy of identity (*Identitätsphilosophie*) and philosophy of nature (*Naturphilosophie*) led to one of the first systematic conceptualizations of the unconscious.

The concept of the abyss (*Ungrund*), however, derives from the theosophic Christianity of Jacob Boehme who (introduced by Plotinus) radically reconceptualized God as the *ens manifestativum sui*, 'the being whose essence is to reveal itself' (Walsh, 1994, p. 16). Indeed, Boehme's impact on Schelling was considerable. Boehme developed an elementary form of dialectic consisting of positive and negative polarities that emerged out of Godhead's original undifferentiated non-being (*das Nichts*) which unfolded through orderly stages of manifestation toward absolute self-consciousness. The term *Ungrund* was once considered to be equated with the Gnostic 'abyss' due to their implicitly shared similarities,[9] but this has been cogently disputed by Koyré, who interprets Boehme's notion of the abyss as the 'ground without a ground' (Weeks, 1991, pp. 148–149). Furthermore, Boehme's *Ungrund* behaves as a subject who desires: it "seeks", it "longs", it "sees", and it "finds" '. Before there emerges the divine *Ungrund*, there is no source of determination, there is *nothing*; it is merely 'unfathomable' and 'incomprehensible'. 'The *Ungrund* is the uncertainty which precedes the divine will's arousing itself to self-awareness' (Weeks, 1991, p. 147). While Hegel did give testimony to Boehme, he was probably more in debt to Proclus (through Creuzer), Erigena, and most notably Schelling (von der Luft, 1994, pp. 37–39).

Unconscious spirit and the feeling soul

In order to understand Hegel's position on the unconscious modes of subjective spirit (viz. universal psychical processes that condition individual subjectivity), we must focus repeatedly on the dialectical organizations, operations, contents and intrapsychic structures that are developed in the evolutionary process of the unconscious. I will show that Hegel's account of the contents and operations of the mind as *aufgehoben* is also the structural foundation of the unconscious. In this respect, the role of subjectivity in Hegel's philosophy is of particular value in its application to the unconscious mind. Throughout his philosophy, Hegel reinforces the point that a subjective ground is the necessary precondition for every act of cognition to experience something as objective.[10] Although the drive toward the Concept (as authentic reason) progressively seeks objective truth, subjectivity as such is never abandoned for a new truth; it is preserved within its new forms and co-exists with universality. Therefore, at various levels of phenomenology, the subjective components of the dialectic will have greater unconscious influence on the vicissitudes of the self in its ascendance towards the Absolute. For Hegel, the abyss is the ultimate ground from which consciousness emerges, and is pure determinate negation which is present throughout the development of spirit. By virtue of its unconscious ontology, the realm of the abyss is a central principle in the phenomenology of spirit.

Hegel gives most of his attention to the unconscious within the stage of presentation (*Vorstellung*), which belongs to the development of theoretical spirit. He refers to a 'nightlike abyss within which a world of infinitely numerous images and presentations is preserved without being in consciousness' (*EG* § 453). Hegel offers no explanation of the nature of this nocturnal abyss; he says only that it is a necessary presupposition for imagination and for higher forms of intelligence. These more complex forms of the psychological would not be possible without the preservation of presentations and images in the abyss. Prior to this stage in the development of theoretical spirit, Hegel makes no specific reference to the unconscious abyss in the Psychology. But even if it is not explicitly mentioned, the occurrence of the abyss is already prepared; its existence already implicit in the most archaic forms of the individual, that of the feeling soul and the nascent ego of consciousness.

> [S]pirit attains to absolute being-for-self, to the form which is completely adequate to it. Through this alone it rouses itself from the somnolent state in which it finds itself as soul, since in this state difference is still shrouded in the form of lack of difference and hence unconsciousness.
>
> (*EG* § 389, *Zusatz*)

In the *Phenomenology*, Hegel initially defines consciousness as the manifestation of the being of the world to a subject who is not self-conscious or reflectively aware of itself as Self. '[C]onsciousness is "*I*", nothing more, a pure "This"; the singular consciousness knows a pure "This", or the single item' (*PS* § 91). In the *Encyclopaedia* Phenomenology, he says the same thing: 'Initially, consciousness is immediate, and its relation to the general object is therefore the simple unmediated certainty it has of it' (*EG* § 418). The presence of subjective spirit, particularly in its initial unfolding as soul and then as ego, is what I shall refer to as the primal domain of *Unconscious Spirit*. The movement of subjective spirit has its genesis in the unconscious, i.e. spirit originally manifests itself as the unconscious. Without equivocation, the abyss is the birthplace of spirit. Hegel makes this clear:

> Spirit has determined itself into the truth of the simple immediate totality of the soul and of consciousness . . . The beginning of spirit is therefore nothing but its own being, and it therefore relates itself only to its own determinations.
>
> (*EG* § 440)

As the natural soul, the unconscious is spirit's initial being, 'the immediacy of spirit' (*EG* § 412).

For Hegel, the unconscious is merely the immediate determinateness of spirit which manifests itself in two primary modes, namely as soul and then as the ego of consciousness. Initially, spirit remains hidden to itself, an enigma, asleep within the abyss of its own inwardness, and thus the unconscious is its presupposition.[11] As incarnate, the soul is the core totality of the nascent Self as the permeation of spirit, making itself known as consciousness, which is spirit's presence as such. Hegel says, 'As soul, spirit has the form of substantial universality' (*EG* § 414), which then assumes its next shape as consciousness. The soul therefore developmentally comes before consciousness. However, consciousness as ego is spirit's ability to make itself an object or reify itself within its own being. Hegel explains: 'As ego, spirit is essence, but since reality is posited in the sphere of essence as immediate being . . . spirit as consciousness is only the appearance of spirit' (*EG* § 414).

Sensuous consciousness only knows itself as being, a 'singular', an 'existing thing' (*EG* § 418). Hegel refers here to the subjective existence of the Self as a personal, singular 'I', with the character of 'self-identity' (*EG* §§ 414, 415). From this standpoint, spirit in its initial shape as *I* takes its form as 'mine' in the mode of personal identity. Within this context, the unconscious is the subjective ground of the most primitive levels of individuality. This pure or original consciousness, the formal 'I', resides within the realm of the abyss, outside our immediate self-conscious awareness of such activity. The soul becomes the formal paradigm for the ego of consciousness because 'the soul is already *implicitly ego* in so far as it is subjectivity or selfhood' (*EG* § 412, *Zusatz*). Although this immediate form of consciousness is not yet elevated to perceptive or understanding consciousness, it contains the primal content of feelings which is the 'material of consciousness' and 'what the soul is and finds in itself in the anthropological sphere' (*EG* § 418). Hence, within the realm of the subject, unconscious spirit resonates within the soul as feeling and ego. The feeling soul becomes the primary domain of the abyss. Not yet explicit or developed, lacking in articulation and structure, what remains is for it to become explicit in theoretical spirit.

Hegel considers feeling in relation to three different stages in the evolution of subjective spirit. First, feeling belongs to the soul awakening from its self-enclosed natural life to discover within itself the 'content-determinations of its sleeping nature' (*EG* § 446, *Zusatz*). The soul comes to feel the totality of its Self and awakens into consciousness as ego. Second, in consciousness, feeling becomes the material content of consciousness, distinct from the soul and appearing as an independent object. Third, feeling becomes the 'initial form assumed by *spirit as such*', which is the truth and unity of the soul and consciousness (*EG* § 446, *Zusatz*). Before spirit's final transition from feeling to reason, every content of consciousness originally exists and is preserved within the mode of feeling. Thus, for Hegel, the life of feeling is inextricably associated with the domain of the unconscious abyss in all its archaic shapes.

Hegel's account of the feeling soul unfolding dialectically is tantamount to the nascent Self as unconscious spirit unified in the soul and expressed as consciousness. Therefore, the natural soul is the heart of unconscious spirit, intuiting itself as such, and feeling its own being. The unconscious awakening of spirit within its own internal slumbers, and thus the feeling of its totality as its essence in consciousness, unites the soul and spirit in the abyss of their own determinations.

The intelligence of the abyss

Subjective spirit, in its theoretical modes, expresses itself as cognition actively concerned with finding reason within itself (*EG* § 445). As the psychological forms of subjective mind unfold, the unconscious abyss is the primary domain of this activity. Hegel points out that intelligence follows a formal course of development to cognition, beginning with (1) intuition of an immediate object (*EG* § 446); moving to (2) presentation (*EG* § 451) as a withdrawal into the unconscious from the relationship to the singularity of the object and thus relating such object to a universal; leading to (3) thought (*EG* § 465), in which intelligence grasps the concrete universals of thinking and being as objectivity. In the stage of intuition or sensation as immediate cognizing, intelligence begins with the sensation of the immediate object, then alters itself by fixing attention on the object while differentiating itself from it. It then posits the material as external to itself, or as 'self-external', which becomes intuition proper. The second main stage of intelligence as presentation (*Vorstellung*) is concerned with recollection, imagination and memory, while the final stage in the unfolding of intelligence is thought, which has its content in understanding, judgment and reason.

As the dialectical forms of intelligence progress, unconscious spirit posits intuition as its own inwardness, recollects itself within it, becomes present to itself, and thus by passing into itself raises itself to the stage of presentation (*EG* § 450). From the standpoint of presentation (*EG* § 451), the various forms of spirit manifest themselves as 'singularized and mutually independent powers or faculties' (*EG* § 451, *Zusatz*). Within recollection, the unconscious content is 'involuntarily' called forth. The presented content is that of intuition, not only intuited as being, but also recollected and posited as 'mine'. This unconscious content of intuition is what Hegel calls 'image' (*Bild*). In the sphere of imagination, the presented content enters into opposition with the intuited content, in which 'imagination works to gain for itself a content which is peculiar to it' and thus seeks to universalize it. As presentation enters into the stage of memory, the unification of the subjective and the objective constitutes the transition to thought (*EG* § 451, *Zusatz*).

Within its initial recollection, however, the 'image' that becomes the focal point of intelligence is posited as feeling the inwardness of its own space and time (*EG* § 452). This is spirit taking up what has been put forth by intuition and positing it as its own content.

> Intelligence is not, however, only the consciousness and the determinate being, but as such the subject and implicitness of its own determinations; recollected within it, the image is no longer existent, but is preserved unconsciously.
>
> (*EG* § 453)

Here, Hegel points to the Concept of intelligence as the being-for-self, capable of presenting itself to itself as a determined object, and preserving such image within the most remote regions of the abyss. 'In another respect therefore, . . . intelligence [is] this unconscious abyss' (*EG* § 453). Unconscious spirit first becomes aware of its existence as feeling; it feels its very life and senses itself as such united in the most rudimentary forms of its intelligibility. Hegel continues:

> The image is mine, it belongs to me: initially however, this is the full extent of its homogeneity with me, for it is still not *thought*, not raised to the *form* of *rationality*, . . . and being not free but a relationship according to which I am merely the *internality*, while the image is something external to me. Initially, therefore, I still have an imperfect control of the images slumbering within the abyss of my inwardness, for I am unable to recall them *at will*. No one knows what an infinite host of images of the past slumbers within him. Although they certainly awaken by chance on various occasions, one cannot, – as it is said, – call them to mind. They are therefore only *ours* in a *formal* manner.
>
> (*EG* § 453, *Zusatz*)

Hegel's characterization of the unconscious life within the subject points to the activity of the unconscious which becomes unified in consciousness as the 'internality' of the self, and yet is a distinct form of consciousness in which the subject does not control. More precisely, it is consciousness that is a modified form of unconscious structure, whereas the degree, content and context of awareness become the critical factor that distinguishes the two. Hegel acknowledges the activity of the unconscious abyss, as limitless, infinite and inaccessible to the conscious will. This conceptualization is similar to psychoanalytic accounts of the unconscious as timeless, in which drives or impulses (*Triebe*) in the form of wishes as 'image' simultaneously press for expression, yet remain repressed or dissociated within one's 'internality' as the abyss of 'inwardness', unavailable to immediate introspective self-reflection.

When theoretical spirit continues on its journey from intuition to thought, the role of imagination within presentation becomes important for understanding the influence of the abyss. For Hegel, as for Kant, imagination mediates between intuition and thought. Therefore, imagination belongs to spirit. More precisely, imagination has its place almost exclusively within psychological spirit. Within the register of presentation, imagination is an intermediate faculty of spirit, surfacing between recollection and memory. As Hegel notes in recollection, the content of intuition in its new form as image is 'preserved' as 'unconsciousness' (*EG* § 453). Therefore, images sleeping in the depths of the abyss can be called forth, related to an intuition, yet separated from both the abyss and intuition. Thereby, the birth of the image for us becomes the contents of imagination. From this standpoint, imagination determines images, first in reproductive imagination (§ 455), as reproducing images called forth by intuition, second, in associative imagination (§ 456), by elevating images as presentations to the level of universality, and third, in phantasy (§ 457), as a determinant being in the forms of symbols and signs. Hegel ultimately sees imagination through to its end. Following a dialectical course, the image becomes surpassed and integrated into higher shapes of cognition.

Hegel's account of spirit's movement within presentation ultimately ends with spirit discovering and sublating itself within 'phantasy as reason'. Thus, for Hegel, imagination is subordinated to cognition as spirit recovers itself in the image. However, the transition from fantasy to reason poses a problem for spirit. Because imagination mediates between intuition and thought, it is susceptible to the powers of the unconscious. Due to the autonomy of unconscious forces and organizations, it is conceivable that the abyss resists the dialectical sublation of its own becoming. John Sallis (1987) raises the question: 'Does phantasy exceed reason? Or, more generally, is imagination in excess of spirit?' (p. 152). This question leads one to envision imagination as being out of the realm of the dialectic, on the periphery of spirit, not susceptible to its movement, transcending spirit's powers to determine the activity and content of the abyss. This has greater implications for understanding the potential faculties of the abyss, independent from spirit. Is it possible that the nocturnal pit of images is beyond the call of spirit? Is it possible that the unconscious abyss can influence the very course of imagination and resist integration into spirit? And even if the abyss were to become subordinated to spirit, would not the pit bring with it its own material, its nightness that would be absorbed in spirit's universalization? Is not the pit bound to leave its residue? And what would this residue be? Could it perhaps be fragments of inclinations and passions that co-exist with spirit in its transcendence toward reason? Is the host of images drawn from the pit susceptible to the sway of desire that seeks life and fulfilment of its own? To what degree is spirit itself influenced by the psychological?

As unconscious spirit dialectically proceeds from consciousness to self-consciousness, desire (*Begierde*) becomes its new shape as drive (*Trieb*). Hegel states, 'desire still has no further determination than that of a drive, in so far as this drive, without being determined by thought, is directed toward an external object in which it seeks satisfaction' (*EG* § 426, *Zusatz*). For Hegel, as for Nietzsche and Freud, the subjective nature of the unconscious, as unconscious spirit, is indissolubly linked to the body, nature, or instinct. Hegel anticipates Freud when he alludes to the instinctual motivations of the unconscious.

> Feeling subjectivity is the totality of all content and the identity of the soul with its content. Although it is not free, neither is it bound, what is present being merely a limitation of it. What we called genius is instinctive [*instinktartig*], active in an unconscious [*bewußtlose*] manner, in opposition to particular determinations. Other oppositions fall within reflection, within consciousness. What we have before us here is feeling subjectivity, which realizes itself, is active, proceeds forth from simple unity to liveliness. This activity belongs to the determination of the liveliness, and although it awakens opposition within itself, it also preserves itself by sublating it and so endowing itself with a determinate

being, with *self-awareness*. This activity is the expression of drive, of desire, its determination or content being drive, inclination, passion, or whatever form this content is given.

(*EG* § 407, *Zusatz*)

In this passage, Hegel points to the dialectical activity of the unconscious whereby it generates its own oppositions and transcends itself within itself as *sublation*, or what we might not inappropriately call sublimation. Recall that for Hegel, subla-tion (*Aufhebung*) is the driving process behind the elevation of spirit. His dialectic is structurally differentiated in that it performs three distinct yet simultaneous tasks: namely, cancelling, annulling or destroying; retaining or preserving; and surpassing, heightening or transcending. As Errol Harris (1993) reminds us, sub-lation 'does not obliterate when it supercedes, but also retains and transmogrifies' (p. 13). Hegel also suggests that self-awareness is born out of such unconscious dialectical activity – an *unconscious self-consciousness*, thus giving the uncon-scious a primary role in psychic organization and conscious motivation. When Hegel says that the feeling soul 'realizes itself' and has '*self-awareness*', he is saying that implicit spirit within the soul is self-conscious of its Self, hence pos-sessing an unconscious self-consciousness. He further attributes this process to 'intro-reflection' or 'self-reflection' (*Reflexion-in-sich*) that is performed inwardly within the unconscious soul before conscious reflection is achieved (*EG* §§ 412, 414). Furthermore, Hegel states that the nature of unconscious content is itself the activity, as drive or desire. This points to the primacy of psychic (unconscious) determination providing the structural organization and the content of its own determinateness which transcends itself in conscious choice. Hegel has paved the way to understanding more precisely the organization, structural integrity and telic operations of the unconscious.

The dialectical structure of the unconscious

It should be clear by now that unconscious spirit is the structural foundation of the Self, as pure activity always in flux and in a state of psychic turbulence. 'It is just this unrest that is the self' (*PS* § 22). Hegel refers here to the unrest of *Aufhebung*, as dialectical process continuously annulled, preserved and transmuted. As Hegel would contend, the dialectic is both the inner organization and the content of unconscious spirit. It is the dialectic that provides the Self with intrapsychic struc-tures and operations that can never be reduced or localized, only conceptualized as pure activity. This pure activity of the dialectic as Self is constantly evolving and redefining itself through such movement. The unconscious forms of spirit (initially as feeling soul then as ego) are thereby necessarily organized around such dialectical activity of the abyss. These structural operations, however, are not mechanistic, reductionistic, or physical as in the natural science framework often attributed to traditional psychoanalysis. They are mental, telic and transcenden-tal, always reshaping spirit's inner contours and the internalized representational world within the night of the mind. Therefore, as a general structure, the unconscious is *aufgehoben*.

For Hegel, the unconscious is pure *process*, a changing, flexible and purposeful activity of becoming. As the very foundation, structure and organizing principles of the unconscious are informed by the movement of the dialectic, the architecture of the abyss is continually being reshaped and exalted as each dialectical conflict is sublated by passing into a new form, that in turn restructures, reorganizes, and refurbishes the interior contours of the core Self. Therefore, the structural foundations of the self are never static or inert, but always in dialectical movement, which has its origin and source in the unconscious, revamping the framework in which spirit emanates. This self-generating dialectical movement of the unconscious is the evoking, responding, sustaining and transcending matrix that is itself the very internal system of subjective spirit.

The concept of the Self as subject in Hegel is of particular importance in understanding the unconscious nature of spirit. Essentially, the stage-by-stage or architectonic progression of the dialectic is expressed as an epigenetic theory of self-development. Recall that as *aufgehoben*, Hegel's notion of the self encompasses a movement in which the subject is opposed to an object and comes to find itself in the object. During the dialectical movement of spirit, the subject recognizes or discovers itself in the object. This entails the mediation of its becoming other to itself, with the reflection into otherness returning back to itself. The process of the development of the self is, therefore, a process of differentiation and integration. For Hegel, Being is characterized by an undifferentiated matrix which undergoes differentiation in the dialectical process of becoming that in turn integrates into its being that which it differentiated through its projection, reclaiming it and making it part of its internal structure.[12] The outcome of the integration is once again differentiated then reintegrated; unification is always reunification. Therefore, it comes to be what it already is; it is the process of its own becoming.[13]

As the darker side of spirit, the unconscious educates itself as it passes through its various dialectical configurations. Parallel to the path of natural consciousness that ascends toward the Absolute, the unconscious also comes to a unity constituted by the bifurcation and rigid opposition that it generates from within itself. Furthermore, it is precisely through such opposition that the unconscious becomes and brings itself into reunification. Thus, the abyss in its evolution undergoes a violence at its own hands. By entering into opposition with itself, it raises this opposition to a higher unity and thus sublates to a new structure. As each unconscious shape or content is confronted with radical opposition, each shape is made to collapse when its non-absolute form is exposed. Indeed, it is always driving the movement on from one shape to the next. Thus, the character of the unconscious is that of negativity and conflict: it is tempestuous, feral, powerful and dynamic. As such, the unconscious is the source of its own negativity as inversion and destruction pave the way of its progression forward.

There is a necessity in the dialectic that informs the internal structures of the abyss; i.e. there is a certain determination to negation. The operation of such determinant negativity comes about through the collapse of each shape. As the negation of a certain content takes place within the realm of the abyss, it derives a certain content from the negation. Therefore, it links shapes into a necessary progression as each form turns into a new one. However, as each form is surpassed, the experience of its alteration is that of death, its end. But for Hegel, death always leads to rebirth. The dialectic is therefore the oscillation between life and death, never separate from one another. Hegel elucidates this point:

> [W]hat is bound and is actual only in its context with others, should attain an existence of its own and a separate freedom – this is the tremendous power of the negative; it is the energy of thought, of the pure 'I'. Death, if that is what we want to call this non-actuality, is of all things the most dreadful, and to hold fast what is dead requires the greatest strength . . . But the life of Spirit is not the life that shrinks from death and keeps itself untouched by devastation, but rather the life that endures it and maintains itself in it. It wins its truth only when, in utter dismemberment, it finds itself.
>
> (*PS* § 32)

As determinate negativity, the unconscious vanquishes itself as it destroys itself. It kills itself as it gives itself life. As each shape alters, however, one assumes that the most primal region of unconscious spirit, that of the feeling soul, experiences, retains and preserves such destruction. It would follow that the abyss itself undergoes a loss of self, and as feeling soul it enters into despair over its death, a suffering it must endure and preserve, a mourning it perpetually encounters. Indeed, it destroys itself in the service of raising itself, albeit it remembers and feels its suffering. Yet, it is precisely through such negativity that there is progression. Perhaps it needs to hold onto its suffering, its death, in order to advance or take pleasure in its elevation.

From this standpoint, we might say that the unconscious is masochistic; it must suffer in order to gain. Perhaps the double edge of the dialectic (as negativity resulting in higher unity) poses a dilemma even for spirit itself. Does spirit fight within itself such a process, thereby leading spirit to retreat back into the nocturnal pit, to withdraw itself from its suffering and return to the warm blanket of the abyss? Is this dilemma a natural inclination of spirit or is it merely the result of disease, that of madness?

Hegel's theory of psychopathology

Perhaps the implicitness of the abyss has been made most clear in its relation to mental illness. In reference to the role of the unconscious, Hegel's theory of mental illness has received the most attention in the literature. For Hegel, the unconscious plays a central role in the development of insanity (*Wahnsinn*), or more broadly conceived, mental derangement (*Zerstreutheit*). Hegel explains:

[T]he spiritually deranged person himself has a lively feeling of the contradiction between his merely subjective presentation and objectivity. He
is however unable to rid himself of this presentation, and is fully intent
either on actualizing it or demolishing what is actual.

(EG § 408, *Zusatz)*

Hegel explains madness in terms that modern psychiatry and psychology would
label as thought disorder or psychosis: the inability to distinguish between inner
subjective states of psychic conflict and the objective reality of the external world.
In madness, the person attempts to cling to the belief that his or her subjective
presentation is objectively valid despite the evidence against it. Thus, the person
is delusional. Hegel continues:

The Concept of madness just given implies that it need not stem from a
vacant imagination, but that if an individual dwells so continually upon
the *past* that he becomes incapable of adjusting to the *present*, feeling it
to be both repulsive and restraining, it can easily be brought about by a
stroke of great misfortune, by the *derangement* of a person's individual
world, or by a *violent upheaval* which puts the world in general out of
joint.

(EG § 408, *Zusatz)*

Hegel comes remarkably close to Freud's general theory of neurosis as the unconscious fixation of conflicted id impulses, feelings and experiences from the past
that are transferred onto the present. This projected conflict, therefore, ultimately
attenuates ego capacities and precludes one from effectively adapting to one's
objective environment. Hegel's notion of madness hinges on the dialectical tumult
that ensues between desire and reason, emphasizing the struggle to gain mastery
over the mind's experience of pain and suffering. Ironically, insanity is a regressive withdrawal back into the abyss; rational consciousness reverted to the life of
feeling as a therapeutic effort to ameliorate the 'wounds of spirit'.[14]

For Hegel, the phenomenon of mental illness is primarily associated to the
domains of the feeling soul, as the result of irreconcilable oppositions between the
subjective and the objective.[15] In the face of perpetual contradiction and disunity,
unconscious spirit engages in a retrogressive withdrawal to the primordial tranquility of the abyss, and thus projects a sense of unity from within itself. Berthold-
Bond has labelled this phenomenon the 'second face of desire', which constitutes
a regression to an earlier nostalgia, a yearning calling consciousness back to the
most archaic depths of its peacefulness. In madness, the archaic world of the
unconscious draws the mind back to its original shape; subjective spirit is once
again an undifferentiated oneness, as a return to the primitive merger within the
symbiosis of its blissful inwardness. No longer driven by rational consciousness in
its search for unity within the external world, spirit resorts back to its earlier form,
hence projecting its desires within fantasy. Perhaps on the most primitive level,

spirit seeks to go to sleep once again, to return to a tensionless state and recover its lost unity with the Absolute. Therefore, the fundamental striving for unity leading to the movement of withdrawal back into the abyss, is the basic structural dynamic of madness. From the abyss spirit emanates, and from the abyss madness is informed. Thus, the unconscious becomes the playing field in both mental health and psychopathology.

Hegel's anticipation of psychoanalysis

Throughout this chapter, I have been primarily concerned with the ground and scope of unconscious spirit and its manifestations in the subjective mind. Although Hegel primarily gave attention to the abyss in the stage of recollection within the intellectual operations of cognition, by showing how it appears in other parts of his philosophy, we have seen that the unconscious plays a central role in his overall system. Throughout the evolution of spirit, there is (1) unconscious spirit, asleep within its nocturnal world only to awaken from its internal slumbers to discover itself as (2) soul, the 'life of feeling', an *'immediate, unconscious totality'* (*EG* § 440, *Zusatz*), only to then sublate itself as (3) consciousness. As consciousness ascends toward the Absolute, every content of consciousness originally exists and is preserved unconsciously within the mode of feeling. Thus, the life of feeling is primordially associated with the domain of the abyss in all its archaic shapes. In its beginning, spirit originally manifests itself as unconscious process.

As a general structure, the unconscious is *aufgehoben*, continually being annulled, preserved and elevated. The unrest of the dialectic perennially provides and reprovides the intrapsychic structures, operations and contents of the unconscious as it redefines and reconfigures itself through such dynamic movements. As a telic structure, 'intelligence as this unconscious abyss', unconscious spirit is grounded in the subject. Thereby, the subjective ground of the abyss continually informs the dialectic throughout spirit's unfolding; transforming into new shapes in its drive toward unity and Truth, preserving old ones within the domain of the psychological.

Hegel prefigures Freud in many remarkable ways, and in my opinion, provides the first theory of the unconscious in the history of western philosophy *in sufficient detail*. Despite many notable thinkers from traditions spanning from antiquity to German Idealism, Hegel's work stands out as a harbinger of the science of unconscious mentation elaborated by the psychoanalytic movement a century later. With the exception of Schelling's notion of the unconscious will generating itself from the materiality of nature, and whose *System of Transcendental Idealism* rivalled Hegel's *Phenomenology*, as well as von Hartmann's *Philosophy of the Unconscious*, which is both an amalgamation of Hegel's philosophy of Spirit and Schopenhauer's philosophy of Will, no other philosopher prior to Freud's time gave the unconscious pivotal status. And what further differentiates Hegel from Schelling and von Hartmann is that he ascribes psychological functions and properties to the very activity of the unconscious itself as it constructs human experience. It may be argued that Hegel's metaphysics situates the role of the unconscious within the very heart of subjectivity, with a particular emphasis on how cognition is conditioned by unconscious forces, as well as how it saturates objective social life. Here I have only focused on the former, which was the initial locus of psychoanalytic inquiry when Freud introduced his radical new science to a world largely conditioned to think only in terms of human consciousness.

The 'underworld' (*PS* § 474) that Hegel explicates, what he also calls the 'power of the nether world' (*PS* § 460), is largely based on delineating the foundation and breath of a subjective ontology, yet one that is universal to all people. In this respect, his metaphysics defines the objective character of the human situation governed by biological and psychosocial life, and the cultural environs that weigh heavily on human experience. In this way, his project anticipates the cultural contributions of psychoanalysis to understanding individual and social psychology.

Having prepared our discussion on the philosophy of the unconscious prior to the rise of modern science, we may now turn our attention to the philosophical presuppositions and commitments inherent in Freud's unconscious ontology. But before doing so, let us tarry briefly with a conundrum introduced by Hegel's system. At this point I wish to raise the question one last time: To what degree does the unconscious resist being exalted or surpassed by the dialectic? Does the abyss resist being integrated into Spirit? This would imply that the abyss would seemingly appear to have a will and a purpose all of its own. Is the urge for unity as the drive toward the Absolute simultaneously in opposition to a competing urge to withdraw in the face of nostalgia within the abyss of spirit's unconscious beginning? As the soul passes through its various configurations on the ladder toward Truth, does it draw itself back toward the pit of its feeling life? Such tendency toward withdrawal, back toward the pit, 'could perhaps broach a wonder that one could never aspire to surpass' (Sallis, 1987, p. 157). And if the abyss resists the call of spirit, to what degree does the unconscious inform reason yet remain behind the back of consciousness? Or is there simply a duality of purpose that spirit fights in-itself? Does desire have a double edge, that of moving forward and backward, of evolution and devolution, transcendence and descendence? Does spirit struggle between competing inclinations of reason and feeling, sublimation and regression, elevation and withdrawal? Is the duality of desire spirit's nature; does it belong to spirit as such, or is spirit its slave?

Perhaps spirit is merely returning to itself, to the symbiotic abyss of its immediate determinant being. Does spirit merely seek to transform or to go to sleep once again? In this sense, the yearning for unity is a return to unity, always its end. Yet for Hegel, this end is always its beginning, the eternal return of the same. Thus, unconscious spirit remains a 'riddle to itself' (*PS* § 365). Perhaps the greatest conflict occurs when spirit attempts to surpass itself. For spirit resists itself, it resists the movement of its own becoming. Perhaps subjective spirit resists such integration for fear of losing its sense of self in the collective; it fights its own process for fear of the loss of its individuality. From this standpoint, spirit can never rid itself of its desire for the recovery of its lost unity, of the yearning to return to its primitive existence, its original condition. Perhaps the Absolute is merely the archetypal image – the call – of spirit's original unity. Perhaps spirit is even empathic to its own dilemma. I wonder. And with wonder comes wonder, as the abyss redefines itself one more time.

Notes

1 Darrel Christensen (1968) may be credited with giving attention to Hegel's theory of mental derangement; however, Daniel Berthhold-Bond's (1991, 1992, 1994, 1995) impressive body of works may be considered the most comprehensive to date. My contributions, *The Unconscious Abyss: Hegel's Anticipation of Psychoanalysis* (2002a) and *Origins: On the Genesis of Psychic Reality* (2010), offer a revisionist extension of Hegel's project to psychoanalytic thought.

2 See Freud's discussion, *SE* 19:24; 20:97; 22:75–76.

3 Hegel's conception of *Geist* is often interpreted to be a supraordinate spiritual force that animates nature and human experience unified by a cosmic process governed by universal logical operations of pure thought, usually attributed to a Godhead. When I speak of spirit, I am referring to the individual and collective mind that is enacted through human subjectivity and that is both consciously and unconsciously informed, thereby generating the social structures we have come to call culture and civilization. Here spirit or mind should not be confused with a hypostatized entity, panpsychism, or a supernatural animating presence, which is neither necessary nor particularly desirable for psychoanalytic inquiry. In order to obviate potential confusion, here spirit, mind and psyche should be viewed as synonymous constructs.

4 In his *Wissenschaftslehre* (*W* §§ 1–3), Fichte (1794) discerns these three fundamental principles or transcendental acts of the mind.

5 See Immanuel Kant's (1781/1787), *Critique of Pure Reason*, second division: *Transcendental Dialectic*, book II, chs I–II. Kant is particularly interested in exposing logical inconsistencies and contradictions as paralogisms and antinomies of human reason, which are 'wrongfully regarded as a science of pure reason' (*CPR*, A345/B403).

6 For our purposes, we may view the striving for self-consciousness as a process of self-actualization that an individual or collective group (society) can never fully achieve, only approximate through laborious dialectical progression. The striving for the fulfilment of an ideal can never completely be attained in actuality (although perhaps it can in theory) because this would mean that the human spirit would no longer need to surpass itself: the dialectic would be complete and thus would no longer desire and, hence, no longer create. We are always oriented towards higher modes of self-fulfilment, whether in action or fantasy. It is the striving, however, that forms a necessary aspect of any transcendental orientation or philosophy of living, and, like the pursuit of wisdom and contentment, it is a process of becoming.

7 Compare to Freud (1923): 'The ego is first and foremost a bodily ego' (*SE* 19:26).

8 John Burbidge (1981, pp. 7–21) provides a nice overview of this process.

9 There are many different systems of Gnosticism that offer varying accounts on the nature of first principles and the coming into being of God and the universe. However, a cardinal element of Gnostic thought is a radical dualism that governs the relation between God and the world. Gnostics conceive of God as the 'Alien' or the 'first' 'Life'. This appears in a standard introduction of Mandaean compositions: 'In the name of the great first alien Life from the worlds of light, the sublime that stands above all', and is reflected throughout gnostic literature such as Marcion's concept of the 'alien God', 'the Other', 'the Nameless', 'the Hidden', 'the Unknown', and the 'unknown Father'. Belonging to another (nether) world, the divine 'alien' is 'strange' and 'unfamiliar', hence 'incomprehensible'. Estranged from the comprehensible world, the 'great first Life' is conceived

of as possessing both positive and negative attributes of superiority and suffering, perfection and tragedy, transcendence and alienation from its original being. Further competing dialectical forces are attributed to the godhead, which are understood differently by various Gnostic myths and theories on cosmology, cosmogony and anthropology. The second century Gnostic, Basilides, is said to have postulated a primal 'non-existent god', which was later taken up by Valentinus who claimed that:

> there is in invisible and ineffable heights a pre-existent perfect aeon [i.e. a supernatural being], whom they also call Pre-beginning, Forefather and Primal Ground (Bythos), that he is inconceivable and invisible, eternal and uncreated (or: begotten) and that he existed in great peace and stillness in unending spaces (aeons).
>
> (Irenaeus, *Adversus Haereses*, 11)

Due to the indescribable nature of the 'divine Absolute', the Valentinians were content with using a few alchemical symbols as 'Abyss' or 'Silence' to represent the ineffable (See Jonas, 1958, pp. 42, 49–50, 199; Rudolph, 1977, p. 62; Irenaeus of Lyons, 1857/1965).

10 Christensen (1968) discusses in depth the role and function of subjectivity in Hegel's philosophy.

11 Hegel discusses this in the Introduction (*Hegel's Philosophy of Nature*, vol. 2) to the *Encyclopaedia*.

12 This dialectical process has become known within psychoanalysis as projective identification. Cf. Jerome Levin (1992), who also discusses this point.

13 In the *Phenomenology*, Hegel tells us: 'As Subject . . . the True . . . is the process of its own becoming, the circle that presupposes its end as its goal, having its end also as its beginning; and only by being worked out to its end, is it actual' (*PS* § 18). Later he says, 'The realized purpose, or the existent actuality, is movement and unfolded becoming . . . ; the self is like that immediacy and simplicity of the beginning because it is the result, that which has returned into itself' (*PS* § 22). In the *Science of Logic*, Hegel further extends the development of the Self to that of the Concept: 'The Concept, when it has developed into a *concrete existence* that is itself free, is none other than the *I* or pure self-consciousness' (*SL*, p. 583). For Hegel, the Self and the Concept are pure becoming: 'The Idea is essentially *process*' (*EL* § 215).

14 Berthold-Bond (1991) points out how Hegel's notion of insanity is spirit's self-attempt at healing itself via regression and withdrawal. This notion runs parallel to Freud's theory of repetition compulsion as an expression of the death drive. For an extended discussion on the role of psychopathology in Hegel's system, refer to my chapter on 'Abnormal Spirit' in *The Unconscious Abyss* (Mills, 2002a).

15 Darrel Christensen (1968) interprets Hegel's central theory of mental derangement as centring on the dialectical opposition between the feeling soul and the physical soul.

2

FREUD'S UNCONSCIOUS ONTOLOGY

Freud never actually used the words 'ego' and 'id' in his German texts; these are English translations into Latin, taken from one of his most famous works, *Das Ich und das Es*. When Freud spoke of the *Ich*, he was referring to the personal pronoun 'I' – as in 'I myself' – a construct that underwent many significant theoretical transformations throughout his lifetime. By the time Freud (1923) advanced his mature model of the psyche, concluding that even a portion of the 'I' was also unconscious, he needed to delimit a region of the mind that remained purely concealed from consciousness. This he designated by the impersonal pronoun *es*, which he used as a noun – the 'It' – a term introduced by Groddeck, originally appropriated from Nietzsche. The translation 'ego' displaces the deep emotional significance tied to personal identity that Freud deliberately tried to convey, while the term 'id' lacks the customary sense of unfamiliarity associated with otherness, thus rendering these concepts antiseptic, clinical and devoid of all personal associations. The 'I' and the 'It' express more precisely the type of antithesis Freud wanted to emphasize between the familiar and the strange, hence the dialectic of the life within.

When we refer to ourselves as 'I', we convey a meaning that is deeply personal, subjective and known, while references to an 'It' convey distance, separateness, objectification and abstraction. The I is familiar while the It is foreign and unknown, hence an alien presence. Because Freud wanted to preserve the individual intimacy associated with a personal sense of self, the I was to stand in firm opposition to the It, which was purely estranged from conscious awareness. But the distinction between the I and the It is not altogether unambiguous, and, as I argue, not theoretically resolved by Freud himself. In fact, even today, psychoanalysis, in all its rich theoretical variations, has not rectified this issue. While Freud (see *SE* 19:24–25, 38; *SE* 20:97; *SE* 22:76–77; *SE* 23:145) eventually conceded that the I developed out of the It, he did not explain with any detail how this activity was accomplished; he merely declared that it just happened.

Conceptualizing the psyche

When Freud refers to the mind, he is referring to the Greek notion *psyche* (ψυχή), which corresponds to the German notion *Seele*. In fact, Freud does not speak of the 'mental apparatus' at all but, rather, of the 'organization of the soul', which

40

he specifically equates with the psyche. Freud (1905b) adopted this usage as early as 1905, when he emphatically stated: '"Psyche" is a Greek word and its German translation is "soul." Psychical treatment hence means "treatment of the soul" [*Seelenbehandlung*]' (*SE* 7:283). Furthermore, Freud equates psychoanalysis with the science of the life of the soul (*wer die Wissenschaft vom Seelenleben liebt*) (*SE* 22:6), which stands in stark contrast to the biological connotations associated with the English word 'mind' (see also Bettelheim 1982, 71–75).

Freud was well read in ancient philosophy, and Plato's notion of the soul, as well as his depiction of Eros, left a lasting impression on his conceptualization of the psyche. Before we proceed, however, it is important to distinguish between what we mean by psyche, self, I or ego, and the It. Psychoanalysis, like other professions, has the propensity of using highly technical jargon to capture the complexities of human mental functioning. This is patently justified, but it poses a problem in conceptual discourse and mutual understanding, especially when concepts remain murky or are presumed to have universal definitions when, in fact, they mean many different things to different theorists and within different philosophic disciplines. So we may avoid equivocation of our terms, let us begin with a conceptual definition of the I.

The I, or ego, has a special significance for Freud, which is associated with personal identity, self-reference, conscious thought, perception, mobility, reality testing, and the higher executive functions of reason and intelligence. *Das Ich* is not a common German expression used in everyday conversation: it is used only by professionals in a quasi-scientific context.[1] Nor are references to the self (*Selbst*) or the subject (*Subjekt*) common parlance. In fact, to refer to oneself as *mein Ich* or *mein Selbst* would be viewed as being exceedingly narcissistic. The term 'ego' also carries negative connotations of inflated self-importance and self-love (as reflected in the words 'egotistical', 'egoistic', and 'egocentric'); hence the terms 'I' and 'ego' have a shared meaning in both German and English. Since the word 'ego' has become immortalized in psychoanalytic literature as well as in popular culture, for customary purposes within this context I refer to the 'I' and the 'ego' interchangeably.

Freud realized that he could not adequately account for the I as being solely conscious; therefore, he introduced a division between conscious and unconscious ego domains and their respective operations. What Freud was mainly concerned about in making this division was to explain how certain ego properties, qualities and tension states affected the nature of wish, defence, drive discharge and self-preservation, and how the I stood in relation to an alien force and presence compartmentalized from the ego itself. The ego became a pivotal concept for Freud because it was the locus of agency, intention and choice (both consciously and unconsciously realized). However, it was an agency that existed alongside competing agencies in the mind. This theoretical move on Freud's part is not without conceptual drawbacks and has led many critics to question the plausibility of competing mental entities. Although Freud used the terms 'provinces', 'domains' and 'realms' to characterize such psychic activity, he in no way meant to evoke the substance ontology characteristic of ancient metaphysics, which is in vogue with some forms of materialism today. Freud explicitly abandoned his earlier neu-rophysiological visions of the mind represented in his *Project for a Scientific Psy-chology* (1895), and, by the time of *The Interpretation of Dreams* (1900), adopted a corpus of the soul that admonished reductionism (see *SE* 5:536; *SE* 15:21). Characterizing Freud's theory of agency in terms of entity or substance ontology further misrepresents his views on the active processes that constitute the psy-che. Freud's purported agencies are active, purposeful, malleable processes – not static, fixed, immobile structures. While Freud (1900, 1923, 1933a) prefers spatial metaphors in his description of these forces, he is quick to remind us they are only heuristic devices: the question of localization becomes a meaningless proposition when, in actuality, we are discussing temporal spacings of mental processes.

Freud's use of the term 'I' imports ambiguity when we compare it to a psycho-analytic conception of the self. In some of Freud's (1914b) intervening works on narcissism, his concept of the ego corresponds to his concept of the self. And, in *Civilization and Its Discontents* (1930), he specifically equates *das Ich* with *das Selbst* (*SE* 21:65). This implies that the self would not contain other portions of the psyche, such as the drives and the region of the repressed. This definition also situates the self in relation to otherness and is thus no different from our reference to the ego, with its conscious and unconscious counterparts. In German, however, the 'self' encompasses the entire human being. But, on a very earthly plain, it represents the core from which the ego acts and relates mostly to the conscious aspects of personal identity. Although a strong case can be made for the Self as a supraordinate (see Meissner 2000) encompassing principle – what Freud calls the Soul (*Seele*) – I believe Freud is justified in conceptualizing the I, ego and self as synonymous constructs. The self stands in relation to its opposite (namely, the Other) as subject stands to object and, hence, evokes a firm point of difference. This is precisely why Freud insisted on the dialectical presence of otherness: the I is *not* the It.

For Freud, the It is *alienus* – both alienated mind and that which is alienat-ing. We know it as conflict and chaos under the pressure, whims and persecutory impulses of the drives, our animal nature. They emanate from within us but are neither consciously willed nor desired. The It does not know and does not say no – *It* knows no negation (*SE* 19:239; *SE* 22:74). Under the force of foreign excita-tions clamouring for discharge, unrest and tumult are *das Es*'s very nature. Yet, by necessity, such chaos is combated by degrees of order emanating from the ego. Freud's introduction of the It preserves that realm of inner reality that we may never directly know in itself. Here Freud insists on the Kantian *Ding an sich*, the Fichtean *Anstoss* – an impenetrable limit, obstacle, or impasse. The mind becomes demarcated by a rigid 'check' that introduces irreconcilable division and contra-diction: in other words, the dialectic.

We may never have direct access to the It, only to the way in which it appears. We know the It through its endless derivatives, such as dreams, fantasies, slips and symptoms, as well as through that which torments us, through that which we wish would remain dead and buried, forever banished to the pit – disowned, renounced and, hence, repressed. But things that are misplaced or forgotten have a way of turning up unexpectedly. With every covering over, with every conceal-ment, there is simultaneously a de-covering, a resurfacing of the old, a return of the dead. Freud crowned the It the king of the underworld – Hades – while the I tra-versed the domains of its earthly surface down into the bowels of its nether regions.

Freud's final paradigm of the mind rests on a basic logic of modification. The I dif-ferentiates itself and develops out of the It; and later, the I modifies itself again and evolves into a critical moral agency, what Freud calls the *Über-Ich*, or that aspect of the I that stands over against itself and holds itself up to a higher authority. Here the I undergoes another doubling function, in fact, a doubling of the doubling – this time turned onto itself. What is familiarly known as the 'superego' is nothing other than a split off portion of the I that stands in relation to a particular form of identifi-cation: namely, a set of values and prohibitions it internalized from attachment fig-ures, familial relations, and cultural experience, ideals and principles the self strives to attain. Freud's logic of modification (the explanatory limits of which he modestly concedes [*SE* 22:77; *SE* 23:145]), however, goes unexplained.

While Freud makes the superego (over-I, or above-I) into a critical agency that besieges the I and defiles the It, the superego is merely an extension of the ego, both the self in its exaltation as an identification and pining for its ideal form as well as the judgment, fury and condemnation that informs our sense of conscience, guilt, shame and moral reproach. The ego and superego are therefore the same agency divided yet internally conjoined. Freud spoke pre-maturely in making the superego a third agency of the psyche, when, properly speaking, it is not: it merely *appears* as an independent agent when, ontologi-cally, the ego and the superego are the same. The ego is *supra* in relation to itself – what it wants to be, hence what it strives to become. And when the ego does not live up to itself – up to its own ideals – it debases itself with as much wrath and force as is brewing in the tempestuous cauldron of the It. It is no coincidence that the It and the superego share the same fist of fury. This is because both are fuelled (with stipulations) by the drives, a point to which I return shortly. But for now it is important to emphasize that the psyche is a divided self, with each division and modification remaining interdependent and ontologically bound.

In the end, Freud gives us a vision of the mind as composed of three onti-cally interrelated forces with varying qualitative degrees of organization and zest, ranging from the most primitive, unmodulated evolutionary impulses to the most refined aspects of intelligence and ethical self-consciousness, all brought together under the rubric of soul. Bettelheim (1982, p. 77) tells us that nowhere in his texts does Freud actually provide us with a direct definition of the soul, although we may infer that he intended for it to stand as an overarching concept that enveloped the three agencies of mental life. We do know, however, that Freud had no inten-tion of implying that the soul is immortal or that it carries any religious connota-tions whatsoever. Freud (1927b, 1933a) was a voluble atheist, thus his use of the term is meant to reflect our shared collective humanity.

Freud's tripartite division of the soul returns us to the Greek vision of the psyche, with one exceptional difference: the soul is largely unconscious. As the seat of the passions (*eros*), reason (*nous*), and moral judgment (*ethos*), the psyche becomes a dynamic organization of competing dialectical forces. Because the notion of consciousness is a modern, not an ancient, concept, Freud is able to enrich the Platonic view by showing that irrationality and emotional forces driven by unconscious processes constantly plague the intellectual and ethical strivings of the ego. Therefore, the logocentrism that is often attributed to Freud must be viewed within the context of the pervasive tenacity of irrational pressures, although there is always a logic to the interior. Left undefined by Freud, we may nevertheless say that the psyche is the composition of competing dialectical processes that inform and sustain the division of the I from the It along with its multifarious derivatives. The psyche is pure process and experiential flow composed of a multiplicity of dialectical organizations – each with varying degrees of opposition, complexity and strands of unification – which form a temporal continuity enduring in embodied space. Although the psyche consists of unifying activity, it itself is not a static unity but, rather, a motional–experiential process of becoming spatio-temporally realized as mediated immediacy. This leads us to a process account of the psyche, or, for our purposes, the Self, as a supraordinate complex whole, including both conscious and unconscious parallel activities.

The dialectics of unconscious experience

Within the history of the phenomenological tradition, the question and meaning of 'experience' is exclusively situated within the realm of consciousness. With the exception of Hegel, Eduard von Hartmann, and Whitehead's process metaphysics, there has been no purported philosophy that attempts to account for the phenomenology of experience outside of conscious states. Here I wish to increasingly draw our attention to the topography of unconscious process, which makes conscious experience possible. Following our dialectical account of the coming into being of the psyche, experience is first constituted on the unconscious level of psychic modification as a process of becoming. Because process is pure activity, unrest, or event, a lesson we have learned from Hegel, by definition it constitutes the ontological movements that define the dialectic; thus, the dialectic itself constitutes the metaphysics of experience.

Freud is a dialectician of the mind: in his final paradigm he envisioned the psyche as an active composition of multifarious, bipolar forces that stand in antithetical relation to one another and are therefore mutually implicative. The I and the It, the dual classification of drives, primary versus secondary process mentation, the pleasure principle versus the reality principle, love and hate, the individual within society – these are but a few of the oppositional processes that inform his dialectical system. However, Freud never clarified his logic of the dialectic; instead, he relied on introspection and self-analysis, clinical observation, and technical judgment based on careful consideration of the data at hand, which, over time, led to radical revisions of his many core theoretical postulates. One of Freud's most modest attributes was his ability to change his mind about previous speculations when new evidence presented itself, thus showing the disciplined persistence of the refined scientific attitude he had revered as *Logos* (*SE* 20:54).

It is not altogether clear how Freud's dialectic is philosophically constituted, a topic about which he said nothing; however, we may draw certain reasonable assumptions. While some dialectical forces seek unification, resolution and synthetic integration, others do not. For example, consciousness and unconsciousness, like the I and the It, are firm oppositions, yet their distinctions become blurred in times of sleep, day-dreaming, and fantasy formation. Even when we are unconscious, such as when asleep, the mind generates impressions and representations from the tableau of images once experienced in conscious sensation and laid down in the deep reservoir of memory within the unconscious configurations of the mind. This suggests that consciousness is on a continuum of presence and absence, disclosure and concealment, with each respective appearance being merely one side or instantiation of its dual nature, a duality highlighted and punctuated by its phenomenal valences and qualities, yet nevertheless ontologically conjoined. Consciousness and unconsciousness could not be ontologically distinct due to the simple fact that each context of being overlaps and participates in the other. If they did not, such duality could not be intelligibly conceived unless each counterpart were to be viewed as having a separate essence. However, if this were the case, neither could participate in the realm of the other, nor could they have mutual causal influence (as they are purported to have) for the simple reason that that which has a distinct ontology or being would, by definition, have a different essence. Just as Aristotle's criticism of Plato's forms still stands as a cogent refutation of ontological dualism based on the incompatibility of different essences, so must we extend this assessment to the split domains of consciousness and unconsciousness. Conscious and unconscious life must have the same ontology, hence the same essence, by virtue of the fact that each informs the reality of the other: their respective differences point to their modified forms.

In order for an essence to be what it is – without which it could not exist – it must stand in relation to what it is not. Freud maintains this division of consciousness and unconsciousness from: (1) an experiential or phenomenological standpoint (that which qualitatively appears); (2) from an epistemological standpoint (that which is known); and (3) as a conceptual, heuristic scheme (that which is conceived). However, despite his dual classification of drives, he does not maintain such duality from an ontological framework: consciousness arises *in* the ego, itself the outgrowth of an unconscious It. I speak more of this later, but suffice it to say that Freud's dialectic permits both integration and impasse, synthesis and disunity, universality and particularity, hence contradiction and paradox. But, as Freud says, the It knows nothing. Above all, it does not know the law of contradiction: 'Contrary impulses exist side by side, without cancelling each other out or diminishing each other: at most they may converge to form compromises' (*SE* 22:73). Mental processes could 'converge' and transmute their original forms only on the condition that they participate in the same essence; that is, in an original ontological ground that makes the conversion of form possible.

Another example of the blurred distinctions of duality and limit in Freud's system may be witnessed in the dialectic of repression (Freud 1915b). That which is denied conscious access, negated and banished to the pit is not totally annulled and, hence, not completely opposed; rather, it is preserved where it festers and seeks discharge through another form. Thus, opposition remains contextual, yet always has the potential of being breached.

Although we may observe a boundary of firm antitheses in Freud's model, there is also a synthetic function to the ego that seeks to mediate, resolve and channel competing desires and conflicts through intentional strategies that find their way into overt behaviour and conscious phenomena. But there is also a regressive function to ego that is potentially mobilized given the particular contingencies that govern psychic economy. On the other hand, the process of sublimation has a unifying, transcending character that combats regression, despite the fact that both can be operative on parallel realms of development. This leaves Freud somewhere between what Kant referred to as the antinomies of reason or the paralogisms of the self, which correspond to irreconcilable contradictions within the mind that meet with no resolve, and the Hegelian notion of *Aufhebung* – a progressive dialectical process that cancels, surpasses and simultaneously preserves opposition within an elevating, unifying procreative self-structure. Despite Freud's lack of clarification surrounding his dialectical logic, we can nevertheless say that his model is compatible with a process account of unconscious experience that is dialectically organized and mediated by oppositional contingent forces exerting equiprimordial pressures that are contextually realized in time.

A common interpretation of Freud's dialectic is to conclude that there are oppositional forces that are never resolved, hence never cancelled, surpassed or transcended. Instead, it is thought that a multiplicity of opposing processes and contents – say, impulses, wishes, fantasies and their counterparts – are preserved in deadlocks, thus maintaining the psychic tension that characterizes the psyche. And there is justification for this argument: Freud himself places a great deal of emphasis on dualism. But this dualism, as I have argued elsewhere (Mills, 2002a, pp. 128–129), is the way in which psychic processes appear or unfold phenomenologically, even if such appearances are movements or modifications within unconscious experience as the transmutation of organizational processes that fuel and sustain psychic structure. Freud is a developmental monistic ontologist, and, in this respect, his dialectic is comparable to (albeit not convergent with) Hegel's. As I point out, Freud's mature theory involves a series of modifications and transmogrifications that are derived from the most primitive unconscious activities to the most exalted self-conscious deliberations; hence, psychic organization is a developmental achievement. In the mind, polarity seeks expression, discharge and resolve. If it does not attain some modicum of compromise, hence negotiated expression, then it can lapse into impasse and, therefore, into a stalemate that can lead to pathology, regression, or fixation at more primitive stages of organization.

This is why dream formation, slips of the tongue or pen, significant forgetting, bungled actions, and symptom manifestation are attempts at dialectical syntheses,[2] just as rational discourse and scientific explorations strive for higher (synthetic) levels of comprehension.[3] But these processes are enacted with varying degrees of success and elevation. For example, it can be argued that a repetition compulsion is a failed attempt at achieving a higher stage of transcendence or sublation, which is aimed at mastery, unification and wholeness, while sublimation is a more successful and cultivated expression of primordial conflict (e.g. through art, culture, religion and social-ethical reform). The mind can never remain 'deadlocked' without falling into chaos and despair, and this is why Freud wants to differentiate the abnormal from more adjusted states of mind.

The mind is dialectical, hence relational; that is, it stands in relation (in both temporal continuity and disjunction) to that which is other than its current form or experience. It is important to note that, regardless of the form of difference we wish to theoretically or experientially highlight, all dialectical organizations of the psyche are simultaneously operative from the vantage point of their own unique constitutions and contextualized perspectives. Therefore, the perspectivism of each inhabited domain of lived (yet at times unformulated) unconscious experience is not to negate the force and presence of competing intentional faculties within the mind.

Freud frowned on metaphysics, yet his theory of mind is a metaphysical treatise replete with quandaries. Although Freud stated that the I develops out of the It and that consciousness arises in the ego, he did not proffer an adequate explanation of how this activity occurs. In fact, there are many problems with the relations between ego activity and the drives, the question of mediation by the drives, the distinctness of the I and the It, and whether they can be distinguished at all (and, if they can be distinguished, this is only in a phenomenological sense; in other words, they do not have separate essences but only different appearances). Freud held that psychic origin commenced in that broad category of the mind labelled *das Es*, what he earlier stipulated as falling under the rubric of the system *Ucs*. Now that we have prepared the context for a process account of the mind, it is time for us to give voice to the logic of modification Freud anticipated but left unexplained. Here we must examine the psyche's most elemental pulse from its natural immediacy, what Freud reified as the indubitable primacy of the drives or pulsions.

Understanding *Trieb*

Freud's (1915a) pivotal work, *Triebe und Triebschicksale*, continues to be a source of misunderstanding among English-speaking audiences almost a century after it appeared in print. Customarily translated as 'Instincts and Their Vicissitudes', this is not only a mistranslation but it also inaccurately implies a set of propositions that Freud neither intended to convey nor espoused – namely, that the human psyche, which Freud referred to as the soul (*Seele*), was composed of behaviourally hard-wired, physiologically determined instincts that formed the edifice for human motivation and action. *Instinkt* was a word Freud rarely used in the context of the human subject; rather, he reserved it for animal species, loathing it for its simple equation to material reduction. This is precisely why he deliberately chose the word *Trieb* – more appropriately translated as drive, pulsion,[4] impulse, or urge – to characterize human motivation. Likewise, *Schicksale*, rendered as 'vicissitudes', is equally misleading because it implies a passionless, staid mechanism of change rather than the dynamic notion of mutability that belongs to the destiny of life experience. This is what Freud had in mind when he envisioned the psyche as a temporal flux of dynamic events that arise from the most archaic fabric of our corporeal nature, which transforms over time through internal mediations we customarily refer to as 'defence mechanisms', itself another unfortunate and misleading term. 'Drives and their Fate' comes much closer to capturing the implied meaning behind the transmogrification of inner forces, a process that extends to the most unrefined and immediate expression or derivative of a drive to the most sublimated aspects of human deed and desire.

George Frank (2003, p. 691) offers another recent challenge to Freud's thesis on 'drives', claiming, like others before him, that we ought to do away with the term altogether, only to replace it with a 'new paradigm' of 'needs, affects, beliefs, etc.'. This seems to be a standard view within contemporary psychoanalysis, yet it does not do justice to the abstruse concept of *Trieb*, which, in my estimate, gets watered down to a theory of consciousness. Not only does Freud's thesis on the nature, activities and transmutations of the *Triebe* answer to the theoretical conundrum of human motivation that still besets psychoanalysis today, but I further show that Freud's concept of drive does not at all contradict competing contemporary models favouring beliefs, needs, wishes and intentionality. On the contrary, he explains how those processes are made possible to begin with.

Freud's technical use of *Trieb* is distinguished from the ordinary usage, which describes an urge, such as a whim or a caprice. For Freud, *Trieb* is the *driving force* behind the mind compelled and fuelled by unconscious desire. While Freud certainly says that the source (*Quelle*) of a drive is biologically informed (hence emanating from constitutionally based somatic tension), this is preceded by his emphasis that the 'essence' (*Wesen*) of a drive is its pressure (*Drang*), namely, internal experiential activity under the press of certain events – events that make themselves felt or known as an urge, wish, desire, or need. It is important to qualify that the source is *not* the motive, as Frank (misinterpreting Freud) implies, only that it is internally derived: motives, on the other hand, are complex phenomena subject to many intervening and emergent interactive effects both internally mediated and externally influenced: 'Although drives are wholly determined by their origin in a somatic source, in the life of the soul [*Seelenleben*] we know them only by their aims' (*SE* 14:123). Note that Freud says a drive is determined by its 'origin' (*Herkunft*), not that all motives are biologically based. Quite simply, the reason Freud logically situates the source of a drive within our biologically determined facticity is that we are embodied beings. We are thrown into a body *a priori*, and hence all internal activity must *originally* arise from within our corpo-reality mediated by internal dynamics. Here Freud is merely asserting an empiri-cal fact grounded in a natural science framework. Those analysts like Mitchell (1988), who wish to abnegate the archaic primacy of the body, are simply mis-guided. As a consequence, many advocates of the American middle group uncriti-cally and naïvely devalue the importance of embodiment in favour of relational motives; however, they do so based on unsophisticated dichotomies that utterly fail to acknowledge the indubitable certainty that relationality is predicated on our embodiment (e.g. Pizer 2006).[5] What is utterly ignored within these circles is the fact that Freud was the first one to pave a theory of object relations and ego psychology that was interpersonally based on the relational motives of the drives. I will explain, but first let us further prepare our discussion.

Freud further analysed the elements of a drive by examining its aim and its object. The aim (*Ziel*) of a drive is to seek satisfaction, hence pleasure, which is achieved by terminating a state of stimulation. This is the *telos* of a drive, its pur-pose. But unlike the mechanical operations of fixed, predetermined tropisms that are genetically hard-wired behavioural patterns belonging to some animals and lower organisms, human drives are determinative. That is, they are endowed with a degree of freedom manipulated by the agency of the ego, an ego that operates on manifold levels of conscious and unconscious activity. Freud specifically tells us that the aim of a drive may take 'different paths' with multiple instantiations, may be inhibited or deflected (perhaps in the service of an ultimate aim), or it can achieve 'intermediate' endeavours, work in tandem with competing goals, and be combined, coalesce, or merge into a confluence all at once, thus being operative on different levels of pressure and meaning (*SE* 14:122). Of course an aim *needs* an object in order to achieve satisfaction, and this is why Freud says an object (*Objekt*) is the 'most variable' aspect to a drive, the avenue through which a drive is able to procure fulfilment. Furthermore, an object is 'assigned', hence it is not 'originally connected' to a drive. In fact, an object can be anything, whether in actuality or in fantasy, and can be both extraneous or internal (e.g. the 'subject's own body' [*des eigenen Körpers*]) (*SE* 14:122). Notice how Freud uses the lan-guage of subjectivity when describing a drive and, specifically, the ego's mediat-ing activity of satisfying its aim. And note that the overarching preponderance of objects are mostly people and the functions they serve. Drives desire others, hence relatedness.[6] Here Freud unequivocally accounts for how interpersonal phenom-ena arise based on the most primordial activities of unconscious desire. Thus, not only does Freud account for a relational theory embedded within the process of drive activity itself, but he also shows the logical necessity and developmental progression from intrapsychic to intersubjective life.

Taken as a whole, drives are pure experiential activity. They are not fixed or static behavioural tropisms (such as instincts); rather, they are dynamic patterns of events that are malleable and flexible instantiations of unconscious occasions. The fate or destiny of a drive is what becomes of its activities, from beginning to end. This is why Freud concludes that *die Triebschicksale* are different 'methods of defence' or resistance (*als Arten der Abwehr*) against a drive and that, due to the competing overdetermined motive forces at work in the psyche, prevent it from satisfying its original unmodified aim (*SE* 14:127). What follows is that a drive must divide or split itself and take itself as its own object.

Freud's careful inspection of the activities and attributes of a drive in his 1915 paper are the result of his changing theoretical system. At this time, Freud was working from the premise that drives derive from a libidinous spring, from a *Lust*-principle. Up until then, *Trieb* was used to describe a number of different activities that arose in consciousness and were applied to intentional self-states belonging to the ego, which he called *die Ich-Triebe*, such as wishes, beliefs, actions, propositions, and so forth. Frank (2003, p. 692) is content to view a drive and a wish as synonymous, but this is inaccurate. A wish, belief, or need is a derivative and transformation of a drive, what is typically considered a conscious manifestation from contemporary perspectives. Of course, Freud wanted to account for the presence and ubiquity of unconscious fantasy, which takes the form of determinate self-states (such as beliefs, needs and propositional attitudes) but only on a pre-reflective level of self-expression or self-certainty that is somatically and affectively realized. While Freud (1912) emphasized the notion that 'every psychical act begins as an unconscious one' (*SE* 12:264), he also showed that, through the transformation of the drives, conscious and self-conscious (hence reflexive) cognition produces various needs, beliefs, and so forth, which are the modification of unconscious structure. Therefore, Freud's 1915 thesis on the nature of a drive is a pivotal step in his move toward his mature theory, in which he concludes that mind is an architectonic, epigenetic achievement that evolves from the most rudimentary expression of the dialectic of life and death – hence from the libidinal activity of Eros and the destructive will of *der Todestrieb* – organized within an unconscious It as alien and alienated desire, executed by the agency of the ego, and sublimated through reason, aesthetics and moral judgment inherent in self-reflective social life. Here we may argue that human subjectivity is predicated on agentic determinacy expressed through the epigenesis of unconscious process as the maturation and actualization of freedom. But before mind can be successful in actualizing its freedom, it must first confront death.

The ontology of death

What could be more banal than death, than the inevitable, something predictable, utterly certain? It is banal by virtue of the fact that it is unimaginatively routine – eternal. Death cannot be waived or amended, what Heidegger (1927) avows 'stands before us – something impending' (*BT* § 250), something imminent – our thrownness – to be postponed, even denied. For Freud, death is much more than that which stands before us; rather, it resides within us, an impulsion toward annihilation. But before the will to murder, there exists an insidious self-implosion, namely, suicidal desire. Here the banality of death is not just something that happens to us, it *is* us – our inner being, only to be experienced in novel fashions, repetitiously, circuitously, ad nauseam.

Death-work for Freud (1933a) was ultimately in the service of restoring or reinstating a previous state of undifferentiated internal being, a drive 'which sought to do away with life once more and to re-establish [an] inorganic state' (*SE* 22:107). Freud did not argue that death was the only aim of life, only that it maintained a dialectical tension in juxtaposition to a life principle under the ancient command of Eros, yet the two forces of mind remained ontologically inseparable.

The force of the negative is so prevalent in psychoanalytic practice that it is perplexing why the death drive would remain a questionable tenet among psychoanalysts today.[7] From a phenomenological standpoint, it is impossible to negate the force and salience of the negative. The world evening news is about nothing but death, destruction, chaos, conflict, tragedy and human agony. Even advocates who champion a pure trauma model of self-destruction or externalized negativity in the service of explaining human aggressivity must contend with inherently destructive organizing elements that imperil the organism from within. Even medical science is perplexed by the internally derived forces (e.g. cancer, AIDS, ALS) that drain the healthy organism of life due to attacks perpetrated by its own immune system or endogenous constitution. Consider the paradoxical processes that result in sleep's being both regressive and restorative and, particularly, how going to sleep is associated with wanting to return to a previously aborted state of peace, tranquility, or oceanic 'quiescence' – perhaps a wish for a tensionless state, perhaps a return to the womb. Excessive sleep is also one of the most salient symptoms of clinical depression and the will toward death. Furthermore, it would be inconceivable to argue that humankind's externalized aggression is not inherently self-destructive for the simple fact that it generates more retaliatory hate, aggression, and mayhem, which threatens world accord and the progression of civil societies. Given the global ubiquity of war, genocide, geopolitical atrocities and the despoliation of our planet, in all likelihood we as a human race will die by actions brought about by our own hands rather than the impersonal forces of nature. *Homo homini lupus est* – 'Man is a wolf to man.'[8]

Contemporary psychoanalysis seems to be uninterested in Freud's classic texts on the primacy of death, to the point that the latter are dismissed without even being read simply because credible authorities in the field say this may be done. Here I have in mind the relational school's anti-drive theory campaign. In my opinion, those who argue against the death drive simply do not grasp the inherent complexity, non-concretization, anti-reductionism and non-linearity of what Freud has to offer us. Critics claim that the death drive defies evolutionary biology, therefore it must be bogus. But this criticism is merely begging the question of what we mean by death. And, more specifically, what we mean by the *function* of death in psychic reality. Or, to be even more precise, how death is organized as unconscious experience. Just because a species is organically impelled to thrive does not mean it is devoid of destructive principles derived from within its own constitution – principles that imperil its existence and proliferation. It can be logically claimed that life is only possible through the force of the negative, which brings about higher developmental achievements through the destruction of the old.[9] This is the positive significance of the negative, an artefact of psychic reality that derives its source from internal negation and anguish while at the same time transcending its descent into psychic pain. Psychoanalysts are often confused by viewing death as merely a physical end-state or the termination of life, when it may be memorialized in the psyche as a primary ontological principle that informs the trajectory of all psychic activity.[10] Here death is phylogenetic (*phulon*, class; *geneia*, born). Death has multiple interpretations and meanings within conscious experience that are radically opposed to the logic of negativity that infiltrates unconscious semiotics. Death is an ontological category for unconscious experience that can never elude psychic existence. This is because what we know or profess to know epistemically as mediated inner experience is always predicated on our felt-relation to death, that is, to the primordial force of repetitive negation, conflict and destruction that alerts us to being and life, a dialectic that is ontologically inseparable and mutually implicative. What we call a life force, drive, urge, or impetus is intimately conjoined with its pulsional opposition, that is, its negation, termination, or lack. Here life = death: being and nothing are the same.

Freud never used the term 'death instinct' to refer to the organism's innate propensity for destruction; rather, he used the term *Todestrieb*, which is more accurately translated as the 'death drive'. Philosophers have placed great importance on the role of death and destruction in the constitution of human subjectivity, but Freud gives it paradigmatic primacy as the ontological force behind the origins of mind. This interpretation may only be properly appreciated after we come to understand how libido, and later Eros, is born/e from death, the details of which are most thoroughly articulated in *Beyond the Pleasure Principle*. Freud's attribution of the centrality of death is the result of laborious theoretical evolution, a notion that gained increasing conceptual and clinical utility as his ideas advanced, based on appropriating new burgeoning clinical data, not to mention the fact that death and decay had a profound personal resonance.[11]

Yet Freud was not always favourably disposed to the primordiality of destruction: his early position was to subordinate aggression to libido or to make it a derivative of it. Freud's ambivalence about the constitutive role of death constituted a visible tension in his thinking from as early as his dispute with Adler regarding the existence of an 'aggressive drive' (*Aggressionsbetrieb*) (see Freud 1909; *SE* 10:140n2). We may further observe his own personal confessions about his unease with the inextricability of sex and death, to the point where it needed to be repressed, a narrative Freud reported as early as 1898 (*SE* 3:292–294), although he later elaborated his views more fully in *The Psychopathology of Everyday Life* (Freud 1901; *SE* 6:3–5). Regardless of his ambivalence, Freud was preoccupied with the nature and meaning of death and its influence on mental functioning since his early psychoanalytic writings. In one of his early communications to Fliess (Draft N, enclosed in Letter 64, 31 May 1897), he discusses how death wishes are 'directed in sons against their father and in daughters against their mother' (Freud 1896b, 255). This passage may arguably be Freud's first allusion to the Oedipus complex.

Death, destruction, anguish and tumult not only become the conflictual properties of the psyche in both content and form, but they also form the ontogenetic ground of the underworld – 'chaos, a cauldron full of seething excitations' (*SE* 22:73) – as Freud puts it. Furthermore, Freud makes death an ontological *a priori* condition of the coming into being of human subjectivity that is 'phylogenetically' (*SE* 22:79) imprinted and laid down within the aboriginal structural processes that constitute our unconscious strivings. Freud situates these strivings within an inherent tendency toward self-destruction that is in combat with the reactionary impetus toward growth and greater unification – in other words, the dialectic of life and death. Yet Freud (1920) ultimately makes death the 'first drive' (*SE* 18:38), a compulsion to return to an original inanimate state. In fact, Freud (1933a) tells us that the death drive 'cannot fail to be present in every vital process' (*SE* 22:107). It is inherent in the whole process of civilization, which is 'perpetually threatened with disintegration' (Freud 1930; *SE* 21:112), just as conspicuously as Eros ensures its survival. Freud built upon his 1920 introduction of the destructive principle and systematically forged his dual classification of the drives in 1923; showed its presence in masochism in 1924; made it a key component of anxiety by 1926; and, in his final days, avowed in his posthumously published monograph, *An Outline of Psycho-Analysis* (1940a), that death is inseparable from Eros, which 'gives rise to the whole variegation of the phenomena of life' (*SE* 23:149). Therefore, death becomes the necessary touchstone and catalyst of psychic existence. Here we have a very grave philosophy indeed.

But how does death acquire such a primary position in the psyche? In other words, how is death interiorized from the beginning? Freud (1920) provides an initial explanation by appealing to what he observed, namely, the phenomenon of repetition. He noticed this in the traumatic neuroses, particularly in people who were suffering from post-traumatic stress due to the baneful effects of the Great War, and who were continuously being resubjected, in horrific dreams, thoughts, fantasies and perceptions, to the traumatic moments they had previously encountered. In fact, here was Freud's first major amendment to his thesis that dreams represented the disguised fulfilment of a wish. On the contrary, traumatic dreams were experienced as a fresh charge of anxiety *against* the fulfilment of a wish. And for good reason. Under these circumstances, the psyche is fighting against what it had internalized through unwanted surprise, ambush and impingement – sheer terror. Anxiety is a bid for survival. But Freud quickly turns to more normative experiences of separation from the primary attachment figure (i.e. one's mother), thus ushering in anxiety, abandonment and loss as an impetus to repetition. In fact, he uses his own grandson, Ernst, as an example – the illustrious *fort-da* narrative – thus canonizing the ambivalence and helplessness associated with the anxiety of uncertainty and anger over the disappearance of a love object. In short, Freud observed his eighteen-month-old grandson invent a game that involved throwing various objects, mainly his toys, and simultaneously saying 'o-o-o' when his mother left him during the day. Freud interpreted this to be the linguistic significa-tion of *fort* (gone). It was only when he discovered a yo-yo that he could make the object return once he had thrown it away, followed by a joyous 'da' (there). Here Freud not only illuminates the motive that drives a repetition (i.e. 'mastery') but also shows the economic element that 'carried along with it a yield of pleasure of another sort' (*SE* 18:16). The inherent aggression involved in throwing the toy away, coupled with the undoing of destruction through the satisfaction of its reappearance, points toward how this childhood game serves to recapitulate loss through return. Freud is suggestive, but he does not actually say that this yield of satisfaction of 'another sort' is achieved in the context of absence, of lack or nothingness, a property of death. Death enters into 'every vital process', and this is certainly the case between the dialectic of presence and absence, being and nothingness, abundance and lack.

The nature of repetition naturally leads Freud to examine the phenomenon of self-destructiveness, what he observes in the nature of psychopathology itself, the 'compulsion to repeat' trauma via symptom formation, a topic he addressed earlier in 'Recollecting, Repeating, and Working Through' (Freud 1914c). Death is manifested in repetitions of thought, fantasy and behaviour; in parapraxes; in mas-ochism and sadism; in symptoms such as melancholia, paranoia and psychosis; and in the uncanny, just to name a few. Death residue impregnates repressed sche-mata that find expression through repeating the unconscious material itself as it is happening in the moment rather than remembering what had been an occurrence in the past. When repressed events take the form of 'fresh experiences' rather than being properly ascribed as reproductions of the past, reality is clouded with nega-tivity, affective contagion, paranoiac fantasy and, subsequently, qualitative suf-fering. These repetitions, driven by inner compulsions, do not bring satisfaction, only 'unpleasure'. This conundrum led Freud to believe that instinctual life was driven by more than just libidinal discharge and 'that there really does exist in the mind a compulsion to repeat which overrides the pleasure principle' (*SE* 18:22). He needed to go deeper than simply relying on his customary economic expla-nations. He needed to find something 'more primitive, more elementary, more instinctual than the pleasure principle which it over-rides' (*SE* 18:23). Moving from the empirical, Freud had no other recourse than to engage inferential logic, what he carefully referred to as 'speculation', and 'often far-fetched speculation' at that (*SE* 18:24). Despite his critics' renunciation of the death drive on evolution-ary grounds, charging that it allegedly betrays Darwinian biology (Sulloway 1979; Webster 1995), there is nothing 'far-fetched' about it at all. From my account, the death drive is Freud's greatest theoretical contribution to understanding the dynamics of the unconscious mind. Let us explore this notion more fully.

Freud situates his argument within the language of embryology and postulates that a living organism in its most simplified form is in a state of undifferentiation yet is 'susceptible to stimulation' from the many forces that comprise the exter-nal world. Freud conjectures that the organism must have an intrinsic capacity to

protect itself from powerful stimuli through a resistive process internally operative and sensitive to intrusive encroachments from externality that threaten its
potential destruction. The human mind is no exception. Here Freud's entire discourse is an economy of energetics designed to transform stimuli in the service
of self-preservation, thus defending them from both external and internal stimuli
that create states of unpleasure. This example from embryology is extended to the
psychical apparatus, once again what Freud later referred to as the soul (*Seele*).[12]
Here the role of trauma becomes paramount,[13] and Freud is specifically referring
to external events that have the capacity to breach the protective barrier and flood
the mental register with excessive states of excitation, thus rendering it unable to
master or bind the breach or to find appropriate modes of discharge. The so-called
'traumatic neurosis' is one such outcome of an extensive breach of the protective
barrier or systems of defence, thus leading to a compulsion to repeat, which Freud
says exhibits a high degree of 'instinctual' (*Triebhaft*) character, by which he means
the degree of felt urgency it assumes in the psyche, what he sometimes equates with
possession by a 'daemonic' power (*SE* 18:36). Here it is interesting to note Freud's
choice of words: 'daemonic' not only signifies possession by a demon but is also
derived from the Greek *daimōn*, which is a creative force or divine power.

Under the pressure of disturbing external forces, a drive becomes an urge, or
pulsion, to repeat itself, the motive being to return to an earlier state of undifferentiation, an 'expression of the inertia inherent in organic life' (*SE* 18:36).
It is here where Freud extends his hypothesis that all drives aim toward a restoration of earlier events or modes of being, namely, unmodified quiescence. Because
drives are 'conservative' – that is, they follow a conservative economy of regulatory energy, are acquired historically and phylogenetically in the species, and tend
toward restorative processes that maintain an original uncomplicated immediacy –
Freud speculates that an 'elementary living entity' would have no desire to change,
only to maintain its current mode of existence. Here Freud attributes the process
of organic development to the disruptive press of external factors that impinge on
the quiescent state of the organism, factors it is obliged to internalize and repeat.
It is here where the organism acquires the *telos* to return to its original inorganic state. Here Freud summons Horace: *mors ultima linea rerum est* – death is
the final goal of things. As Freud concisely puts it: '*the aim of all life is death*'
(*SE* 18:38, emphasis in original).[14] Therefore, the first drive comes into being as a
tension introduced by an extrinsic force that stimulates the impulse to cancel itself
out. It is here that the genesis of organic life becomes death, itself the 'origin and
aim of life' (*SE* 19:39).

It is important to note that Freud is attempting to delineate a philosophy of
organic process by isolating the 'origin' (*Herkunft*) of life within a psychic ontology constituted by death. What Freud does with death is to make it an inner
attribute and impetus, originally summoned from within the psyche itself, that
is awakened by an external stimulus. According to Freud, all living organisms
die for 'internal reasons', that is, death is brought about from the cessation of
internally derived activity. In other words, death is not merely executed by an

extraneous force; rather, it is activated by endogenous motives. But death does not happen any which way: it must be executed by the agent itself, more specifically, by the unconscious ego aligned with fulfilling the wish for its own destruction. Here the psyche is given determinate degrees of freedom to 'follow its own path to death' (SE 18:39), that is, to bring about its end fashioned according to its own hands.[15] But this end is actually a return to its beginning, a recapturing, a recapitulation of its quiescent inorganic immediacy. This is why Freud thought that the unconscious forces operative in repetition were ultimately in the service of self-destruction in the form of a wish to return to an original undifferentiated condition. However, because the impetus towards death is internally derived, the ego can seize upon many choices in its death-work, which is accomplished through the circuitous routes and detours that often accompany the variegated phenomena of life. Although the ultimate *telos* of a drive, and hence its final cause, is death, it may only be enjoyed via postponement through unconscious volition. This is why *Todestrieb* is beyond the pleasure principle: not only does it precede the life-preserving drives but it also stands over them as a supraordinate organizational thrust. And this is how the life instincts, or Eros, harness the power of death to serve their own transformative evolutionary purposes. Here evolution is not merely unquestioned conformity to Darwinian principles oriented toward a single aim; rather, it is a modified internal organization oriented toward higher modes of existence and self-development via defensive adaptation forged through forays into conflict, negativity and death.

But what is to become of death if life supersedes it? What Freud concludes particularly highlights his genius, for death is ultimately in the service of the pleasure principle. This is a very delicate theoretical move and is only successful when you observe the logic of the dialectic as the confluence of mutually implicative oppositions that share a common unity. Following the laws of psychic economy, the pleasure principle is a tendency to free the psyche of excitation, or at least to minimize stimulation levels so that there is a tolerable degree of constancy. The ultimate condition of pleasure would therefore be a state that is free of tension: through this end, cessation of tension would represent its fulfilment, hence its completion. From this impersonal account of unconscious teleology, what could be more pleasurable than death, than non-being? Death is a tensionless state, unadulterated peace. But Freud's teleology is not strictly Aristotlean: although the unconscious mind aims toward death, it has the capacity to choose its own path toward self-destruction. It is only under this condition of determinate freedom that the psyche can bring about its own end, which makes death-work inherent in the life-enhancing processes that repudiate the will toward self-destruction while embracing it. Here we may observe two opposing forces operative within the single purpose of the pleasure principle: death and life are ontologically conjoined yet differentiated from one another. It is here that Freud's dual classification of the drives is solidified.

Recall that, for Freud, death is the 'original drive' or urge in the embryonic psyche, and it is transformed by the life forces that emerge from it and then combat it, hence bringing about a doubling of the negative. Freud is clear in telling us that death and its derivatives or representatives, such as aggression and destruction as well as Eros and its manifestations of libido or the life-enhancing processes that promote self-preservation and advance, are 'struggling with each other from the very first' (*SE* 18:61–62n1). Harnessing and diverting the internal powers of death, the destructive principle must be deflected outwards, which serves the libidinal progression of the psyche in its ascendance toward self-development. The sexual or libidinal impulses thus become defined and refined in opposition to competing forces that seek to bring about their demise or premature decay. Here the life force is at odds with its destructive antithesis, both conjoined in conflict yet punctuated by oscillating moments of self-manifestation. Freud could not bifurcate Eros and Thanatos, despite their dual forms of appearance, because he observed that each always interpenetrates the other, hence they are not ontologically separated.

Freud (1930) vacillated, even waffled, with regard to his tendency toward a dualistic view of the drives verses a monistic developmental ontology, and, in this way, he remained a thorough dialectician in conceiving the mind as 'an original bipolarity in its own nature' (*SE* 21:119). Melanie Klein continued this tradition of juxtaposing oppositions but gave the death drive an even more exalted status: death became the meridian of mental organization. In Klein's (1932) first book, *The Psycho-Analysis of Children*, she makes her first reference to the death drive, which she takes over wholeheartedly from Freud. Under the influence of Abraham's views on orality, Klein becomes interested in the phenomenon of infantile sadism, which she attributes to the tension between the polarity of the life and death instincts. It is specifically in the context of the early development of the origin of the superego that Klein annexes the death drive and makes it a key catalyst in the emerging process of the infant's mental functioning. Klein sees the fusion of the dual drives as occurring at birth, the destructive forces further emanating from within the infant and in response to unsatisfied libido, thus culminating in anxiety and rage, which only strengthens the sadistic impulses. Here Klein sees the source of anxiety as directly flowing from the destructive principle directed toward the organism, thus reactively alerting the ego to danger and helplessness in the face of annihilation. As Klein states: 'anxiety would originate from aggression' (p. 126). Not only does the infant experience anxiety in response to its own self-destructive urges, but it also fears external objects that are the locus of its sadism, now acquiring a secondary source of danger. Here Klein introduces the splitting of the ego as a defensive attempt to deny and repress the acknowledgment of its internal sources of anxiety fuelled by the death drive: objects of frustration, hate, rage and sadism are now seen as the exclusive source of danger, thus diverting the dual nature of anxiety by transposing internality onto externality. This is the earliest manoeuvre of splitting, projection and paranoia that transpires in the ego, which 'seeks to defend itself by destroying the object' (p. 128).

Klein radicalizes the presence of the death drive and anxiety in the embryonic mind. Death creates anxiety, thus leading to the developmental processes of schizoid, paranoiac and depressive positions, later recaptured in awakening

Oedipal tendencies but first originating within the organism itself and defensively deflected onto external objects. This process thereby becomes the antediluvian cycle of projective identification: the entire architectonic function of psychic maturation is predicated on the instantiation and transformation of death.

Death-work suffuses the ontology of subjectivity instantiated through its experiential unfolding, what Hegel attributes to the dialectic of mind in both its maturation and decay. Death permeates being, from its archaic nether regions to the triumph *Geist* enjoys in vanquishing earlier moments of experience, itself the result of annulment and supersession, only to devolve back into darkness – the abyss. Freud (1925d) tells us that death largely works 'in silence' (*SE* 20:57), a position he was later to recast. Yet for Klein, there is nothing silent about death: it screams violently upon the initial inception of the psyche, an intrinsic predetermined barrage of negation, onslaught and desolation, an inferno besieged by it own flames. Here Freud is radicalized: mind becomes apocalyptic. Active at the moment of birth, death lends structure to the embryonic mind, a facticity that saturates all aspects of early ego development. In Klein, death finds its pinnacle as the fountainhead of psychic life.

Even if critics find the death drive theoretically untenable, I still believe it is a useful clinical heuristic that guides therapeutic practice. What we as analysts face everyday is the inherent self-destructiveness of patients who can find neither amity nor reprieve from psychic conflict and the repetitions that fuel their suffering. These inherent capacities for self-destruction are not merely located in external sources as they are both *interiorized* and *internalized*, thus becoming the organizing death principles at work on myriad levels of unconscious experience. Inherent capacities for self-destruction take many circuitous and compromised paths, something the modern conflict theorists would ascribe to symptom formation, addictions, self-victimization, pernicious patterns of recurrence, and harmful behaviours that hasten physical deterioration or poor health. All of these tragedies may be further compounded by external trauma and affliction, which Freud first identified in his trauma model of hysteria; however, this does not necessarily negate the presence of internally derived deleterious aggressions turned on the self. We see it everyday in the consulting room. From oppressive guilt, disabling shame, explosive rage, contagious hate, self-loathing and unbearable symptomatic agony, there is a perverse appeal to suffering, to embracing our masochistic *jouissance* – our ecstasy in pain. Whether in the form of an addict's craving for a bottle or a drag off a cigarette, there is an inherent destructiveness imbued in the very act of the pursuit of pleasure. All aspects of the progression of civilization and its decay are the determinate teleological fulfilment of death-work.

The transmogrification of drives

The inner pulsion, urge, or locomotive pressure of a drive becomes a more descriptive way of emphasizing the notion of intrinsic unrest, desire and compulsion often associated with impersonal, non-intentional forces impelling the individual from within. We may initially see why Freud's concept of drive has descriptive utility: it is an unconscious process that fuels and propels the organism. But, more important, Freud conceives of a drive as a malleable, plastic, transformative activity – not as a static, genetically imprinted or determined pressure that cannot be mediated or amended. For Freud, a drive can be altered and permutated, while an instinct, being stagnant and unchangeable, cannot. Whereas the expression of a drive can be mitigated if not changed entirely, an instinct cannot undergo modification at all. In English, the term 'instinct' also typifies something that is innate. Therefore, in order to avoid duplicating confusion about the nature of drive and instinct, it should be clear by now that all references to instinctual processes should be viewed within this stipulated context of drives.

As we have seen, Freud's theory of the drives went through many significant transformations throughout his career, at one time focusing solely on libido (*Lust*), then on many different competing urges belonging to both unconscious and conscious processes (e.g. *die Ich-Triebe*), before finally settling on the primacy of two antithetical yet interpenetrable classifications: sex and death. Many contemporary analysts can't buy this central tenet, what Mitchell (1992, p. 3) calls the 'outmoded concept of drives'; namely, that the mind is driven and influenced by multifarious, overdetermined unconscious forces that, originally, are biologically based pressures impinging on the conscious subject and clamouring for release. But the main objection among these schools, echoing Jung, is the concentrated refutation of the role of libido with regard to relational and intersubjective motives. Here we see the first big turn-off (and subsequent resistance from the anti-classical field): everything boils down to sex.

This unfortunate attitude is based on Freud's (1905a) early work on infantile sexuality; it does not take into account his mature theoretical advances (see Freud 1933a, 1940b). As mentioned earlier, Freud was not particularly impressed with having to think the same thing all the time: by the end of his life he had incorporated libido, or the sex drive, into his conception of Eros – an encompassing life principle, similar to that of the Greeks, who saw the pursuit of Eros as life's supreme aim (i.e. the holistic attainment of sensual, aesthetic, ethical and intellectual fulfilment). In this sense, mind and body are contiguous. Blindly focusing on Freud's early work at the expense of his mature theory leads not only to misunderstanding him but also to distorting his theoretical corpus. It also leads one to incorrectly presume that Freud was committed to a genetic fallacy; namely, that all psychic life can be *reduced* to its developmental origins.[16] Eros is the sublimation (*Sublimierung*) of natural desire, first materializing as drive then progressing to the cultivated activities of the ego (i.e. rational self-conscious life).

As we have seen, for Freud (1915a), the source of a drive is unequivocally biological and somatic. This is the second big turn-off: humanity is viewed as a physical–instinctual machine that is turned on by the environment. But this attitude misunderstands the nature of drives and the role of biology and human embodiment in psychic economy. Why sex and aggression? Because they are part of our animal evolutionary past and are the essence of being human. The notion of drive underscores Freud's natural science foundation, which is inextricably bound to evolutionary currents: sex and aggression are the two fundamental forces behind the inception, course and progression of civilization, without which there would arguably be no human race.[17] Unconsciousness precedes consciousness, hence subjective experience is internally mediated prior to one's encounter with the object world, including other subjects. In fact, drive becomes an ontological *a priori* that cannot be annulled or denied: moreover, it precedes interpersonal interaction by virtue of the fact that drive is constitutionally predicated.

We can never escape from the fact that we are embodied. Freud's insistence that the source of a drive is biologically given is simply an acceptance of the brute facticity of our natural corporeality. The mistake many psychoanalytic theorists make involves interpreting biology as reduction and assuming that drive discharge precludes relational activity, when, contrarily, Freud's conception of drive makes reduction impossible and relatedness possible. Let me explain.

Freud has to account for embodiment – our natural immediacy – within which urges and impulses arise, thus he focuses on the body as initially providing form, content and structure to internal experience. This is why erogenous zones are corporeally emphasized. But, more important, Freud has to show how ego activity and consciousness are also sensuous processes: attention, perception and the greater faculties of cognition are sentient experiential actions. This is why Freud (1923) says that the ego is a body-ego, itself the projection of a surface: *It* projects itself *onto* its surface, the surface of its immediate feeling and sensuous embodiment. Therefore drive is constituted as ego, but not at first. While Freud does not say this directly, it may nevertheless be inferred: drive becomes ego, which first knows itself as a feeling, craving, desirous corporeal being. But how does this occur? Freud says very little.

It is important to reiterate that Freud (1915a) distinguishes between four constituents of a drive: source, pressure, aim and object. While the source (*Quelle*) is somatically organized, Freud is very clear that the pressure (*Drang*), thrust, or force of a drive is its very 'essence' (*Wesen*). Here he unquestionably situates the nature of *Trieb* in its activity: drive is pulsation, unrest – pure desire. The aim (*Ziel*) or motive of a drive is to satisfy itself, to achieve pleasure as tension reduction, to end the craving; and the means by which a drive is sated is through an object (*Objekt*). Objects, especially people, are coveted for the functions they serve, and these functional objects may fulfil many competing aims as psychic life becomes more rich and variegated. In fact, drives transmogrify through many circuitous routes and take many derivative forms: what we commonly refer to as a 'defence mechanism' is the teleological fate of a drive. This is an unfortunate term because 'mechanism' evokes images of stasis, rigidity and fixed predetermined movements when, instead, defences are fluid, mutable and teleologically directed expressions of desire as *process systems*. As transformed drive, a defence is a particular piece of desire, often unconsciously intended and differentiated by its function in relation to a competing urge, impulse, or counter-intention, internal danger, environmental threat, and/or potential conscious realization that must

60

be combated. Some defences urge the psyche to regress while others urge it to progress, and this is why a drive cannot simply be seen as biological reduction or devolve back to its original state. Because drives transform, they cannot return to their original form: we can never know a drive in itself, only as a psychical representative, presentation, or idea (*Vorstellung*). Furthermore, what we often experience as drive is its aim – the craving for satisfaction. Moreover, because drives modify themselves through a process of epigenesis, they make the more sophisticated forms of conscious and self-conscious life possible: from the archaic to the refined, unconscious drive manifests itself through relatedness to objects.

Freud's theory of *Trieb* is not without difficulty, and many critics proclaim that, because his model of tension reduction was ultimately a hydraulic component of biological–homeostasis theory, the aim or *telos* of a drive overrides relational motivations. But this conclusion is not justified, especially when others become the objects of our satisfaction and search for personal fulfilment and meaning. Freud (1915a) specifically says that the object of a drive is its most variable aspect and that it may serve multiple simultaneous motives (*SE* 14:123). Nowhere are we led to believe that relation is subordinated to biology when a drive is mediated (by the ego) though object relatedness. Furthermore, Freud's later theory of Eros ultimately speaks to the desire for love and the pursuit of our most cherished ideals, which he specifically equates with the Eros of Plato in the *Symposium* (Freud 1925a; *SE* 19:218). As a result, Eros becomes a relational principle (see Reisner, 1992), a relation toward ourselves and others through the exaltation of human value. From the most primitive mind to the most civilized societies, we are *attached* to our ideals through others.

But let us return to a conceptual dilemma for Freud: how could a drive have an object? Put another way, how could a drive take an object as its aim without possessing some form of agency? As a teleological process, a drive has a purpose constituted through its aim; but how could it also be guided in its ability to *choose* objects for its satisfaction without accounting for intentionality on the part of an unconscious agent? Here we see why Freud had to introduce the notion of unconscious agency as constituted through the alien presence of the It. The It constitutes the realm of the dual classification of drives as well as the realm of the repressed. But is Freud justified in making the It into an agency? Could it be possible that unconscious actions of the ego are actually performing object choice, while the drives and repressed material merely act as a constant pressure the ego must mediate? This is particularly problematic for Freud given that he specifically tells us that the I logically and temporally proceeds from the It. Freud is very clear in his final specifications of how the psyche develops in this fashion. In *Inhibitions, Symptoms and Anxiety*, Freud (1926a) states:

> We were justified, I think, in dividing the ego from the id, for there are certain considerations which necessitate that step. On the other hand *the ego is identical with the id, and is merely a specially differentiated part of it*. If we think of this part by itself in contradistinction to the whole, or if a

real split has occurred between the two, the weakness of the ego becomes apparent. But if the ego remains bound up with the id and indistinguishable from it, then it displays its strength. The same is true of the relation between the ego and the super-ego. In many situations the two are merged; and as a rule we can only distinguish one from the other when there is a tension or conflict between them . . . [T]he ego is an *organization* and the id is not. *The ego is, indeed, the organized portion of the id.*
(*SE* 20:97, emphasis added)[18]

Freud (1933a) clearly explains that the I is a modally differentiated aspect of the It, which becomes the mental organization of its prior shape. Elsewhere he says: 'the ego is that portion of the id that was modified . . . tak[ing] on the task of representing the external world to the id' (*SE* 22:75). This corresponds to the ego of consciousness, where the materials of sensuous perception and thought are mediated, stored and retrieved from the inner world, hence underscoring the contiguous and interdependent levels of unconscious and conscious processes. Freud's theory of mind adheres to an architectonic process: the ego develops out of its natural immediacy, then acquires increased dynamic complexity and organization as modally differentiated shapes of earlier processes assume new forms. As previously stated, Freud's recognition that organized psychic processes develop from unorganized hence undifferentiated natural determinations insulates him from criticism that his theory of mind purports three ontologically distinct agents that participate in mutual causal relations. Because the trinity of the three provinces are modally differentiated forms or shapes of its original undifferentiated being, each participates in the same essence and, thus, none is an independent nominal agent; rather they are interdependent forces that *appear* as separate agencies, when they in fact together form the unification of the dynamic temporal processes that govern mental life.

Although Freud admonished Jung for allegedly 'watering-down' libido to a monistic energy, Freud's model of the psyche conforms to a developmental monistic ontology: higher instantiations of mental order evolve from more primordial forces of psychic life through a process of differentiation and modification. Although the I and the It are modifications of the same ontology, it is only the I that appears, itself an unconscious derivative. The specific process of differentiation, however, goes unexplained. All we are told is that the ego becomes the higher organizing agency of the mind derived from primitive processes. In fact, Freud (1940a) concedes that, while drives find their first psychical expressions in the It, they are 'in forms unknown to us' (*SE* 23:145). But why did not Freud isolate the moments of differentiation and modification within the It itself? Given that drive is the basic constituent of mind, which even precedes the organization of the It as a thoroughly unconscious agent, why did he not address modification at this level? Furthermore, if the ego is a secondary modification from a primary unconscious ground, then, by Freud's account, drive mediation would have to take place before the ego emerges. But how could a drive possess such agency? Freud does not say.

From my account, the transmogrification of the drives gives rise to psychic agency, and it is through a careful inspection of the process of modification that we can potentially resolve the genesis problem. I believe that Freud was mistaken when he made the It into an agency without accounting for how the unconscious portion of the I performs the executive functions of object choice for the drives and competing unconscious material pressing for discharge. The It cannot be understood as an unconscious agency (if at all) without the implicit inclusion of the I, unless the nature of a drive includes the capacity to choose objects, which is highly improbable given that only the ego is organized and synthetic with regard to its executive tasks. In fact, Freud (1915a) tells us that the object of a drive is '*assigned* to it only in consequence of being peculiarly fitted to make satisfaction possible' (*SE* 14:122, emphasis added). What does the assigning, ego or drive? If the I is ontologically undifferentiated from the It, it makes the question of unconscious agency more delicate when attempting to account for teleology and intentional object choice. Rather than the I developing from the It, the ego may be properly said to develop from drive. But even more important, as we can infer from Freud's thesis on the identity of the I and the It, we have reason to believe that drive and ego are the same.

As it stands, there are many problems associated with Freud's contrast between the I and the It. The It is impersonal but it allegedly picks an object for the drives: how is this so? According to Freud, only the ego can do this; hence, we have a problem with an executive agency, and we have a problem with the definition of a drive. Although a drive needs an object for its satisfaction, are we justified in saying that an object is a proper characteristic of a drive? This implies that an object inheres in the drive as a property of it, when this is unlikely. An object stands in relation or absence to the *telos* or aim of a drive, but it does not follow that an object is necessarily a part of a drive's constitution, only that it requires an object for its satisfaction. In order to procure an object, the drive requires mediation. Here enters the I. The unconscious ego, not drive, mediates object choice, hence Freud introduces a contradiction in his model. He further confounds the issue by making the ego a developmental agent that does not materialize until the formative stages of early Oedipalization, a postulate corrected by Klein and many post-Kleinians, and today confirmed by developmental researchers who recognize the existence of the ego or the self at the moment of birth.

Freud attempts to resolve his own contradiction by making the It a separate agent. But how does it have any organizing agency without the ego, which lends it structure and direction? Yet Freud equivocates by saying that the I is 'identical' with the It. In Freud's final tripartite model (the Freudian trinity), the ego becomes the locus of mind because of its synthetic and dynamic functions, which stand in mediatory relation to the other two competing agencies. Yet, because these other two agencies are ontologically, and hence inextricably, conjoined, we cannot separate any one agency from the others.

Ego as unconscious modification

It can be argued that Freud's theoretical vision of the ego underwent more modifications than any other theoretical construct, experiencing important refinements through diligent attempts to work out problematics inherent in the ego's relation to the other competing psychical agencies that govern mental life. In my estimation, Freud's mature model of the mind is represented in three primary texts: *The Ego and the Id* (1923); *New Introductory Lectures on Psycho-Analysis* (1933a); and the posthumously published uncompleted manuscript *An Outline of Psycho-Analysis* (1940a). Here we can observe the overdetermined functions and processes at work in ego activity. For Freud, the ego is developmental (*SE* 14:77), both externalizing and internalizing, projective and incorporative. It is both information-emitting and information-processing, born/e from the unconscious. In Freud's mature system, the ego can be characterized in the following fashions:

1   The ego is the heart of subjectivity and selfhood. As Freud says, 'the ego is in its very essence a subject (*Subjekt*)' (*SE* 22:58). Elsewhere he states: 'There is nothing of which we are more certain than the feeling of our self (*Selbst*), of our own ego (*Ich*)' (*SE* 21:65). Here Freud emphasizes the conscious elements of the ontology of the ego. The ego develops out of the unconscious It and becomes a conscious organization that mediates perception, motility, conscious thought, affect and action (*SE* 20:195–196). However, as Freud reminds us, 'the ego is also unconscious' (*SE* 19:23). In 1923, he believed that the ego '*starts out* . . . from the system *Pcpt* [the perceptual apparatus], which is its nucleus, and *begins* by embracing the *Pcs* [preconscious system]' (*SE* 19:23, emphasis added). Note how Freud refers to points of origination when describing the coming into being of the ego. But he had stated in his earlier 1914 paper that the ego developed out of a narcissistic self-enclosed unity. In 1923, he situates this birth as having its 'nucleus' in perception and preconscious functioning. But, by 1926, Freud amends his position to conclude that the ego is a 'specially differentiated part of . . . [and] organized portion of the It' (*SE* 20:97). Therefore, the ego is conditioned on unconscious processes and emerges from the unconsciously derived activities of differentiation and modification. Hence, the ego attains the acquired properties of freedom and executive agency that derive from its original primitive form.

2   The ego develops into an organized agency that must mediate between internal and external forces, those springing forth from the drives and impulses, and those that force their effects on the ego, which it is obliged to receive and mediate: 'The ego is an organization. It is based on the maintenance of free intercourse and of the possibility of reciprocal influence between all its parts' (*SE* 20:98). Here Freud is referring to the tripartite functions of the soul (*Seele*). Notice he uses the term 'free' (*freien*). Hence, both internal and external reality can present as autonomous forces the ego must register and to which it must respond.

3   The ego's tasks are multifaceted: it processes all the cognitive functions that belong to perceptual consciousness, information processing, motor- and goal-directed activities, affect regulation and linguistic productions. It retrieves and bars memory. It censors, defends, finds compromises, reduces tensions, secures pleasure outlets and 'adapts' to symptoms. It is the conduit to unconscious life and resides in parallel realms of psychic spacing. It heeds external reality while attempting to fulfil the dialectic and vicissitudes of desire. It allows reason to surface, is pragmatically concerned with environmental forces that affect it, and maintains functional adaptation. It adjusts to the laws of secondary process thinking while subduing primary process mentation, despite the fact that it mediates and finds avenues for the fulfilment of pleasure. In short, the ego is the hub of the psyche.[19]

4   One motivational and functional aim the ego possesses is the act of synthetic mediation. This synthetic function is central to its agentic organization. What distinguishes the ego from the It is its tendency toward synthesizing contents and unifying mental processes (*SE* 22:76). Freud further tells us that the ego 'shows *traces of its origin* in its impulsion to bind together and unify, and this necessity to synthesize grows stronger in proportion as the strength of the ego increases' (*SE* 20:98, emphasis added). For the most part, Freud saw this synthetic function as an attempt to restore or reconcile tension or conflict generated among the competing forces that populate mental life and that pressure the ego for resolution. Here we see an underlying defensive purpose to ego activity, one aim of which is to control the passions (*SE* 22:76). Also note how Freud refers to a 'trace' of the ego's 'origin' (*Herkunft*), which he situates in the act of synthesizing. To be more accurate, the origin of ego activity bears its mark – hence its *semeion* – in the act of splitting.

5   For Freud, an ancillary albeit rudimentary aim of the ego is constituted through the act of splitting. In fact, this is more basic and primary in the ego, occurring long before synthetic functions monopolize psychic connections. Here it is important to underscore the logical priority of splitting as determinate negation. This is the initial act of its dialectical activity, while the attempt to unify is technically the third movement or consequence of the previous determinate events. The second action is in the process of incorporation, which simultaneously subsumes otherness and unifies opposition within its active process of becoming. Freud recognized that the ego takes itself as an object. In this sense, it is 'setting itself over against the rest. So the ego can be split; it splits itself during a number of its functions' (*SE* 22:58). Earlier Freud (1924a) commented on how the ego submits to 'encroachments on its own unity . . . by effecting a cleavage or division of itself' (*SE* 19:152–153). He specifically focused on cases of fetishism and psychosis, where a disavowal of external reality is employed, but he eventually attributed this process to the normative childhood ego whose attempts to detach from reality are simultaneously met with the obligation to acknowledge certain elements of the world around us. Splitting is operative in the defensive functions of

inversion and turning the aim of a drive into its opposite form, as articulated in Freud's 1915(a) metapsychological paper entitled 'Instincts and Their Vicissitudes'. Ultimately, however, Freud (1940a) highlights the inherently conflictual nature of splitting as a set of implicative dialectical relations: 'two contrary and independent attitudes always arise and result in the situation of there being a splitting of the ego' (*SE* 23:204). The act of synthesis or integration is an attempt to unify opposition.

As we can see, Freud is the true founder of ego psychology, a direction of thought that was further taken up by Anna Freud and advanced by the American ego psychology movement. A concept advanced by this school of thought is the assumption, introduced by Hartmann (1939), that there is a 'conflict-free sphere' or 'autonomous' portions of the ego that are exempt from negativity and that allow the subject to function adaptively. From a pragmatic point of view, we can appreciate this functional attribute of human resilience; however, this is only the case on the phenomenological level. Formally, the ego is never free from conflict because it is part of the ontological fabric of negativity inherent in unconscious process. During moments of autonomy that are seemingly devoid of conflict, the ego lives in a certain experiential realm, casting a certain shadow or appearance that defines its character at that time. It is merely a moment in the process of its own becoming, and, consequently, it does not reveal its whole truth. Structurally, conflict drives human experience and human relatedness. The ego must adapt to the constant bombardment of multiple conflicts. This is why Freud spoke of 'self-preservation' as one task the ego must set for itself.

From psychoanalysis to existentialism

Throughout this chapter, we have been preoccupied with attending to the philosophical parameters of Freud's unconscious ontology that represents his mature model of the mind. In this way, we have traced his early work on the biologicalization and economics of drive theory to the complex role of the negative and increased dynamicism that lends dialectical structure to unconscious organization, modification and differentiation, eventually leading to the centrality of the ego as the executive agency governing psychic reality. As with Spirit's ascendance toward the refined regions of self-conscious life, we may readily observe parallels in Hegel's and Freud's theoretic visions that articulate the developmental progression of the ego from its primitive unconscious beginnings, even though their projects are radically different in aim and scope.

While Hegel was chiefly concerned with the metaphysics of human experience, Freud was preoccupied with the 'tyrant' of human psychology. But regardless of their divergent theoretical systems, both thinkers saw value in the role of the unconscious, gave it the metaphysical status of being or presence underlying psychic structure, and described how the greater faculties of mind emerged and developed from an archaic and primordial underworld. Freud (1933a) believed this 'psychical underworld' (*SE* 22:58) was inhabited by three differentiated aspects of the soul that corresponded to his mature tripartite model of mental functioning. In his final theoretical paradigm, he accounted for the existential complexities of subjectivity and the throes of becoming a subject within a cultural milieu that during his era was plagued by anxiety, war, alienation and the search for meaning in an increasingly discontented world.

The struggle of the existential subject was very much a focus during Hegel's and Freud's time, although it is usually identified as a different yet parallel and contemporaneous movement that began during Freud's lifetime in Germany yet was more fully realized in France as a distinct movement in philosophy that grew out of phenomenology. Because the questions of human existence, suffering, social malaise and living an enlightened life span a range from antiquity to Christendom, we will now focus our attention on competing theories of human nature that prospered during the rise of psychoanalysis. Here our inquiry will centre primarily on the ontological structures of subjectivity represented in the works of Heidegger and Sartre, which ultimately engage the greater questions of agency, human value, authenticity and the quest for meaning in an uncertain world.

Notes

1 The noun *Ich* stands in philosophic relation to German Idealism, particularly Fichte's (1993 [1794]) absolute self-positing self: '*The self exists for itself* [and] *begins by an absolute positing of its own existence*' (*W* § 1: I, 98, emphasis in original). Today it is almost exclusively a Freudian term.

2 Here unconscious phantasy appears to be operative as an unarticulated form of agentic enactment under the *telos* of negotiating some compromise in intrapsychic conflict.

3 For Freud (1940a), the ultimate aim of Eros is to integrate differentiations of mind under the rubric of a synthetic unity, or, in his words, 'to establish ever greater unities and to preserve them, thus – in short, to bind together' (*SE* 23:148–149). Notice here that Freud stresses the preservative aspect of unification.

4 This is the term preferred by Antoine Vergote to emphasize the pulsations of urges emanating from the lived body.

5 To be fair to my relational colleagues, there have been some recent attempts to amend earlier views that the body is of less importance than human relatedness (see Aron and Anderson's [1998] *Relational Perspectives of the Body*). However, regardless of some relational authors' views on embodiment, the books that launched the relational movement – namely, Greenberg and Mitchell's (1983) *Object Relations in Psychoanalytic Theory*, Mitchell's (1988) *Relational Concepts in Psychoanalysis*, and Greenberg's (1991) *Oedipus and Beyond* – all position a relational theory by abnegating drive (hence embodiment). Consequently, I maintain that my critique of their work is still legitimate (see Mills, 2005, 2012).

6 We must acknowledge the multiple motivations and overdetermined processes operative within the drives, including economic and regulatory teleonomic functions as well as adaptation and defence under the influence of evolutionary currents. Objects are not only coveted for pleasure but also for the function and purpose they serve. And derived modes of relatedness, such as emotional connection and love, are based on early bonds and identifications with attachment figures.

7 In this relational age, the death drive appears to be a drowning man. Even many classical analysts have difficulty accepting this central postulate in Freud's theoretical corpus.

From my account, these attitudes appear to be either based on unfamiliarity with what Freud actually said in his texts, are based on theoretical incompatibilities, or are the result of reactionary defences. It is incumbent on any critic to know exactly what he or she is criticizing, and that means delving into the nuances of what Freud truly had to say, not to mention what he implied or the logical inferences that may be deduced from it. Freud's seminal work on the primacy of death particularly highlights his ability to think as a philosophical scientist using the discipline of logical rigour wedded to clinical observation. Recall that Freud had aspirations to become a philosopher before deciding on medicine, was tutored by Franz Brentano at university, and said to Fliess: 'Through the detour of being a physician . . . I most secretly nourish the hope of reaching my original goal, philosophy' (see Letter to Fliess, 1 January 1896 [Freud 1896b, 159]). Regardless of what opinion contemporary psychoanalysts have of Freud's conception of the death drive, for historical, clinical and philosophical reasons it is worthwhile to engage Freud's thoughts on the matter. Here I am mainly interested in offering an exegetical reflection on Freud's introduction of the destructive principle to psychoanalytic theory; therefore, I do not address all the controversy, dissension and detractors who have debunked his contributions largely on evolutionary grounds. If psychoanalysis is destined to prosper and advance, it must be open to revisiting the controversial ideas that gave it radical prominence to begin with.

8 Derived from Plautus, *Asinaria* II, iv, 88; see Freud (1930, p. 111).

9 Recall that the impetus, loci and movement behind the force of the negative is the basis of Hegel's entire logic of the dialectic. This is exemplified in his treatise on the evolution of cognition, self-consciousness and the ethical development of the human race in the *Phenomenology of Spirit* (1807), and it is ontologically grounded in his formal system, which is introduced in the *Science of Logic* (1812).

10 I realize that many readers are not sympathetic to the death drive, but it is essential for understanding the interiorization of death as a metaphysical principle of negation and conflict that saturates the global universal structures of the dialectic. To dismiss death qua negation as an ontological structure would be to reject the dialectic, something I cannot theoretically justify. Here my views on death and desire are not a pure endorsement of Freud but, rather, a revisionist perspective on the death drive within the context of the processual nature of the dialectic. Unlike other contemporary Freudians, who privilege libido or explain aggression within the context of desire and trauma, I argue that life and death, being and nothing, are ontologically the same.

11 Recall that Freud had lived through the savagery of the First World War, lost his daughter Sophie to influenza the same year he published *Beyond the Pleasure Principle*, and was in the early stages of cancer of the palate, which was formally diagnosed three years later, the same year he formally classified his dual drive theory.

12 It should be noted that, when describing mental functions, the language of energetics, homeostasis and hydraulics has been replaced in contemporary discourse by equivalent metaphors that stress activity, experience, process and action. Even physicists use the language of quantum mechanics, but they stress non-material reduction, highlight the energetic stratification of material interactions via systemic and holistic paradigms, and use the poetics of determinate possibilities when describing the emerging processes of cosmology.

13 It should be observed that Freud's original theory of neurosis is based on defensive, albeit adaptive, reactions to trauma. Here, in his mature theory, he cannot escape the resonance of his earlier position by privileging the role of traumatic interference on psychic organization introduced by the forces of external reality. In fact, the death drive is constituted in the immediacy of trauma, itself a defence against annihilation. Here Freud may be begging the question as to whether death is constitutive or reactionary, but it is nevertheless present in the genesis of the self-preservative drive toward life. Paradoxically, it is this defensive psychic order that is also inherently oriented

toward destruction, whether this be internally or externally manifested. Proponents of an extrinsic trauma model may have no need to posit the primacy of a death drive when external intrusions give an adequate explanation. Freud, however, felt the theoretical need to explain the internal processes operative within unconscious mentation before incurring external trauma. Therefore, in my opinion, he attempts to logically prepare the psyche's response to trauma by accounting for a priori forces that govern the mind's primordial activity. Here Freud not only interiorizes death qua trauma but also privileges its sequence as an exogenous intrusive act that simultaneously arouses and institutes the psyche's aim toward self-destruction, albeit in routes it chooses through its own determinate teleology.

14 An Aristotelian interpretation can be supported by assigning death a final cause inherent in drive.

15 It is interesting to note that, as we will see in a future chapter, Whitehead's (1929) entire cosmology of process explains how each 'actual entity' that comprises the universe is oriented toward seizing upon its inherent freedom to actualize its potential possibilities and actions, which are ultimately destined toward 'perishing' into the next events that constitute an ongoing process. Hence, the *telos* of all living entities, or 'occasions', is death. This is compatible with the beliefs of many contemporary theoretical physicists who postulate an inherent entropy to the cosmos.

16 Here we must stipulate that, while early life predisposes one to neurosis, it does not predetermine a hard-and-fast developmental sequence: personal maturation is radically moulded by context and contingency. Like Freud's concept of drive, which is mobile and transmutational, the notion of psychic adaptation requires a certain margin of freedom.

17 In evolutionary biology, as in history and in nature, sex and aggression are necessary conditions for an organismic survival and self-preservation. Insofar as species could not continue without natural copulation, aggression must be harnessed in order to ensure survival. In fact, the whole historical narrative of the human race may be viewed as a 'slaughterbench' (Hegel 1833; *RH* 27) in order to advance human civilization, which still requires aggression to enforce law and order (Freud 1930).

18 In Freud's *Gesammelte Werke*, vol. 14, the actual German words for the Latin *ego* and *id* are I (*Ich*) and It (*Es*), respectively (see *GW* 14:124). I have quoted the customary English translation here.

19 Freud gives a very lucid description of the ego in its relation to the It and superego in Lecture 31, 'The Dissection of the Psychical Personality', in *New Introductory Lectures* (*SE* 22:57–80).

3

EXISTENTIALISM AND THE UNCONSCIOUS SUBJECT

Existentialism in a postmodern world

The term 'existentialism' is so ambiguous that it has essentially become a meaningless word. It is associated with a number of disparate philosophical doctrines, social–political movements and artistic sensibilities, that it becomes slippery to pin down its core philosophical tenets to such a degree that an undertaking of this kind would be no less rendered moot. We may nevertheless say that existentialism is a form of phenomenological philosophy that relies on certain reflective methods of studying human consciousness instantiated in the individual, society and culture, which emerged as a popular general movement characteristic of twentieth-century European thought represented across many disciplines including literature, the humanities and the social sciences.

Sartre is often heralded the father of existentialism, but surely philosophical preoccupation with the question and meaning of human existence dates back to antiquity. In philosophy there is often a distinction made between the nature of 'being', a broad ontological category, and that of 'existence', what we generally confine to the study of human subjectivity. From the Platonic notion of the soul to medieval Aristotelian theology, to modern materialism and transcendental idealism, there has always been a primary fascination with the longings and mysteries of human experience.

Sartre (1943) formally inaugurated the existential movement with its first principle in his magnum opus *Being and Nothingness* when he stated that 'existence precedes essence'. What he meant was that existence is prior to essence, and that essence is what man makes of his life through his lived, subjective concrete acts. But this dictum goes back to Descartes (1641) three centuries earlier in his *Meditations* where he avows that 'I am, I exist' (p. 17). The cogito knows itself to be necessarily and indubitably true whenever it puts itself forward or is conceived in the mind. Hence Descartes showed that we know that we exist long before we know who or what we are in our essence. Even the medievalists believed in the necessity of starting with the experiential givens of the sensuous world and then proceeding by induction and abstraction to the ultimate intuitive awareness of unchanging essences and internal truths – thus if anyone was an existentialist, it was surely St Thomas (Grene,1948). And here enters modernism. All modern philosophers from Descartes to Kant were preoccupied with the reconciliation between nature and mind, science and religion, self and society, and causality and freedom, thus giving rise to the late modern philosophies of the will and our continued preoccupation with the transcendence of the ego. For Fichte (1794), the father of German Idealism, the absolute self-positing self was a pure assertion – *I!* Schopenhauer (1818) was so enamoured with the I that he believed it was the foundation for that which is both determined and that which is determining, thus *The World as Will and Representation* – the fundamental reality is will, a will that suffers. And as we have seen, Hegel meticulously argues that *Geist* is a self-articulated process of becoming: essence must appear in order for anything to exist, hence to be made actual (*PS* § 147; *EL* § 131).

What does this all have to do with psychoanalysis? Everything! Anxiety and death, alienation and responsibility, meaning and possibility – the very ontological conditions that inform human subjectivity as both normative and pathological. For Kierkegaard, we live in extreme anxiety and trembling over death and dread, and despair over who we are, the very thing that defines our being, the very thing that orients us toward our future, hence our possibilities; and for Kierkegaard, that meant the ethical and spiritual life of man. Nietzsche also could not tolerate the herd mentality, where truth was far from being found in 'the crowd'; but unlike Kierkegaard, he saw life as meaningless and in need of nihilistic revolt, of the transvaluation of values – to create oneself afresh – through a will to power. But the single most unremitting question for our existential man is the nature of freedom. Sartre was an extremist: human subjectivity was radical freedom, the unabated obligation to choose how one is to be. For Sartre, we are condemned to freedom – we cannot not choose, or else we plummet into self-deception or bad faith (*mauvaise foi*). The human being is not a thing, but a process of transcendence that must seize upon its freedom in order to become and define itself via its authentic choices. Psychopathology is a failure to seize upon one's freedom. Sartre's magnum opus is a treatise on existential analysis, and in many ways shares affinities with psychoanalysis, but he had one beef: Sartre could not accept nor tolerate the idea of an unconscious mind because it fractured his very thesis that we are all unconditionally self-determining. How could we be free if choice was governed by alien forces from within? Despite enjoying wide popularity, perhaps for this single attack on Freud, Sartre was not destined to find many followers among psychoanalysts of his day.

It was with Heidegger (1927) that existential analysis began to find a broader voice, and this was largely due to the dissemination of his thought by Swiss psychiatrists Ludwig Binswanger and Medard Boss. Heidegger's influential work, *Being and Time*, one of the most celebrated texts of the twentieth century, is essentially about the throes of human existence, what he refers to as *Dasein* – the concretely existing human being who is there in the world.[1] Dasein has a relationship with itself, others and its environment which is constitutive of its facticity – as a being thrown into a pre-existing social ontology. Like Sartre, Heidegger was preoccupied with explicating the essential elements of human existence as being in relation to its own struggles with anxiety and death, freedom and inauthenticity, and transcendence as a temporal phenomena of seizing one's possibilities. Like Sartre's notion of bad faith, Heidegger showed that human beings have a propensity for being neurotic and living in self-deception as the fallen *Das Man*, those who gravitate toward the herd and fail to live their lives genuinely. But as with Sartre, Heidegger could neither accept the primacy of the unconscious nor the governing causality it implicitly brings forth in our conscious lives. And here, in my opinion, is a cardinal reason why existentialism remains foreclosed and underappreciated by the psychoanalytic community. While psychoanalysis underscores the primacy and ubiquity of unconscious mentation, existentialism cannot bear to have its freedom curtailed.

But this did not stop existential analysis from flourishing in Europe, and to some extent in the United States, at least for a time. The novelists, poets, journalists and playwrights, from Dostoevsky to Rilke, Kafka, Ortega and Camus, many of whom were contemporaries of Sartre and Heidegger, swept over the masses, also drawn to the philosophical–religious aspirations of Martin Buber, Gabriel Marcel, Paul Tillich, Frieda Fromm-Reichmann and Erich Fromm; and in the field of mental health, Jaspers, Binswanger, Boss, Bally, Laing, Saasz, Van den Berg, Frankl, Minkowski, Ellenberger, Rollo May and Yalom, just to name a few, did much to pave the way toward appreciating existential analysis and phenomenological psychopathology. In fact, Boss and Bally were classically trained analysts, while Binswanger, although in Switzerland, became a member of the Vienna Psychoanalytic Society at Freud's recommendation when the Zurich group split off from the International Psychoanalytic Association (May, 1983); although many existential therapists were under Jungian influence.

In the States, there was much more interest in existential analysis during the 1950s, perhaps in part due to burgeoning interest in humanism, social–political thought, critical theory and neo-Marxism, the marginalized anti-psychiatry movement, the backlash against positivism, the seduction of Eastern spirituality, and the dehumanization of industrialized, materialistic culture. In the end, existentialism remains a multitudinous set of precepts, some systematized, but mainly recalcitrant to systematic reduction. But one irrefutable premise is that we as subjective agents are never static or inert creatures, rather we are a process of becoming, an observation made by the ancients from Heraclitus to Laotzu.

One could argue that psychoanalysis has always been an existential enterprise, and nowhere do we see this more poignantly realized than in Freud. Freud's entire metapsychology could be said to be an existential treatise on the scope, breadth and limits to human freedom. Freud was profoundly engaged with the questions of life and death, determinism and choice, self and other, alienation and causality, so much so that his mature model of the mind is none other than a return to the Greek concept of the soul. But what Freud is capable of showing that the existentialists and phenomenologists refuse to accept, is that the unconscious is also self-determining, hence the coming to presence and actualization of freedom.

Now we seem to live in a postmodern time of scepticism concerning the existence of the self (Frie, 2003). While postmodernism has no unified body of theory, one unanimous claim is the demise of the subject. Although postmodern thought has propitiously criticized the pervasive historical, gendered and ethnocentric character of our understanding of the world, it has done so at the expense of displacing several key modern philosophical tenets that celebrate the nature of subjectivity, consciousness and the teleology of the will. Consequently, the transcendental notions of freedom, autonomy and authentic choice that comprise the fundamental activities of personal agency are altogether dismantled (Mills, 2003).

In the empirically driven world of contemporary scientific psychology, postmodernism may appear as an interesting yet marginalized phenomenon. In this sense it shares the eccentricity historically associated with existential, phenomenological and psychoanalytic accounts that have fought for recognition from traditional psychological paradigms. However, within the larger intellectual community that comprises the humanities and behavioural sciences, we may observe a divide between science on the one side, and postmodernism on the other, each with its purported critics and adherents. Yet strangely enough, scientific and postmodern approaches yield similar implications for the fate of the self. Because scientific psychology is largely entrenched in empirically and biologically based materialistic frameworks, the dynamic activities of mind – including consciousness, cognition and subjectivity – are imperilled by reductionist strategies. While postmodernism boasts to have subverted the subject, materialists have reduced it to a brain state. Either way, subjectivity, selfhood and personal agency are displaced.

Eclipsed by postmodernism, psychoanalysis is even beset from within its own discipline. Hell bent on displacing classical psychoanalysis, the relational and intersubjective schools, or what has been called the American Middle Group, is content with chucking Freud altogether, while in my view, this movement is mainly a reinvention of the analytic wheel. While Freud has been largely discarded in the States, albeit subsumed by the rest of the world, relational and intersubjective approaches are at least turning to philosophy to find a fresh breath of ideas, despite it merely being a return of old paradigms under a new guise. Contemporary psychoanalysis may become a friend to existential thought, for it is much more open to developing an appreciation for philosophy in general. With the recent translation of Heidegger's *Zollikon Seminars*, given at Boss's invitation to the psychiatrists of Zurich over a ten-year period between 1959 and 1969, we may anticipate renewed interest in reiterating the question of *Dasein* in the consulting room. But how is Heidegger as a professor of psychiatry? Let us look at a brief passage from his *Seminars*.

HEIDEGGER: How does Dr. R. relate to the table before him?

LISTENER A: He is sitting behind it and looking at it.

HEIDEGGER: At one with this, the 'nature' of Dr. R.'s Dasein also reveals itself – but as what?

[Five minutes of silence]

HEIDEGGER: I remain silent because it is senseless to want to lecture you about Dr. R's existing. Everything depends on your learning to *see* the matter for yourselves, that you are patiently attentive to the matter, so that it may reveal itself to you in the totality of its own proper meaningfulness.

LISTENER C: Dr. R is separated from the table by an interval of space.

HEIDEGGER: What, then, is space?

LISTENER D: The distance between Dr. R. and the table.

HEIDEGGER: What is distance?

LISTENER E: A definition of space.

HEIDEGGER: What, then, is space as such?

[Ten long minutes of silence . . .]

(cited in Boss, 1978–79, pp. 10–11)

From this example, perhaps I am a little overly optimistic that Daseinsanalysis will make a comeback; but I am still rather hopeful. Nevertheless, existential, phenomenological and continental perspectives in philosophy complement psychoanalytic discourse, thus providing a fecundity of overlap in conceptual thought and practice that contemporary schools have been increasingly acknowledging over the past few decades. It can be said that psychoanalysis is fundamentally a theory and method geared toward insight, truth and the amelioration of human suffering, while philosophy is the pursuit of wisdom, truth, human excellence and rational meaning, what Freud himself identifies as *Logos*. I see these two disciples as embracing similar convictions that human existence is ultimately about developing our potential, fulfilling our possibilities, and living an authentic life through the liberation from ignorance and the malicious forces that threaten our happiness. This takes courage and fortitude, but it first and foremost takes awareness. In this way, therapy is a *liberation struggle* – Know thyself! This Delphic decree is the psychoanalytic motto. Insight or self-knowledge takes a commitment to educating oneself to what truly lies within – the complexity and competing flux of the inner world, and this is never an easy endeavour. It takes another to nurture and draw this out, to validate and reinforce, to encourage and to guide, to hold and reassure. This begins with the most primary of all relations, the relation of the embryonic self to that of its mother, then to its family and community at large, and finally to the social institutions that foster and beget the cultivation of self-consciousness.

Despite the postmodern trend that displaces personal agency and the self, from Hegel to Freud we have seen that human subjectivity is an indispensable and emergent experiential process of becoming. Although some Heidegger scholars may argue that Dasein is technically not a subject, which is a minority opinion, for our purposes, as Heidegger elucidates, Dasein is the concretely existing human being. Heidegger is very clear that 'Dasein exists', not as an epiphenomenon of larger cultural and linguistic forces, but as a subject who emerges within them equiprimordially. Dasein is the subjective human being who lives in a world composed of multiple dynamic organizations that are psychologically, socially and temporally realized in relation to the past, the present, and future possibilities.

And just as Sartre emphasizes our subjectivity as radical freedom, and psychoanalysis is the pursuit of bringing to light that which lies hidden from our immediate conscious awareness, we exist in relation to what we can become. Ultimately in both the existential and psychoanalytic traditions, we can only become more free through knowledge.

Throughout this chapter I will attempt to defend a concept of the self as an experiential process of becoming that challenges postmodern and scientific ideologies. In order to do so, I will largely draw on Heidegger's existential philosophy and show how his concept of Dasein constitutes a phenomenology of becoming that preserves the notions of freedom, choice and subjective agency. Juxtaposed to Sartrean and psychoanalytic accounts, Heidegger's philosophy allows us to engage the question of authenticity, which is a central task in the process of Dasein's own becoming. By closely examining the work of Heidegger and Sartre, I will seek to demonstrate the relevance of existential–phenomenological approaches to contemporary psychoanalysis. The phenomenology of becoming is a fundamental pursuit of the human condition, and it is precisely the process and quality of the lived experience that becomes important within a therapeutic and philosophical context. Therapy is a process of becoming, and like life, it must be embraced, endured and transcended. In order to become, we must first confront the possibility of authenticity and its existential–psychodynamic contingencies.

The enigma of authenticity

What does it mean to be authentic? Perhaps this is a question one can never adequately answer. As illusive as the meaning of being, the question of authenticity existentially moans for a response. Although Heidegger was primarily concerned with the question of Being (*Sein*) rather than the nature of beings (*Seiende*), he was deeply interested in the interface between philosophy and psychology (Boss, 1978–1979; Guignon, 1993; Richardson, 1993).[2] Despite Heidegger's apathy toward Freudian psychoanalysis (see Craig, 1988; Richardson, 1993), his conceptualization of Dasein has direct and significant contributions for psychoanalytic thought. While there are potential conceptual quandaries between the technical, 'ontological' discourse of Heideggerian theory and the applied, 'ontical' discourse of psychodynamic approaches,[3] Heidegger's existential ontology has profound implications for understanding the role of the unconscious and the questions of authenticity, truth and agency.

For Heidegger, authenticity is a uniquely temporal structure and a process of unfolding possibility. It is a state of being that is active, teleological, contemplative and congruent – an agency burgeoning with quiescent potentiality. As such, authenticity is the process of becoming one's possibilities: by nature it is idiosyncratic and uniquely subjective. Thus the pursuit of authenticity becomes a key therapeutic endeavour. Generally we might say that selfhood vacillates between authentic and inauthentic modes; that it tarries with genuine inauthenticity only to find itself genuinely authentic. Selfhood therefore participates in many forms on its acclivity toward apprehending its possibilities. Perhaps selfhood is beyond this antithetical distinction; it merely is what it is. Perhaps authenticity is beyond the individual; it ultimately belongs to the very ontology that constitutes Being itself. This becomes particularly relevant to how Being is actualized within the process of therapy as the personal attainment of one's possibilities.

Heidegger tells us that humankind has the recalcitrant need to divulge itself as inauthenticity. Not only does Dasein unveil itself in the everyday mundane modes of existence, but it does so in a false manner. But what does it mean for Dasein to be false, that is, what are the conditions that influence the development of inauthenticity? Within this context, truth and falsity are regarded not in terms of their epistemic verity, but in reference to Dasein's states of authentic and inauthentic disclosedness. From this standpoint, is it possible that the very ontological structures of Dasein itself are false? Can the human being be thrown into a deficit world, a world tainted by fallenness and inauthenticity, so much so that it predetermines Dasein's Being-in-the-world as a falsehood? To what degree is our social environment structurally differentiated into various existential modalities that are themselves pathological, thereby affecting the very ways in which the self is disclosed? I will demonstrate that selfhood encompasses a dialectical course undulating through experiential modes of authenticity and inauthenticity, in which this very process itself is an authentic one; this is the necessary *a priori* condition of Dasein itself as Being-toward-possibility.

Dasein and fallenness

In his philosophical treatise *Being and Time* (1927), Heidegger offers an existential ontology of selfhood as *Dasein* (being there), the actual human subject who is there, as part of a world. In Dasein's original disclosedness as Being-in-the-world, one is thrust into the ontological contingency of 'Being-in' an environment (*Umwelt*) and 'Being-with' others (*Mitwelt*) and with-oneself (*Eigenwelt*), which underlies all participation, engagement and concrete involvement with the world that is *given* in one's immediate preoccupations and concerns. Thus, the world itself is constitutive of Dasein's Being for 'Being-in-the-world is a state of Dasein which is necessary *a priori*, but it is far from sufficient for completely determining Dasein's Being' (*BT* § 54). As Heidegger explicates, Dasein's Being takes on a particular character a priori, and exists within the modes of authentic and inauthentic disclosedness.

> Dasein exists. Furthermore, Dasein is an entity which in each case I myself am. Mineness belongs to any existent Dasein, and belongs to it as the condition which makes authenticity and inauthenticity possible.

> (*BT* § 53)

The modes of Dasein's disclosedness are already structurally constituted in Dasein's Being-in-the-world. However, they are only the existential conditions that make authenticity and inauthenticity possible. As Heidegger points out, these two modes of disclosedness must have ownership, that is, they necessarily belong to the subjective, singular Dasein. For our purposes, Dasein is to be understood within the context of *selfhood*.

As the self, Heidegger delineates the factuality of Dasein characterized by humankind's naked 'thereness', one's abandonment as thrown into the publicness of 'the they'. As human beings disclose themselves in the everydayness of Being-in-the-world, they discover that they have been thrust into an environment without any consultation or choice in the matter whatsoever, and by definition have been abandoned to chance factors which already constitute their Being. Therefore, there is a fundamental propensity of Dasein, one which belongs to everydayness and manifests itself as *das Man*. Das Man, one among 'the they', is Dasein's ontological destiny. The world is a world in which one shares with others in communal proximity. Thus, Dasein's communal structure lends itself to a participation that cannot be annulled, namely, that of *they*ness. By virtue of Dasein's communal character, one cannot *not* participate in a world determined by the pragmatics of society and the everyday concerns that structure Dasein's activities.

For Heidegger, the question of authenticity becomes intimately associated with the existential character of Dasein as concern and solicitude. He states:

> If Dasein-with remains existentially constitutive for Being-in-the-world, then . . . it must be interpreted in terms of the phenomenon of *care*; for as 'care' the Being of Dasein in general is to be defined.
>
> (*BT* § 121)

Just as Dasein's relation to the environment is that of practical concern, Dasein's relation to the communal world is that of personal concern. As Heidegger explains, this form of concern belonging to everydayness by necessity will ultimately lead to modes of inauthenticity. As the 'anonymous one', the uniqueness of selfhood is diffused and lost in depersonalization and 'averageness'.

> Being for, against, or without one another, passing one another by, not 'mattering' to one another – these are possible ways of solicitude. And it is precisely these last-named deficient and indifferent modes that characterize everyday, average Being-with-one-another.
>
> (*BT* § 121)

Heidegger expounds upon another structural element in the ontological constitution of Dasein, that of 'fallenness'. This is the universal tendency of human beings to lose themselves in the everydayness of present concerns and preoccupations to such a degree that it does nothing but alienate them from their personal and unique future possibilities, thus reducing the fallen *das Man* to a mere 'presence-at-hand'. He posits:

> This 'absorption in . . . ' [*Aufgehen bei*] has mostly the character of Being-lost in the publicness of the 'they'. Dasein has, in the first instance, fallen

away [*abgefallen*] from itself as an authentic potentiality for Being its Self, and has fallen into the 'world'.

(*BT* § 176)

Everydayness and fallenness are ontological and natural predispositions of Dasein, therefore devoid of any value judgments attached to them; nevertheless, they are modes of inauthenticity that cannot be avoided nor refused. The degree to which one participates in these inauthentic modes has a direct bearing on the existential status of falsehood.

As a perpetual mode of inauthenticity, the falseness of Dasein becomes manifested as a ' "levelling down" [*Einebnung*] of all possibilities of Being' (*BT* § 127). The fallenness of Dasein is expressed most ostensively through idle talk, curiosity and ambiguity. Gossip is an inauthentic use of discourse which simply repeats what is heard and accepted by the public without critically examining the grounds or validity of the subject matter under question. Idle talk is merely a repetition of the conventional, an unscrutinized acceptance of the interpretations of the public. The fallen *das Man* is not concerned with understanding the ontological priorities of what is blindly accepted as truth or fact, only in reiterating the public clichés of the 'anonymous one'. Curiosity, which parallels gossip, underscores Dasein's hunger to explore one's environment merely for the sake of discovering novelty that provides excitement, a pleasurable distraction, and knowledge simply in order to have known. Curiosity, therefore, is not motivated by the need for authentic understanding; it is merely an inauthentic form of solicitude. Ambiguity, on the other hand, is the dubious nature of information which is disseminated by 'the they', which makes it impossible to determine what was disclosed in genuine understanding and what was not. This ambiguity is not only about the public gossip, but also in reference to Being-with-one-another, and Dasein's Being-toward-itself, hence, an inauthentic relatedness.

At this point, we must further clarify what we mean by Dasein's falsehood. In section 44 of *Being and Time*, Heidegger (1927) discusses the relationship between Dasein, disclosedness and truth. This was the beginning of his later preoccupation with the pre-Socratic notion of ἀλήθεια, which he translates as *Unverborgenheit* or 'unconcealedness'. Truth or *aletheia* is a form of disclosure, unconcealment, or uncoveredness that reveals itself through that which appears. Heidegger continues his analysis in 'On the Essence of Truth' (1930), where he offers a more comprehensive engagement of this subject. Truth may only be disclosed from its hiddenness in a clearing that opens a space for unconcealment. Equally, as each space reveals the potentiality for truth to be made known, there is also conversely a closing, in that truth may only be revealed in the wake of concealment. Such movement of uncovering in the presence of covering underlies the dialectical participation of the nature of truth. Given Heidegger's very careful analysis of *aletheia*, how can Dasein be false? From this standpoint, truth and falsity are in reference to unconcealed states of Dasein's disclosedness, not in terms of their epistemological status. Therefore, the anonymous one, the fallen *das Man*, the identification with 'the they' of everydayness as averageness is a direct allusion to a constricted Dasein. This inauthentic mode of Being is a retreat from the ontological obligations that Dasein demands. In these extreme modes, Dasein is a reduced self, a stifled existence, a false Being. In addition, the false Dasein as Being-in and Being-with 'the they', starts to take on an existential character which is more negative, similar to Kierkegaard's notion of 'the crowd', or even more pejoratively, the Nietzschean 'herd'. The Dasein who has fallen into falsehood closes itself off from authentically Being-in-the-world, and even more significantly of Being-with and Being-toward itself. In psychoanalysis, this might be chalked up to the defence mechanism of denial, that is, people need to deny the ontological obligations of Dasein in the service of more primordial psychological needs or conflicts, such as psychodynamic motivations surrounding security, attachment and, as Heidegger points out, 'tranquility'. But as he continues to point out, this tranquility leads to an 'aggravation' and alienation of Dasein from itself. Heidegger states:

> When Dasein, tranquilized, and 'understanding' everything, thus compares itself with everything, it drifts along towards an alienation [*Entfremdung*] in which its ownmost potentiality-for-Being is hidden from it.
>
> (*BT* § 178)

Fallenness leads to the 'downward plunge' into the inauthentic Being of 'the they' in which authentic possibility is lost in obscurity and under the guise of 'ascending' and 'living concretely'. Is it possible, however, that this downhill plunge is a necessary one which provides the dialectical movement toward the fulfilment of Dasein's possibilities? Perhaps this turbulent necessity is the very authentic movement of Dasein toward itself as *becoming*. Rather than falling away from itself, Dasein is falling into itself. But this is only possible if Dasein becomes aware of its possibilities that it hides from itself. At this point we must ask, Why does Dasein close off its possibilities in the tranquility of fallenness rather than seize them authentically? In other words, why do we hide ourselves from our own potentiality-for-Being? Perhaps Dasein is afraid, afraid of its freedom.

Dasein in bad faith

In offering an existential analysis of authenticity, we have determined that Dasein's fundamental structure is ontologically oriented toward fallenness. In the case of the false Dasein, fallenness is exacerbated in that the subject constricts its comportment primarily to the modes of the inauthentic, thereby abdicating its potentiality-for-Being. Why would Dasein abnegate its potentiality? While theoretically distinct from Heidegger's existential ontology, Sartre's conception of inauthenticity further contributes to our understanding of the psychological–ontical processes immersed in Dasein's falsehood.[4]

In his magnum opus, *Being and Nothingness* (1943), Sartre introduced the notion of *mauvaise foi*, or bad faith. For Sartre, consciousness is Being, 'a being, the nature of which is to question its own being, that being implying a being other than itself'; that is, 'to be conscious of the nothingness of its being' (*BN*, p. 86). In other words, authentic Being is literally *no-thing*. Conversely, self-negation is the pinnacle of inauthenticity. The failure to define oneself as *other-than* what one is, is to reify oneself as a thing and thus deny the possibility of a future transcendence. Sartre asserts that 'consciousness instead of directing its negation outward turns it toward itself. This attitude, it seems to me, is *bad faith [mauvaise foi]*' (*BN*, p. 87).

Broadly stated, bad faith is characterized by self-deception, a lie to oneself. But how can one lie to oneself? Only if one is not consciously aware of such intentions to lie or to deceive. For the individual in bad faith, the nature of such a lie 'is not recognized by the liar as *his* intention' (*BN*, p. 88, original emphasis). While a genuine lie is a 'behaviour of transcendence', the bad faith lie is a denial of such possibility. Such is the case that liars find themselves as the victim of their own self-deception and live in falsehood.

> By the lie consciousness affirms that it exists by nature as *hidden from the Other*; it utilizes for its own profit the ontological duality of myself and myself in the eyes of the Other. The situation can not be the same for bad faith if this, as we have said, is indeed a lie to oneself. To be sure, the one who practices bad faith is hiding a displeasing truth or presenting as truth a pleasing untruth. Bad faith then has in appearance the structure of falsehood. Only what changes everything is the fact than in bad faith it is from myself that I am hiding the truth.
>
> (*BN*, pp. 88–89, original emphasis)

Sartre's notion of bad faith is intimately linked to his model of consciousness. He recognized two levels of consciousness: (1) consciousness as intentionality and self-reflection, and (2) prereflective consciousness. The former is consciousness as such and encompasses awareness of the self as a human subject. Prereflective consciousness, on the other hand, is the form of consciousness prior to being aware (of) an object for reflection. This is similar to Freud's notion of pre-consciousness, that is, one is not immediately aware of an internal event or object but could be if one's attention were drawn to that particular object for reflection. But we could say that self-deception is always informed by unconscious defence. Sartre vociferously repudiated the notion of the Freudian unconscious; instead, his model espouses Brentano's concept of intentionality. Consciousness is always conscious *of* or *about* something – conscious of some object we posit or place before us for reflection. Therefore, there is no inertia to consciousness; consciousness is not an object nor does it exist in itself. For Sartre, consciousness can be positional or non-positional. Consciousness that posits places an object before it for immediate reflection. Non-positional consciousness is consciousness by itself. Consciousness is experienced as a 'lack', a *hole* in being. In Sartre's view, consciousness is nothingness, a freedom compelled to fill its own lack through future projects. Therefore, consciousness is what it is not and is not what it is. For Sartre, we are more than what we can be if we are reduced to what we are. What we are is freedom, and as freedom we are transcendence.[5]

Bad faith can manifest in various existential modalities, from singular situational choices to patterns of self-deception, or as one could argue, character structure. Nevertheless, there is a double face to bad faith, namely (1) *facticity* and (2) *transcendence*. In the first case, bad faith is the failure to accept one's facticity. In the second, it is a failure of transcendence. For example, Sartre portrays a woman who consents to go out with a man for the first time and in her bad faith she denies his intentions behind the seductions of his conduct. 'She does not want to realize the urgency' of the moment and 'refuses to apprehend the desire for what it is' (*BN*, pp. 96–97). Throughout the flirtations, her companion places her in such a position as to require an immediate decision, only to be protracted and disguised by the various procedures she uses to maintain herself in this self-deception. Her 'aim is to postpone the moment of decision as long as possible' (*BN*, p. 97). In Sartre's example, the woman has failed to project a future, and has allowed herself not to take notice of the reality of the situation. Her decision rests in the locus of prereflective consciousness: she chose not to posit a future with her suitor, thus deceiving herself of such possibility.

> She has disarmed the actions of her companion by reducing them to being only what they are; that is, to existing in the mode of the in-itself. But she permits herself to enjoy his desire, to the extent that she will apprehend it as not being what it is, will recognize its transcendence.
>
> (*BN*, pp. 97–98)

According to Sartre, the woman has reduced herself to a thing, a passive object in which events happen to her that she can neither provoke nor avoid. In bad faith, the person is in possession of the truth, but fails to acknowledge it as such, thereby avoiding the responsibility it requires.

For Sartre, authenticity or good faith is when you represent yourself to yourself in the mode of being what you are not. The bad faith attitude is one in which the individual seeks to flee from their freedom and the obligations it demands by construing oneself as a thing, a Being-in-itself, rather than a Being-for-itself. Instead of, 'I am in the mode of being what I am *not*', the bad faith attitude is 'I am in the mode of being what I am', thus, a thing-in-itself. In short, as human agents we *must* choose. As long as one consciously chooses in freedom and accepts full responsibility for one's actions, one is in good faith. Human beings define and redefine themselves via their choices. Decisions are made in the interest of a value or one is in bad faith. This is the case when one fails to choose, or more appropriately, when one *chooses not to choose* authentically.

Sartre's portrayal of bad faith elucidates the psychological nuances of self-deception that are structurally instantiated in Dasein's ontical practices. For

Heidegger, bad faith would be a deficient mode of Dasein's Being-in-the-world; more specifically, Being-with-oneself and Being-toward one's future authentic possibilities. Within this general context, Dasein's fallenness is bad faith, a falsehood, a retreat into the everydayness of theyness, cloaked by self-deception. Furthermore, to deny our human reality as freedom by defining ourselves as a thing is Dasein's propensity to reduce itself to a mere 'presence-at-hand'.

If Sartre's depiction of bad faith is accurate, then every human being is in self-deception at one time or another. In fact, this is a necessary ontical condition of Dasein itself. Due to our penchant to fall into inauthentic modes of Being-in-the-world, Dasein will inevitably engage in such deceptive practices. For Sartre, we are condemned to freedom, which necessitates radical responsibility for our Being-for-itself. However, choices are made in the context of our ontological facticity and thus are affected by a milieu which, by definition, is deficient or inauthentic. Sartre's position ultimately demands for Being to transcend its ontological structures via choice. To what degree is this possible? Furthermore, he ostensibly denies the primordial motivations attributed to a dynamic unconscious. While Sartre rejected the psychoanalytic project, his delineation of inauthenticity contributes to the psychodynamic conceptualization of the primacy of ego organization in personality development. Again, we might say that bad faith is a defensive form of denial, a disavowal in the service of unconscious motivations, conflicts and wishes. Sartre assumes that *every* Being has the *same* developmental capacities and intrapsychic structures to choose authentically as free agents. But what if one's freedom to recognize authentic choices has been truncated due to structural deficits in psychological development? Here, is it possible that Being itself is robbed of its full potential for authenticity?

The false self

While the predisposition toward inauthenticity is an elemental condition of Dasein's facticity, the specific psychological dimensions of Dasein's falseness require further exploration. Dasein's psychological structures become more lucid with the assistance of a psychoanalytic explication of the self. What would it be like to not know who you are, to be alienated from your true sense of self? What would it be like to have to construct an identity that is ingenuine and artifically manufactured? What would it be like to not feel real? Within psychoanalysis, there has been a burgeoning interest in the clinical literature on the concept of the false self (Cassimatis, 1984; Chescheir, 1985; Khan, 1971; Lerner, 1985; Mitchell, 1992; Naso, 2010; Schacht, 1988). The inauthentic self, or the 'as if' personality, further deepens our understanding of the false Dasein.

Winnicott (1960) formally introduced the notion of the false self. While some parallels exist between Heidegger's exposition of the fallen Dasein and Sartre's depiction of bad faith, Winnicott's contributions to understanding the question of authenticity deserve special merit. For Winnicott, a false self is the result of developmental conflict encountered in the child–maternal relationship. As a result, a false self is constructed as a defensive system which remains unconsciously maintained. Winnicott's theoretical framework falls within a defence model that is ultimately tied to drive theory within the interpersonal context of the mother–child dyad. While having a ground in Freudian metapsychology, Winnicott's conceptualization of the false self is essentially a relational theory centring on ego defensive manoeuvres that arise in response to environmental demands. More specifically, within the infant–mother milieu, the child struggles to manage libidinal/creative impulses that are solely intrapsychic; however, this takes place within the context of the relational matrix or intersubjective field. Therefore, within the stage of the first object relationships, various defences are constructed in response to external demands, and particularly that of the maternal object. Ego organization is in the service of adaptation to the environment and procurement of object attachment. Repeated compliance to such demands, concomitant with a withdrawal from self-generated spontaneity, leads to an increased stifling of impulses constitutive of the natural drive for spontaneous expression, thereby culminating in a false self development.

For Winnicott (1960), the idea of a true self originates in the capacity of the infant to recognize and enact spontaneous needs for self-expression. 'Only the True Self can be creative and only the True Self can feel real' (p. 148). The notion of the self as the centre of spontaneity that has the 'experience of aliveness' constitutes the core or heart of authenticity. However, this ability to enact such spontaneous gestures is contingent upon the responsiveness of the 'good-enough mother' within an appropriate 'holding environment'. Thus, the aetiology of the true and false self is contingent upon the quality of maternal responsiveness. Winnicott postulates:

> The good-enough mother meets the omnipotence of the infant and to some extent makes sense of it. She does this repeatedly. A True Self begins to have life, through the strength given to the infant's weak ego by the mother's implementation of the infant's omnipotent expressions.
>
> (p. 145)

The true self flourishes only in response to the repeated success of the mother's optimal responsiveness to the infant's spontaneous expressions. If the mother is 'not good-enough', she does not facilitate the infant's omnipotence and repeatedly fails to meet the child's spontaneous gestures with appropriate responsiveness. Instead she substitutes her own gestures with which the infant complies. This repeated compliance becomes the ground for the earliest modes of a false self existence due to the mother's inability to sense and respond optimally to her baby's needs.

Like Heidegger's hermeneutical treatment of Dasein's ontology, Winnicott obviates the subject–object dichotomy with regards to the ontical structures of the self. The maternal holding environment is part of the very ontic structure of Dasein: it is constitutive of Dasein's Being. Failure in empathic attunement, mirroring and optimal reponsiveness is a deficient mode of Being-with, a precondition of the false Dasein's inauthenticity. Within this context, freedom becomes abridged and affects the true self development *as it would have unfolded* if Dasein's ontological constitution of Being-with had been different. Authenticity is curtailed by the demands of others. In this sense, there is no authentic self distinct from Being-with others. Winnicott supports this claim:

> This compliance on the part of the infant is the earliest stage of the False Self, and belongs to the mother's inability to sense her infant's needs.
>
> (p. 145)

Under these circumstances, perhaps a false self is not false at all. The false structures are authentic ones, that is, they are superimposed and constitutive of a true self, albeit a deficient one. Due to the historicity of various ontological contingencies that are themselves deficient modes of Being-in-the-world, Dasein is subjected to power relations by the very ontological positioning of worldhood itself. Dasein's Being-with others and toward-oneself will be greatly affected by other's deficiencies. Winnicott (1960) explains that:

> the infant gets seduced into compliance, and a compliant False Self reacts to environmental demands and the infant seems to accept them. Through this False Self the infant builds up a false set of relationships, and by means of introjections even attains a show of being real, so that the child may grow up to be just like mother, nurse, aunt, brother, or whoever at the time dominates the scene.
>
> (p. 146)

The defensive functions of the false self are constructed for one cardinal purpose, namely, 'to hide and protect the True Self' (p. 142). 'The False Self defends the True Self; the True Self is, however, acknowledged as a potential and is allowed a secret life' (p. 143). But what is the nature of this true or authentic self which is allowed a secret life? Winnicott does not offer an adequate explanation, he only points to the ability to enact spontaneous gestures of self-expression:

> The True Self appears as soon as there is any mental organization of the individual at all, and it means little more than the summation of sensory-motor aliveness.
>
> (p. 149)

But is this a sufficient understanding of authenticity? Doesn't the notion of authenticity carry with it, if not demand of it, that Dasein *can* to some degree transcend its mere thrownness; that is, choose actively to seize upon its subjective agency despite its environment?

Clearly Dasein is more than its physiological contingencies. On one level, to be authentic or true is to act in accord with one's genuine and congruent, innate strivings and yearnings. Within the various psychoanalytic domains, authenticity may conform to the influence of unconscious drive determinants, ego mastery of the self and the environment, object relatedness and the pining for relational attachments, and the psychic need for mirroring and idealizing selfobject experiences that form the rudimentary basis of a vital and cohesive self. Whatever the nature or *being* of these authentic strivings are, Winnicott assumes they exist, are hidden, and are preserved unconsciously due to the character structure of defence.

Winnicott concludes that the false self takes on a role which appears to be 'real', when in fact it is artificial. Indeed, this pseudo-real appearance takes on a 'personal living through imitation' in which the child may 'act a special role, that of the True Self *as it would be if it had had existence*' (p. 147, original emphasis). However, for Winnicott, the true self always exists behind the mask of the false persona, lying dormant, concealed and protected. The false self, as defence, is 'a defence against that which is unthinkable, the exploitation of the True Self, which would result in its annihilation' (p. 147). Thus, the aetiology of the false self may be said to arise out of the deficient modes of other Daseins, which were foisted upon the child with various ontological and psychological exigencies to comply with or perish under. It may be said that a false personality constellation is constructed in reaction to the fear of death of the self. Such fear of annihilation is the most archaic form of existential anxiety, a primordial denial of Dasein's Being-toward-death.

The unconscious displacement of the emerging annihilation anxiety is organized within the interpersonal matrix of the infant's earliest object relations. Within this context, Masterson (1981) defines the false self as 'a collection of behaviors, thoughts and feelings that are motivated by the need to cling to the object', and thus suppress the longings for separateness and individuation (p. 101). Within contemporary object relations theory, the false self functions defensively as a means to ward off separation anxiety and abandonment fears which ultimately represent the inability to integrate whole self and object representations, which in turn become the formative basis of a cohesive self. As a result, the capacity for spontaneity, autonomous self-assertion and the expression of creativity is stymied and lost in falsehood.

Winnicott's developmental model anticipates Kohut's (1971, 1977, 1984) psychoanalytic self psychology. For Kohut, the self is a bipolar structure composed of two dimensions: (1) the pole of ambitions and strivings, and (2) the pole of values and ideals. The former constitutes mirroring selfobject experiences in which the authentic core self is the centre of initiative, self-assertion, autonomy and vitality. The second pole is attained via the identification process and merger with omnipotent, calming, infallible selfobjects that are in turn internalized and become the intrapsychic structural foundation of the self. As Kohut (1978) theoretically moved away from the metapsychology of classical theory, the primacy of the self replaced the vicissitudes of the drives as 'the center of our being from which all initiative springs and where all experience ends' (p. 95). The self, as the centre of initiative and psychic motivation, depends upon the quality of selfobject experiences for its structural integrity and cohesion. Within this context, a false self would develop out of repeated failure in empathic attunement and optimal responsiveness in the early selfobject milieu. If the self becomes defined in the context of others' narcissistic needs, capacities for self-soothing and self-esteem regulation are thwarted due to a depleted or fragmented self structure.

The false self can manifest in various modalities and in degrees of its falseness. The more psychologically adjusted false self organization may be represented by the overly compliant, obsequious, acquiescent, interpersonally polite attitudes that accompany the expectations of social convention. This may be similar to Heidegger's description of Dasein's everydayness as fallenness in the modes of idle talk, curiosity and ambiguity. In terms of Sartrean bad faith, one makes inauthentic choices which are situational, repetitious, or characterological in the service of avoiding one's responsibility to accept freedom. In other words, by choosing not to choose authentically, we reside in the everyday inauthentic mode of 'theyness' as fallen *das Man*.

For contemporary psychoanalysis, Dasein's tendency toward fallenness serves primary motivations for relational attachment, emotional–interpersonal involvement, and validation of the self. In the case of the false Dasein, such wishes are inordinately intensified due to intrapsychic structural vulnerabilities of the self. Alice Miller (1981) discusses a particular form of false development, that of individuals who are raised by narcissistic parents and are cajoled into being responsive and attuned to everyone else's needs at the expense of their own. Children who are treated as objects to meet the narcissistic fulfilments of their parents may develop a virtuous yet tragic gift, the gift of empathy. Gifted children in this sense may develop skills of empathic attunement to anticipate, respond to, and meet the wishes of others in order to gain love and attention of their own; but only at the steep price of sacrificing their true self.

Still more toward maladjustment, one could say the false self is the 'actor' who puts on a theatrical facade but is unable to remove such persona; the actor becomes over-identified in the role and loses one's authenticity in one-sidedness.[6] Under the rubric of such one-sidedness, individuals seek to make themselves into a 'thing', a Being-in-itself rather than a Being-for-Self. Winnicott (1960) asserts, 'Whereas a True Self feels real, the existence of a False Self results in a feeling unreal or a sense of futility' (p. 148). He continues: 'The best example I can give is that of a middle-aged woman who had a very successful False Self but who had the feeling all her life that she had not started to exist' (p. 142). In the severe forms of the psychiatrically impaired, a false self system consists of an organization of various part-selves, none of which are so fully developed as to have a comprehensive personality of their own. This clinical phenomenon is what Laing (1959) spoke of as the *divided self*. In a divided self, there is no single false self, rather only partially elaborated fragments which might constitute a personality. In the Daseinsanalytic tradition (see Kockelmans, 1978), for Laing, as well as for Ludwig Binswanger, Medard Boss, Karl Jaspers, and more contemporarily Rollo May, a false self develops out of ontological insecurity, thereby leading to an overall constricted Dasein. To the extreme, the false or divided self may experience a dissociation of personality or a radical splitting of its embodied and disembodied aspects.

The call of conscience

Up until now, we have delineated the ontological and psychological structures of the false Dasein as inauthenticity maintains itself in the throes of selfhood. By virtue of Dasein's ontological predisposition as Being-in-the-world, selfhood is subjected to inauthentic existential modalities already constitutive of its Being. Such disclosedness to worldhood is formatively installed in Dasein's constitution. Dasein's propensity toward fallenness is therefore necessary and unavoidable. However, if environmental conditions are such that Dasein's ordinary ontological structure is subject to more extreme forms of inauthenticity, the false development of the subject may not be eluded. The false Dasein results from interactions with pre-existing deficient modes of Being-in-the-world that are thrust upon selfhood as its facticity. These pathogenic ontological structures lead to further vulnerabilities that predispose Dasein to develop psychological deficiencies as well. Such intrapsychic conflicts and structural limitations of the self further contribute to Dasein's *pathos* as deficient modes of Being-in-the-world and Being-toward-Self.

Given these assumptions, worldhood itself may be said to be a falsehood, plagued by bad faith and copious forms of psychopathology. Can Dasein transcend its predicament, or is it destined to live inauthentically? As Heidegger and Sartre would contend (albeit conceptualized differently), ultimately the self is free. However, freedom exists within the context of Dasein's ontological constitution. For Ricoeur (1965, 1966), Dasein primarily exists as fallenness in the sense that the will is enslaved by its actual conditions. In the case of the false self, Dasein is constricted by virtue of its ontological relation to a deficient environment that contributes to deficits in one's psychological development. Assuming this is the case, does this imperfect condition lead to another proclivity of Dasein to fall even further into inauthenticity? That is, if the environment into which one was hurled was ontologically inadequate to begin with, is not this bound to affect one's future overall Being-in-the-world? Is not the subject's Being-in and Being-with others and with-oneself greatly precluded from genuine authenticity, or at least the full possibility of such? And where do freedom and responsibility fit in for Dasein's future possibilities?

We as human beings have no control whatsoever over our thrownness (as authenticity in the toils of inauthenticity). However, as Heidegger and Sartre would insist, Dasein has the capacity and responsibility to choose authentically, thereby actualizing its freedom to become and fulfil its possibilities. However, is this a correct assumption? Winnicott and Kohut underscore the point that one's true self or authentic Dasein may be structurally deficient, hence false. This structural deficiency is due not merely to Dasein's historicity, which may bring about self-deception, but also to developmental interactions that form the psychological

basis of a cohesive self. That is, the very intrapsychic foundation of the self is deficit and replete with tumultuous unconscious activity, thereby influencing choices
and the modes Dasein assumes in the pursuit of authenticity. Perhaps the false
Dasein does not have these capacities that are more authentically developed in
other people, thereby encumbering the ability to form genuine good faith com-
portments characteristic of an authentic posture. Is it possible that the individual's
intrapsychic structures are so deficient that the emergence of a false character
organization is not false at all, only deficient in comparison to others' whose ontological and developmental constitutions are less false? Is the false Dasein destined to make choices that are dynamically informed by such limitations under
the influence of psychic determinism? Are these processes set firmly in place as
unwavering constitutional vulnerabilities, or is there an inner motivation, so that
underdeveloped structures would resume their appropriate developmental trajectory if given the opportunity? And what would constitute this opportunity – a
modification of Dasein's introspective capacities as recognizing and then actualizing its freedom within the context of its thrownness? Would this also require a
modification from the social environment as well? Does the hidden true self strive
for authentic expression despite its false structure, or is this false structure its very
true or authentic mode to begin with?

If selfhood is abandoned to falsehood that is already constitutive *a priori* of
its Being, then the false Dasein will structurally exist (both ontologically and
developmentally) in authenticity, but in deficient modes. In other words, false self
structure is authentic given Dasein's ontological contingencies that inform these
deficient modes of Being. However, these constitutional deficiencies may lead
the false Dasein to develop even further deficient modes of Being-in-the-world,
including, at the extreme, psychopathology. The false Dasein is a real system; it
is primary and true although it is stifled in its development. Due to these partially
underdeveloped psychic structures, it is unformed in its potential, whereby its
internal states directly perpetuate inauthentic modes of Being. Although the false
Dasein is real, it is deficient and impedes more healthy aspects of the self from
flourishing. Therefore, the *lie* or the falsehood is experienced as psychically real
albeit in the modes of the inauthentic.

At this point we must ask: To what degree does the false Dasein have responsibility to its authentic possibilities? Can the false subject overcome its fallenness and its psychological vulnerabilities as well? Can it alter its ontological and
developmental status? Heidegger differentiates: 'The Self of everyday Dasein is
the *they-self*, which we distinguish from the *authentic Self* – that is, from the Self
which has been taken hold of in its own way [*eigens ergriffenen*]' (*BT* § 129).
Can the false Dasein take hold of its true nature as transcendental possibility?
Like Sartre's position on self-deception, Winnicott would maintain that the false
self hides the inner realities of the true self. In this interpretation, unlike Sartre's,
the unconscious cannot be denied. These authentic strivings, wishes and yearnings will always be allowed to have a secret life in the night-like abyss of the
unconscious mind, and their disillusionments will be endured. But what resonates

within the nocturnal pit of Dasein's core Being? Perhaps it is Dasein's transcendental authenticity as the 'potentiality-for-Being which must be made free in one's *ownmost* Dasein alone' (*BT* § 178).

For Heidegger, authenticity is ultimately self-relatedness (within world-relatedness) marked by the embracing of Dasein's responsibility toward genuine care. This care, in other words, is an ownership of Dasein's freedom that, in turn, opens a space for sublimated authenticity, which perennially exalts itself in its self–world relation. For Heidegger, this necessitates the 'call of conscience', the voice of Dasein within Dasein that summons us to respond to an authentic appeal to transcend the corrupted public everydayness of Being and to call Dasein to a new possibility of Being. It is the voice of authentic Dasein's Being-toward authentic possibility. It summons *me*, it commands me toward myself. Such authentic relationship to our true possibilities of Being-toward-possibility must be born/e out of our own experience, clamouring for a higher unity of Being. Authentic Being-one's-Self requires an existentiell modification of the 'they' in which 'Dasein specifically brings itself back to itself from its lostness' (*BT* § 268). Authentic Dasein must 'make up' for not living and choosing genuinely and must first make possible its authentic potentiality-for-Being. Dasein comes to find itself through the disclosure of conscience as an inner voice. The receptivity of the voice calls Dasein to a 'giving-to-understand' the authentic self, in which the call 'passes over' the they-self and finds its true home in its enlightened understanding of itself. Heidegger articulates:

> One must keep in mind that when we designate the conscience as a 'call', this call is an appeal to the they-self in its Self; as such an appeal, it summons the Self to its potentiality-for-Being-its-Self, and thus calls Dasein forth to its possibilities.
>
> (*BT* § 274)

As conscience, Dasein calls itself; it is both the caller and the one being called. The voice of conscience has the character of an appeal '*summoning* to its ownmost Being-guilty' (*BT* § 269). Such guilt, however, is not a moral or psychological guilt, rather an indebted, beholden obligation Dasein has toward its responsibility to become and fulfil itself as Being-in-the-world. Dasein must seize upon such guilt in that it 'owes' something to itself and to others. It is the call of care, in which its lostness is recovered in its apprehension of its obligation to be *other-than* what it is in its everydayness.

But what does the voice say? It says nothing. The content or substance of such a call is empty; it is the inner voice without words, an appeal without authority, a summons without a notice, merely the 'call of care'. The call is the inner guidance of truth, an enlightenment that 'points *forward* to Dasein's potentiality-for-Being' (*BT* § 280). This call comes from the uncanniness it experiences in its guilt, which makes Dasein inextricably responsible for its own authentic becoming. Such uncanniness arouses a ubiquitous anxiety, directed toward its truth as 'resoluteness'. As a distinctive mode of Dasein's disclosedness, resoluteness is the truth of Dasein's authenticity as Being-one's-Self, as concern for Being-alongside what is ready-to-hand and the solicitous care of Being-with-others. As positive solicitude in Dasein's Being-with, authenticity is a special form of concern, that which is a 'leap ahead' of the Other, a genuine care that helps the Other 'become transparent to himself *in* his care and to become *free for* it' (*BT* § 122). Equiprimordially, such transparency must apply to Dasein's Being-toward-itself as care.

On one level, the truly authentic Dasein is idiosyncratic, it is uniquely subjective and personal. Heidegger supports this position:

> When the call gives us a potentiality-for-Being to understand, it does not give us one which is ideal and universal; it discloses it as that which has been currently individualized and which belongs to that particular Dasein.
>
> (*BT* § 280)

Within this context, authenticity is a Being who contemplates itself, a Being who transforms itself. As authenticity, Dasein is care. Authenticity is Dasein's possibility *as such*; a fundamental relatedness of possibility-toward-becoming as an indeterminate openness to oneself. Authenticity is then, simply, *to be*, to be in selfhood that is a fundamental openness, rather than a self-enclosed, self-enslaved participation in everydayness. It is the relatedness of Being-toward-transcendence in its purist form.

But what are we to make of Heidegger's final determination of authenticity? One is left with a sense of generic ambiguity. Authenticity is opaque and equivocal. It follows a voice that does not speak, it points to a direction that is not visible, it summons us to respond to a calling we cannot identify; yet it appeals to an obligation that cannot be disowned. Perhaps authenticity is *beyond* what words can define, only Dasein knows its truth. Yet this conclusion always runs the risk of collapsing into relativism or radical subjectivism. Despite Heidegger's insistence that the authentic call is 'individualized', we may nevertheless say it is in the *form* of care, which becomes a *subjectivity universality* belonging to a phenomenology of becoming.

Is there such a clear cut demarcation between authenticity and inauthenticity? I think not. Instead of these antipodes, we need to understand selfhood as an epigenetic development on a continuum of authenticity, in a state of becoming as emerging freedom. How are we really to determine the criteria of what constitutes an authentic from an inauthentic Dasein when these ontic–existentiell conditions are indissolubly determined in Dasein's own Being? If Dasein is its disclosedness, in that we disclose ourselves and then discover ourselves in our disclosing or unconcealment, then the false Dasein is only one mode of Being-in-the-world capable of finding itself in its lostness and recovering its authenticity in its freedom. Therefore, the false Dasein is capable of hearing the call, understanding the message, responding to the subpoena by following the path of possibility, and transcending its thrownness in its Being-toward-becoming. The horizon of possibility is Dasein.

Toward a discourse of the other

Throughout our quest for authenticity, we have seen how inauthenticity is maintained within an authentic falsehood ontologically constituted in Dasein's existential disclosedness. Despite the false Dasein's inauthentic comportment as Being-in-the-world, we have determined that it *is* indeed possible for Dasein to transcend its inauthenticity, even in the case of the false self, by apprehending its authentic Being-toward-possibility in its potentiality-for-Self. In other words, despite intrapsychic deficits characteristic of the psychoanalytic description of the false self, Dasein *can* ennoble itself in actualizing its freedom. Perhaps the interface between Heideggerian philosophy and psychoanalysis provides us with a clearer window into the possibilities for selfhood and gives us a more profound grasp on what it is to be.

In conclusion, I believe there is, for Dasein, a *double edge of centredness*: namely, the authentic centre of selfhood is one in the same, inseparable and ontologically undifferentiated in that authenticity and inauthenticity exist in symbiosis as the core dialectical function of Dasein's Being. Dasein is beyond the authentic and the impure; a disclosure of such unification is its wholeness. In the phenomenon of falsehood, everydayness is a deficient mode, yet a necessary complement to the dialectical organization of selfhood. In this sense, existence is neutral: it discloses the conditions not only for fallenness, but also for transcendence as Dasein's emphatic destiny. The choice can only be Dasein's. As a temporal structure, authentic Dasein is a *movement*, an incessant opening and closing of itself to itself, entering into the mode of the inauthentic only to discover its authenticity in such violent process. Indeed, this process is an authentic one, a continual movement on the continuum, sublimating and elevating itself in awareness, understanding and action. Authenticity is therefore merely a moment, the indeterminate immediate. Bound within its temporal unfolding, authenticity is *Being-in-becoming* one's possibilities. As the possibility-for-Self, authenticity is only one appearance among many appearances. It emerges from itself and passes away back into itself, coming to be what it already is, the process of its own becoming. As an existentiell, the discovery or realization of one's inauthentic modes of Being necessitates, if not commands, a dialectical progression toward the fulfilment of one's authentic possibilities in the endless search of the true self. This double edge is Dasein.

In Heidegger's 'turning' (*Kehre*) or transition from the question and meaning of Being, to the truth of Being, he was to initiate an ontological discourse that situated language as the 'house of Being'. The repositioning of Dasein as language developed alongside the Anglo–American linguistic turn in philosophy, which was simultaneously taken up in France by the structuralist movement. Here enters Lacan. Lacan read Heidegger (in German) and referenced his work repeatedly throughout his *Écrits*. Lacan was to emphasize how the human being largely is constituted by language as the discourse of the Other (*discours de l'Autre*), which is broadly subsumed within a social ontology that comprises the symbolic order within culture. But unlike the existentialists, Lacan was not particularly invested in defending a notion of human freedom or agency because, as a result of his philosophical positions, the subject is subverted by the dominion of language, and hence is *caused* by linguistic forces instituted by the Other. Rather than following the psychoanalytic tradition that emphasizes the agency of the unconscious as intrapsychic activity derived from the ego's modification out of biological pulsions, Lacan places causal emphasis on three psychic registers that derive from forces outside of the subject, namely, the Imaginary, Symbolic, and Real. Let us now turn to the metaphysical implications of Lacan's environmental determinism and see how this infiltrates his particular form of epistemology as paranoiac knowledge.

Notes

1 Because the ordinary German word 'Dasein' is used by Heidegger as a technical term to connote a complex set of inner experiences, intrapersonal organizations and external relations that inform its ontological structure, I have retained the use of the word Dasein rather than attempt an English translation (such as self or subject), which would cripple its original meaning.

2 Heidegger's close friendship with the Swiss psychiatrist Medard Boss is well known. At Boss's invitation, Heidegger gave seminars to psychiatrists in Zurich for over ten years on his existential–ontological treatment of Dasein and its theoretical applications to psychological practice. As the founder of Daseinsanalysis, Boss was instrumental in introducing Heideggerian philosophy to the mental health profession in Europe, which eventually made its way into the American existential psychology movement in the 1950s and 1960s. From the published Heidegger seminars, Boss (1978–1979) informs us that Heidegger expressed the hope that his thinking could break away from purely philosophical inquiry to benefit those in human suffering including psychiatric populations. An interesting historical note is that Heidegger was hospitalized in Boss' clinic (Haus Baden Sanatorium) after he suffered a mental breakdown and a purported suicide attempt following interrogations by the denazification commission surrounding his involvement in the National Socialist Party prior to World War II, where he received treatment by psychoanalyst Dr Viktor von Gebsattel (see Askay and Farquhar, 2011).

3 Some may argue that psychology is not ontology and the conceptual link between the two is illegitimate. Although Husserl (1950) entertained ontological psychology (see *Cartesian Meditations*, § 59), this was not a problem for Hegel, so I am proceeding with the assumption that our understanding of the human condition is grounded in a structural ontology. However, I do not wish to equivocate the ontological–ontical terminology or treat them as though they are interchangeable. My aim is to proceed with a clear respect for the line between ontological/ontical and existential/existentiell. For Heidegger, '*Understanding of Being is itself a definite characteristic of Dasein's Being*. Dasein is ontically distinctive in that it *is* ontological' (*BT* § 12, italics in original). The ontic, that which concerns beings, and the ontological, that which concerns ways of being, are differentiated by virtue of their apophantical and hermeneutical referents. Existential understanding, on the other hand, is an understanding of the ontological structures of existence, that is, what it is to be Dasein, while existentiell understanding is a person's

self-understanding, that is, an understanding of his or her own way to be or what he or she is. Although Heidegger does differentiate the ontological from the ontical, the ontical can only be possible vis-à-vis the ontological, thus, our social and individual practices embody an ontology. Also see Dreyfus (1991) for a general commentary.

4 Although Heidegger's and Sartre's phenomenological ontologies are conceptually distinct with variegated subtleties, the question of authenticity is central to both of their philosophies. Albeit conceived differently from Heidegger's inauthentic Dasein, Sartre's notion of bad faith, as the renunciation of human freedom in the service of self-deception, contributes to our understanding of selfhood enthralled in the toils of inauthenticity and further anticipates the psychodynamic exploration of underlying defensive processes characteristic of the dynamic unconscious. While Heidegger offers a comprehensive hermeneutical treatment of Dasein in its relation to selfhood, Sartre depicts more acutely the psychological processes involved in the formation and maintenance of inauthenticity. While respecting the distinctions and divergences between Heidegger's and Sartre's ontological discourses, it becomes important to illuminate Dasein's falsehood in terms of its inauthentic ontical relations, which is the primary task of psychoanalysis. The equivocation of these different terminologies is therefore intended to facilitate the conceptual bridge between the existential–ontological structures of Dasein and their relation to the existentiell–ontical manifestations of inauthenticity that will be further addressed within a psychoanalytic account of the self.

5 Sartre's (1963) later notion of freedom stressed the 'practico-inert', demarcating the scope of freedom as always being situated (as determined) within concrete historical, social, cultural and economic limits. This parallels Heidegger's notion of thrownness.

6 In Jung's analytical psychology, one-sidedness is generally used to denote a mental construction of the self that is false. Within a Jungian context, one-sidedness with one's persona would be an over-identification with the archetypal nature of the collective unconscious that is constricted. Following Jung's notion of the Principles of Equivalence and Entropy, one-sidedness would be an over-emphasis and incompensatory discharge of mental energy, hence unequally distributed within the psyche.

4

LACAN'S EPISTEMOLOGY

If you were to randomly open any text of Lacan's and begin to read, you might immediately think that the man is mad. In a word, his writing is psychotic: it is fragmentary, chaotic, and at times incoherent. First of all, his style of spoken discourse, given in lecture format before appearing in print, is infamously troublesome. Second, his fragmented texts obstinately oppose conforming to formal articulate systematization. As a result, Lacan is not very accessible, either as a stylist or a theoretician. For these reasons he invites controversy and is often misinterpreted.[1]

Because Lacan was a fearsome polemicist, radical eccentric, and unorthodox practitioner bordering on the scandalous, within mainstream psychoanalysis his name has become a dirty word. Although he was hailed as the 'master' by his adherents, vociferous criticism of the 'French Freud' mounted vast condemnation for his exploitation of psychoanalytic technique labelled as manipulative, abusive, unethical and perverted. It comes as no surprise that he would be inevitably blamed (perhaps unfairly) for the suicide of some of his analysands, thus leading to his eventual expulsion from the psychoanalytic community (Haddad, 1981; Lacan, 1964a). Although the recognized genius that often accompanies his legend has by no means vanished from academic circles, due to the arcane and inconsistent nature of his writings, Lacan's theoretical oeuvre has been dismissed by some as a 'delusion' (Roustang, 1990).

It is rather ironic that Lacan's theoretical innovations are sometimes characterized by the language of the psychoses, for his theory of knowledge is tinged with a psychotic hermeneutics. 'Paranoia' is derived from the Greek, *para* – outside of or beside – as in '*beside* oneself' – and mind (*nous*, νόος), thus beyond intelligible thought (*noēsis*), hence madness. It can also be said that Lacan's splintered, disparate and often implicit theoretical structure personifies his very notion of desire: desire is beyond structure, beyond words – it is merely the unutterable, ineffable. That which remains nameless, indescribable – unknown – is surely that which haunts us; and it is ominous precisely because it is alien.

For Lacan, all knowledge is imbued with paranoia. Like Lacan's conception of the *Real*, which has no formal text, his comments on paranoiac knowledge are limited to only a few fragments in his *Écrits* and his *Seminars*, thus lacking clarification and systematic rigour. Because his scant remarks on the subject have genuine theoretical and clinical value, it is my intention in this chapter to provide a conceptual model explicating the scope, breadth and process of paranoiac knowledge, thus showing how Lacan's insights have clinical utility. By way of illustration, I will examine a case of paranoia.

Developmentally, knowledge is paranoiac because it is acquired through our *imaginary* relation to the other as a primordial misidentification or illusory self-recognition of autonomy, control and mastery, thus leading to persecutory anxiety and self-alienation. Secondarily, through the *symbolic* structures of language and speech, desire is foisted upon us as a foreboding demand threatening to invade and destroy our uniquely subjective inner experiences. And finally, the process of knowing itself is paranoiac because it horrifically confronts the *real*, namely, the unknown. Through our examination of a clinical case study, paranoiac knowledge manifests itself as the desire not to know.

Prolegomena to Lacan's system: the relation between knowledge and paranoia

Lacan is very difficult to understand, which makes the interpreter's task ever so daunting. Such difficulty is in no doubt why, in part, most psychoanalytic clinicians in North America and Britain remain confused about – if not oblivious to – his theoretical visions. Even worse, there is no unified agreement among Lacanians on how we should interpret Lacan. His invented jargon is highly esoteric, drawing on and reappropriating concepts from many different fields of study including philosophy, anthropology, semiotics and mathematics, and thus can evoke both admiration and dismissal. Here I am reminded of a decorative centrepiece: it's nice to look at, but no one dares to touch it. The confusional aspects of Lacan's discourse become particularly vexing when Lacan himself declares that he is intentionally trying to confound the very audience that seeks to understand him (Lacan, 1955–1956d, p. 164). For these reasons, Lacan's technical jargon cannot be easily converted into a user-friendly guide. Moreover, many of his concepts have multiple meanings that even oppose each other when viewed from different contexts within his system. Although I attempt to mitigate some of the confusion surrounding his discourse, it will be necessary for me, throughout this chapter, to retain much of his technical language, without which many of his theoretical distinctions would go unrecognized.

It is not necessary to adopt Lacan's entire system, which is neither essential nor desirable, in order to appreciate what he has to offer to our topic at hand. In fact, many of Lacan's positions – such as the decentring of subjectivity for the reification of language – radically oppose contemporary psychoanalytic thought to the degree that Lacan becomes essentially incompatible. Notwithstanding, with the ever increasing linguistic turn in psychoanalysis, Lacan becomes an important figure to engage. Because language is a necessary condition (albeit not a sufficient one) for conceptual thought, comprehension and meaning to manifest (see

Frie, 1997; Mills, 1999), human knowledge is linguistically mediated. But the epistemological question – that is, the origin of knowledge – requires us to consider prelinguistic development, intrapsychic and interpersonal experience, and the extra- or non-linguistic processes that permeate psychic reality, such as the constitutional pressures of the drives (*Triebe*) and affective states (from the monstrous to the sublime) that remain linguistically foreclosed as unformulated unconscious experience. When these aspects of human life are broadly considered, it becomes easier to see how our linguistic–epistemological dependency has paranoiac *a priori* conditions. From Hegel to Freud, Heidegger and Lacan, knowledge is a dialectical enterprise that stands in relation to fear – to the horror of possibility – the possibility of the *not*: negation, conflict and suffering saturate our very beings, beings whose self-identities are linguistically constructed.

The relation between knowledge and paranoia is a fundamental one, and perhaps nowhere do we see this dynamic so poignantly realized than in childhood. From the 'psychotic-like' universe of the newborn infant (e.g. see Klein, 1946); to the relational deficiencies and selfobject failures that impede the process of human attachment; to the primal scene and/or subsequent anxieties that characterize the Oedipal period, leading to the inherent rivalry, competition and overt aggression of even our most sublimated object relations – fear, trepidation and dread hover over the very process of knowing itself. What is paranoid is that which stands in relation to opposition, hence that which is alien to the self. Paranoia is not simply that which is beyond the rational mind, but it is a generic process of *noēsis* – 'I take thought, I perceive, I intellectually grasp, I apprehend', and hence have *apprehension* for what I encounter in consciousness. With qualitative degrees of difference, we are all paranoid simply because others hurt us, a lesson we learn in early childhood. Others hurt us with their knowledge, with what they say, as do we. And we hurt knowing. 'What will the Other do next?' We are both pacified yet cower in extreme trembling over what we may and may not know – what we may and may not find out; and this is why our relation to knowledge is fundamentally paranoiac.

For Aristotle, 'All men by nature desire to know' (*Metaphysics*, I(A):980a22). This philosophic attitude is kindled by our educational systems perhaps informing the popular trite adage, 'knowledge is power'. But whose? There is no doubt that the acquisition of knowledge involves a power differential, but what if knowledge itself is seen as too powerful because it threatens our psychic integrity? In the gathering of knowledge there is simultaneously a covering-over, a blinding to what one is exposed to; moreover, an erasure. I know (No)! Unequivocally, there are things we desire to know nothing about at all; hence the psychoanalytic attitude places unconscious defence – negation/denial (*Verneinung*) and repression – in the foreground of human knowledge, the desire not to know.

When we engage epistemology – the question and meaning of knowledge – we are intimately confronted with paranoia. For example, there is nothing more disturbing when after a lifetime of successful inquiry into a particular field of study it may be entirely debunked by the simple, arrogant question: 'How do you know?' Uncertainty, doubt, ambiguity, hesitation, insecurity – anxiety!: the process of knowing exposes us all to immense discomfort. And any epistemological claim is equally a metaphysical one. Metaphysics deals with first principles, the fundamental, ultimate questions that preoccupy our collective humanity: 'What is real? Why do I exist? Will I *really* die?' Metaphysics is paranoia – and we are all terrified by its questions: 'Is there God, freedom, agency, immortality?' *Is? Why? Why not? Yes but why?!* When the potential meaning and quality of one's personal existence hinge on the response to these questions, it is no wonder why most theists say only God is omniscient. And although Freud (1927b) tells us that the very concept of God is an illusory derivative of the Oedipal situation – a wish to be rescued and comforted from the anxieties of childhood helplessness, He – our exalted Father in the sky – is *always* watching, judging. Knowing this, the true believer has every reason to be petrified. For those in prayer or in the madhouse, I can think of no greater paranoia.

Three realms of being

Human knowledge is paranoiac – it torments, persecutes, *cuts*. This is essentially what Lacan (1953–1954) means when he says 'my knowledge started off from paranoiac knowledge' (p. 163), because there are 'paranoid affinities between all knowledge of objects as such' (1955–1956b, p. 39). In order to understand what Lacan means, it is necessary to provide a preliminary overview of his ontological treatment of the human condition, which he situates in three realms or contexts of being, namely, the Imaginary, Symbolic, and Real. By closely examining a few of Lacan's key works, it will become increasingly clear that aggressivity suffuses the very fabric of human knowledge, a paranoiac residue of the dialectic of desire.

It may be useful to think of three main periods that characterize Lacan's work. Although his early period (1932–1948) focused on the role of the imago, his middle period (1948–1960) concentrated on the nature of language that subordinated the world of images to linguistic structures and practices. During his late period (1960–1980), Lacan was preoccupied with a formal systematization of psychoanalysis via logic and mathematics that sought to provide a coherent explanatory framework involving the three realms or registers of mental life. As a cursory definition, we might say that the Imaginary (*imaginaire*) is the realm of illusion, of fantasy, belonging to the sensuous world of perception. In contrast, the Symbolic (*symbolique*) is the formal organization of psychic life that is structured through language and linguistic internalizations implemented as semiotic functions, thus becoming the ground of the subject; while the Real (*réel*) remains foreclosed from epistemic awareness within the abyss of unconscious desire. The real is delimited – the *Ding an sich*: it remains the mysterious beyond, the heart of desire. For Lacan, desire is persecutory by virtue of belonging to the Other, first originating in a specular imago, then constituted through the domain of language and speech.

These three domains of mental functioning constitute psychical reality and compose the fundamental basis or ground of the human being, which may be metaphorically viewed as a Borromean knot: each realm may operate autonomously on parallel planes but they are entirely interdependent and intersect at any given moment. The three registers are held together in tension by a negative dialectic that fundamentally opposes each other, yet at times may coalesce; but there is no Hegelian *Aufhebung* or ultimate synthetic progression. Instead we can envision a pressure-cooker held together by conflict. Together as a whole these opposing domains form a dynamic structure or process system that accounts for all human experience through their interrelatedness.

Imaginary forms of relating to the world fundamentally comprise what Lacan (1936–1949) refers to as the 'mirror stage' in the early formative development of the I or ego (*moi*). The infant sees itself in the mirror, face, or actions of the other but mistakes the other for itself as an imaginary relation. In other words, following Hegel (1807), the nascent mind comes to recognize itself through the other, which produces a crude semblance of self-definition. The visual (mirroring) imago lends a degree of coherence and organic wholeness to the infant's hitherto internal state of undifferentiated experience or primary narcissism, and hence introduces for the first time the notion of a separate sense of self from others, which provides definitional form and structure to ego development. The imaginary therefore belongs to the realm of spurious identifications and idealizations based on the interplay between images and fantasies that are necessary (albeit insufficient) for the construction of the self, which is the initial unfolding of self-identity.

In essence, for Lacan, there is no real self or ego because the infant's internal world is determined by external images it internalizes through identificatory mergers; and this early form of ego development conditions all subsequent organizations of the self. This process largely consists of identifications with (idealized) images that ingress (from the outside as alien activities) into the infant's incipient sense of self, which result in failures of recognition of self and subject. Rather than view ego development through a Freudian lens, which situates intrapsychic activity as the locus of mental life, Lacan instrumentally endows externality with determinate powers of psychic causation. In effect, the ego is a fantasy of self-relation defined by the Other. What this means is that all forms of epistemology are derived from external sources and are caused from without. An imaginary mode of relating to the world is fundamental to psychosis, but it is also a general basis of self-knowledge, which Lacan (1936–1949) states always has an alienated and paranoid quality.

The symbolic plays a central role in Lacan's system, which, in my assessment, is ultimately the *cause* of the subject's being. Lacan believes that the unconscious is 'structured like a language' and, indeed, he equates the unconscious with language itself (see Lacan 1955–56a, p. 11; 1955–56b, p. 119; 1955–56c, pp. 166–167), which is predicated on consciousness and cultural determinism. For Lacan, because the symbolic temporally exists prior to the contingent birth of the subject, this, in turn, determines the essence of the subject. Therefore, the subject is constituted by the symbolic function. For Lacan, the subject is conditioned upon its 'entrance into language' under the symbolic Law (*E* 1957, p. 148), which ultimately makes the unconscious a cultural category captured by his formula: 'the unconscious is *"discours de l'Autre"* [discourse of the Other]' (*E* 1960, p. 312).

Because the symbolic order, namely, the Other (as familial and communal interaction, language, culture, and so forth) is causally superimposed, this corresponds to the creation or constitution of the human subject. Here Lacan precariously subverts the notion of freedom within psychic agency as if everything is conditioned on language. This commits him to a particular brand of external determinism, rather than the internal (psychic) determinism of classical theory. Furthermore, for Lacan, the ego is an 'illusion of autonomy' based on its *méconnaissances* and imaginary relations to others (*E* 1936–1949, p. 6); and, unlike Freud, who places natural desire within an internal burgeoning process of unconscious expression, for Lacan, even 'man's desire is the *désir de l'Autre* [the desire of the Other]' (*E* 1960, p. 312). In Lacan, we may call into question whether human agency even exists, for he sees agency as belonging to the authority of the Letter. Although we may attempt to salvage a notion of agency in Lacan by the way we choose to (re)interpret his text, or by redirecting shifts in emphasis that recast his positions within a framework compatible with the ontology of freedom, if we follow Lacan to the letter, the human subject is determined by the structures and parameters of speech. Here there is no intrapsychic mediation that confers meaning, rather signification is conferred through the act of speech itself. As Vanheule (2011) describes, 'the process of generating meaning also has the effect of producing subjectivity' for 'subjectivity is generated via the signifying chain' (p. 44). In other words, we don't simply employ language, we *are* language. Language creates being, hence the signifier and the act of speech determines the subject.

This particular facet of Lacan's theory may be the single most philosophical conundrum in his metaphysical system. If speech produces the subject, then, I suggest, he hypostatizes the signifying chain (language) as a being or creator entity (which implies agency through causal imposition). Through the reification of language, he specifically gives semiotics – the laws of language, signification and speech production – the ontological status of Being caused by the qualitative particularity of the signifying chain. Here the chain (i.e. the structure of speech and its infinite deferral of signifiers) is attributed agency as some overarching causal (although not fixed) law(s) that presides over the subject superimposed from an omnipotent external force, which creates the subject at any given moment. The subject is therefore the epiphenomenon of an inscripted linguistic act that is fleeting and ephemeral, but paradoxically contains no ontological status of its own. Here speech – not the subject – has the determinate power to create, yet it possesses no real agency.

Instead of viewing speech and the laws of grammar, syntax, sign and signification, and so forth as an invention and production of human subjectivity, Lacan turns the table. Rather than the human being who has agency and creates linguistic expression and meaning, language is granted the exalted status of supreme Order that determines the contours of intrapsychic life. How can the structural mechanisms of speech, such as metonymy, cause the subject when we are accustomed to conceptualizing the experiential ego as the agent responsible for speaking? Here, like Fichte's Absolute Self as pure self-posit, language institutes itself; in other words, it brings about its own being. But language does not think itself into existence or institute itself *ex nihilo*; rather, it is the anthropological product of human creation. If language is fundamentally a human activity born of psychic creativity and cultural expression, then how can it cause anything independent of the linguist or user of language? If language is the invention of human thought and ideation mediated through mind, then how could it exist outside of human consciousness? Words don't think. This would require a special ontological status, as if it were some cosmic macroanthropos. For Lacan, human subjectivity is always composed by something outside of itself. What this means is that Lacan's entire metaphysics is conditioned on an environmental determinism that is the functional basis of the human being.[2]

The real surfaces as the third order, standing in juxtaposition to the imaginary and the symbolic, intimately intertwined yet beyond the previous domains. The real has no formal text, it is deliberately undecided. It is neither symbolic nor imaginary, rather it remains foreclosed from the analytic experience which relies on speech. The real is the domain of the unconscious, that realm of psychic territory we can never know as such in itself; it remains beyond the epistemic limitations of the symbolic, yet is disclosed in every utterance. We may say that the real is the seat of desire whereas the imaginary and symbolic orders devolve into it. The real is the presupposed psychical reality, the raw substrate of the subject awaiting structure through linguistic acquisitions. Lacan's notion of the real should not be confused with 'reality', which is in some ways knowable (at least theoretically), yet the subject of desire may only suppose the real – the *thing in itself* – as reality for the subject is merely phantasmatic. For Lacan, the real is the 'impossible', it is the realm of the unthinkable, the unimaginable; and this is precisely why the real cannot be penetrated by imagination or the senses. The real is that which is missing in the symbolic order, that which is untouchable, indescribable by language, yet 'the ineliminable residue of all articulation' (*E* 1977, p. x).

According to Malcolm Bowie (1991), the imaginary, the symbolic and the real are not mental entities, rather they are *orders* that serve to position the individual within a field that traverses and intersects her. The word 'order' suggests a number of important connotations for Lacan. Analogous to botanical or zoological taxonomy, (a) there is a hierarchical arrangement of classes whereby (b) internal principles of similarity and congruence govern membership in each class. Furthermore, (c) higher levels of classification have superior cognitive status, suggesting that (d) a series of commands or orders are being issued from some undetected source – presumably the real – the night of the mind. No limitations are placed on the Lacanian orders; they may be used to explain any form of human condition from the most banal mental mechanism to the most severe forms of psychopathology. Within the three Lacanian orders, each perspective is realized from its own unique vantage point, revealing an insight into psychic organization that forecloses the others, yet envelops them. However, by themselves, each fails to fully represent and articulate the greater dynamic complexity that characterizes the parallel processes and temporal unification of the three orders.

As multiple processes, the Lacanian three orders are not stable, fixed entities; rather they are under the constant pressure of evolution, vacillating between antithetical movements of progression and regression, construction and decay. The three orders pressurize each other constantly, having short-term moratoriums. In other words, the three orders are in conflict with each other and, when operative, attempt to exert their own unique influence over the other orders. This in turn creates overdetermined and multiple, dynamic levels of psychic reality. In their dialectical transitions, each order encroaches on the other – the symbolic defining and organizing the imaginary, the imaginary hallucinating the real. Furthermore, the real always wedges its way through the gaps of conscious intentionality, giving desire a voice through the medium of perception and speech. At any given moment we live in all three realms of being, each operative and dynamic within their own orders parallel to each other, yet they are integrative, structured and complex. Although the real is the most obscure concept for Lacan, it reintroduces a vibrant theoretical life to psychoanalytic inquiry that underscores the primacy of an unconscious ontology which Freud was so instrumental in advancing. Despite its mysterious appeal shrouded in inconceivability, the real is the reverberation of its own truth disclosed on its own terms and understood through its own language, the idiom of desire.

Through the looking glass

Lacan's inaugural theory of the self was formally introduced in 1936 to the 14th International Psychoanalytic Congress and published the following year under the title 'The Looking-Glass Phase'. This single contribution launched a radical new portrait of ego formation in psychoanalytic thought. One reason why his theory is so radical and controversial is that, for Lacan, the ego, with qualifications, does not exist – at least not in the ordinary sense that psychoanalysis has come to view the notion. The ego is a mistake (*méconnaissance*), thus it is merely an illusory projection of autonomy and control. In other words, the ego (*moi, Ich*) or 'I' is merely a *wish* – itself the product of social construction.

At this point, it may be useful to distinguish between what Lacan means by the self, the ego, and the subject. The 'self', 'ego', or 'I', which is used synonymously throughout much of Lacan's writings, is typically equated with our conscious perceptions and definitions of ourselves. Therefore, when Lacan (1955–1956b) says that 'meaning is imaginary' (p. 65), he is saying that our ego is conceptually bound to our conscious self-*image* or self-representations. The term 'subject' (*Sujet*), on the other hand, refers to the unconscious – that which is alien and lies outside of conscious self-awareness; however, we conventionally refer to a person when we use the term subject, as Lacan did throughout his writings. Lacan, as does Freud, privileges the unconscious over the conscious ego, and hence emphasizes that all foreign desires, thoughts, parapraxes, and so on, which slip out during acts of speech are tantamount to revealed id (*Es*) processes (Fink, 1997). However, Lacan does not make the distinction between the conscious and unconscious portions of the ego as Freud (1923) does, nor is he inclined to attribute 'agency' to the unconscious, even though he concedes we have a tendency to attribute subjectivity to it. While Freud (1933a, p. 6) spoke of the trichotomy of the psyche or 'Soul' (*Seele*) – not the 'mental apparatus', which is a mistranslation – as the temporal unification of the dynamic processes that constitute psychic life, Lacan makes the unconscious subject completely non-personal. For our purposes here, however, it may be less confusing if we think of the subject as the whole human being composed of both conscious and unconscious organizations.

The mirror stage is the initial point of self-discovery, hence the dawn of the nascent ego insofar as the 'I' is discovered in the eyes of the other. From the recognition of the self through the looking glass, or through another as its metaphorical representation, the emergence of self-consciousness is constituted in and through alienation. Taken over from Hegel's (1807) theory of desire and recognition, Lacan (1953–1954) states that 'the original, specular foundation of the relation to the other, in so far as it is rooted in the imaginary, [is] the first alienation of desire' (p. 176). In the realm of the imaginary, the budding ego first recognizes itself in an object outside of itself, in the mirror image of the other. This illusory order is the initial constitution of the self, as the first matrix of the ego, which is the psychically formative period that occurs between the ages of six to eighteen months of infancy.

Through Kojève, Lacan was deeply influenced by Hegel, especially by his lordship and bondage chapter outlined in the *Phenomenology of Spirit*. For Hegel, one's sense of self is contingent on the recognition of the other, and this contingency itself fosters a paranoid dynamic. We all seek recognition, this is a basic human need. The ego is affirmed by the other, but not at first. There is originally the experience of inequality, whether this be the child's relation to the parent or the servant's relation to the master. Ultimately the desire for recognition becomes a fundamental battle for dominance and validation in which each subject struggles to overcome the objectification of the other. From this standpoint, the sense of one's fundamental contingency on recognition is basically paranoiac and may regress to that paranoid state whenever one becomes acutely aware of that contingency.

Drawing on the ethological research of Tinbergen and Lorenz regarding the perceptual functions of animal behaviour, and on Freud's thesis of identification, Lacan emphasizes the organizing function of the imago as the perceptual *Gestalten* that forms the most elemental contours of psychical structure. For Lacan, as for Hegel, the initial recognition of the 'I' does not entail the subject's self-awareness of itself as a fully self-conscious agent. This is a developmental achievement mediated by its burgeoning modes of identification. For Lacan, however, this primordial form of identification 'situates the agency of the ego . . . in a fictional direction' (1936–1949, p. 2), namely, in the gaze of the other which gives the illusory semblance of self. In other words, images symbolize, reflect the 'I', and thus resemble a constituted self that are the initial stimuli for ego-boundaries and body differentiation to be forged. The mirror phase is therefore the world of perception, forever cast under the penumbra of the imaginary.

As early as his essay on 'The Mirror Stage', Lacan's mature theory of desire is already implicit, it is already prepared. The mirror experience functions as the coming into being of identity, the initial formation of the self – a self that is dialectically and intersubjectively constructed through desire, as the relation of being to *lack* (*manque*). Lacan emphasizes the 'internal thrust' of desire within the presupposed subject, yet desire is always *caused* or given over, through internalization, by the Other. As a result, desire is always characterized by absence and incompleteness. Such a void, such a hole in being clamours in 'anticipation' for presence, for fulfilment of its lack, facilitated by the parental imagos that the premature ego identifies with, thus giving an illusory sense of totality and completeness. We may say that such illusory completeness is fantasized, hallucinated *as* reality, thus the fulfilment of a wish. However, the dislocated images mirrored in the other subjected to the illusion of cohesiveness of identity, are in fact *defensive* processes enacted to ward off fragmentation anxiety: the genesis of ego development is the life of desire.

The other as persecutory

Lost in its alienation, the Lacanian subject discovers itself in the imaginary, recovered through the mediation of the other, giving itself meaning through the symbolic, struggling on the threshold of the real. But for Lacan, there can never be an absolute self, no autonomous 'I' or transcendental ego that exists apart from the Other; the 'I' is always linked 'to socially elaborated situations' (1936–1949, p. 5) mediated by linguistic structures ontologically constituted *a priori* within its social facticity. Thus the *I* is the *Other*.

It is through the image of the other that the infant comes to grasp awareness of its own corporeal integrity and seize the first measure of control over its body movements. The imago serves as an 'alter-ego', an organizing, stabilizing function which coordinates cohesiveness out of internal chaos and provides homogeneity out of primal discord. Through the imaginary, the ego is no more than a return of an image to itself. The paradoxical structure of the imaginary is therefore the polarity between alienation and recognition. Lacan sees recognition as the recovery of the alienated image facilitated through the mirroring of the other. As the subject finds or recognizes itself through an image (insofar as recognition is the misrecognition of its autonomous ego as an illusory mastery), it is concurrently confronted with its own alienated and alienating image; hence this process becomes an aggressive relation.

Lacan describes the degree of 'aggressive disintegration' that torments the inchoate ego in 'the form of disjointed limbs, or of those organs represented in exoscopy, growing wings and taking up arms for intestinal persecutions'

(1936–1949, p. 4). The persecutory fantasies that accompany early ego development may indeed take the form of 'images of castration, mutilation, dismemberment, dislocation, evisceration, devouring, bursting open of the body, in short, the . . . *imagos of the fragmented body*' (1948, p. 11). Feldstein (1996) notes that the imago allows the infant to elide a fundamental rupture in which 'anxiety-producing images of the fragmented body are disavowed because such untotalizable self-differences could give rise to paranoid perceptions; . . . [thus] paranoia is related to the mirror-stage attempt to manufacture a future-perfect mastery' (p. 135). It becomes essential for the ego to split, compartmentalize, and/or project its negative introjects from its internal experiences and internalize soothing ministrations in order to defend against such hostile intrusions. Therefore, the stabilizing and 'fixating' quality of the positive imago serves a cohesive function. As the imago (accompanied by maternal ministrations and validating presentations) helps constitute the burgeoning I, the salutary power of the specular image becomes a unifying and integrating activity.

The organizing and synthesizing functions internalized over maturation become unifying yet mobile fixtures of the child's inner representational world. Such internalizations are fortified through ongoing identifications that provide the illusion of self-cohesion, which further serve to ward off primordial anxiety associated with fragmentation, decomposition, and loss of undifferentiated bliss with the imago. This is also a prevalent theme for Klein (1946) and post-Kleinians (Bion, 1959; Segal, 1957): ego organization is besieged by the horrors of persecutory–annihilation anxiety. Unlike Klein, however, the self is the introjection of the other, not the projection of the self discovered in the other. For Lacan, the self is causally given over by the other; thus the self is the Other internalized in all its variegated forms.

Given the plethora of images and fantasies that populate the early stages of the imaginary, it becomes increasingly clearer to see how the other becomes a persecutory object. The other, and particularly the other's desire, is always a potential threat to the subject because it is an alien force that stands in firm opposition to the subject, an antithesis that evokes rivalry and competition. This is why Lacan (1955–1956b) says that 'all human knowledge stems from the dialectic of jealousy, which is a primordial manifestation of communication' (p. 39). The subject first encounters the other as *opposition* – an opposition that *desires*. As such, the other is in possession of something the subject lacks. We are jealous of what the other has, which naturally evokes feelings of rivalry, competition and envy. This naturally leads Lacan to conclude that 'the object of human interest is the object of the other's desire' (p. 39). What the subject desires in otherness is the other's desire, thus bringing about a primordial confrontation with death: in opposition there is always the possibility of being annulled. 'The dialectic of the unconscious always implies struggle, the impossibility of co-existence with the other [is] one of its possibilities' (p. 40). Whether the other is the object of desire that enjoys a degree of liberty which the subject lacks, or whether the Other is the symbolic order imposing an austere reality on the subject's inner world through the violation and demands of speech, the acquisition of knowledge becomes a paranoiac enterprise.

Aggressivity and identification

Within the initial phases of the imaginary, aggressivity becomes paramount for Lacan. The image as an alienating presence may be an ominous, rivalrous threat that the subject fears as dangerous. Although the imago may be a validating–soothing–sustaining introject that provides the self with illusory stability, it may also become coloured by the projection of one's own innate destructive impulses organized in one's paranoiac relation to the imago. The doubling function of the imaginary, as the medium for both self-recognition and self-alienation, serves as the initial developmental impetus behind the dialectical unfolding of desire.

The interface between identification, aggression, and the captivation of the specular imago in the imaginary register serves paradoxical functions. For Lacan, the 'captation' of the mirror image is both entrancing and intrusive; it fascinates yet it captures. As the image of oneself is given over by the other, there is a new psychical action, that of identification, which for Lacan is the moment of the inception of the ego. While Freud (1921, 1933a) envisions identification as the development of an emotional bond with a significant figure, Lacan focuses on the dialectical capacity to form judgments of identity and difference. Through identification, the baby finds the image a captivating albeit imprisoning force chained to the pull of the imaginary. For Lacan, this incarcerating point of attraction implies that the ego momentarily becomes fixed and static. Unconscious fantasy systems largely serve a defensive function in the pre-oedipal child, fuelling illusory misrecognitions as a way of fending off the aggressive violation of the imago's encroachment.[3]

There is an *a priori* manifestation of destruction within the imaginary order: aggressivity is ontologically constituted within any dyadic relation. The imaginary capture of the mirror is mired in destruction, for as Lacan emphasizes, any imaginary relation generates rivalry and conflict. Recall that what we identify in opposition is the other's desire which we long to possess. Identification therefore generates an ambivalent tension between possession and lack. Identification with a rival evokes the dialectic of presence and absence, mastery and servitude; thus the initial point of confrontation entails the recognition of what one has not yet procured or mastered. For example, we may say that the mother's image is castrating because it is more powerful. Fear, dread, or shame may be evoked by a simple look: the other's desire is exposed through a gaze. Thus, the boundary of the imaginary becomes difference. For Lacan, this dual relation between the infant–mother dyad encases desire within an interminable narcissistic battlefield.

It is important to note that aggressivity and aggression are not the same. For Lacan, aggression is a derivative of the death drive (*Todestrieb*) while aggressivity is the acting out of aggression through the symbolic and imaginary orders. Following Freud (1920), aggressivity is both the deflection of self-destruction and a defensive, protective reaction to an external threat. Lacan (1948) shows that aggressivity is immured within the structures of subjectivity 'by its very constitution' (p. 9), and avouches that 'aggressivity in experience is given to us as intended aggression and as an image of corporeal dislocation' (p. 10). As we have said, imagos can be noxious and disfiguring, thus leading to fragmentation and a fracturing of the body. The ego attempts to fantasize the illusion of mastery and unity in the face of these dislocated and contrary experiences characteristic of the child's fragmented bodily states which are displaced as aggressivity directed toward others. Richard Boothby (1991) argues that:

> aggressivity is a drive toward violation of the imaginary form of the body that models the ego. It is because aggressivity represents a will to rebellion against the imago that aggressivity is specifically linked in fantasy to violations of the bodily integrity.
>
> (p. 39)

Thus, for Lacan (1966), 'the notion of aggressivity corresponds . . . to the splitting of the subject against himself' (p. 344). Such 'dehiscence' in the nascent ego gives rise to persecutory anxiety, hence the origins of knowledge are paranoiac in their 'most general structure'.

> What I have called paranoiac knowledge is shown, therefore, to correspond in its more or less archaic forms to certain critical moments that mark the history of man's mental genesis, each representing a stage in objectifying identification.
>
> (Lacan, 1948, p. 17)

Knowledge – the other's knowledge – is always lurking with pernicious intent to get in and *kill* the ego. The objects of identification are inherently baneful: they eviscerate desire simply because they are the other's desire. As the child's identificatory powers increase, so does the capacity for aggressivity. When the burgeoning ego identifies with the other's desire, it models the other and hence enters into an aggressive rivalry over the object of the other's desire. Following Hegel (1807), Lacan (1953–1954) sees this process as a competition for recognition:

> The subject's desire can only be confirmed in this relation through a competition, through an absolute rivalry with the other, in view of the object towards which it is directed. And each time we get close, in a given subject, to this primitive alienation, the most radical aggression arises – the desire for the disappearance of the other.
>
> (p. 170)

Lee (1990) aptly tells us that 'aggression directed toward others is found at the very center of the *moi's* structure, as it comes into being through the dialectic of the child's narcissistic identifications with various visual images' (p. 27). Such identification, says Lacan (1948), is also an:

erotic relation, in which the human individual fixes upon himself an image that alienates him from himself, that are to be found the energy and the form on which this organization of the passions that he will call his ego is based.

(p. 19)

For Lacan, the aggressivity injected into the very process of ego identification itself 'determines the awakening of his desire for the object of the other's desire' (1948, p. 19). Lacan essentializes aggression as an ontologically indispensable psychic process that infuses narcissistic ego development. Aggressivity breaches the margin of libidinal self-investment as it falls on the fringe of self-destruction. Such 'narcissistic suicidal aggression' operative with the formation of the ego is due to the alienated and lethal assault of the imago, which unleashes a violence on the subject to the point of self-extinction. As the other, *objet a* (sometimes referred to as *objet-petit-a*) is the signifier of desire; thus the subject is an-*other* plundered by the object's desire. Bowie (1991) explains that 'the original act of identification is the original narcissistic declaration too; into the very constitution of the ego its destruction is already woven; the only escape from alienation is an aggravation of the alienated state' (p. 34).

For Freud, narcissistic object-choice is the process of conversion (*Umwandlung*) of aggressivity into love, a process that hinges on the repression of the drive toward aggression in the face of socialization and object attachment. For Lacan, this two-phase process is compressed into one: narcissism and aggressivity are correlatives. Julien (1994) expatiates on this claim:

Narcissism, in which the image of one's own body is sustained by the image of the other, in fact introduces a *tension*: the other in his image both attracts and rejects me. I am indeed nothing but the other, yet at the same time, he remains *alienus*, a stranger. This other who is myself is other than myself.

(p. 34)

As the ego is formally laid down in the imaginary relations of the mirror stage, aggressivity is embedded in love by virtue of this dual relationship. Duality implies difference, exclusion, antithesis. My desire is *their* desire! – it is already tainted with ugliness. A fundamental dichotomy is already constituted by this *a priori* relation, a rigid *either/or* leading to what Lacan calls the 'fraternal complex': *either* I kill the other *or* the other will kill me. As the immature ego is imperilled by perceived hostile and persecutory advances by the other's desire, the child is immersed in a destructive reality, which it must endeavour to deflect, project and keep at bay. At the same time aggressivity contaminates the inner I, the ego is subjected to its own libidinal and relational strivings to attach to an ideal love object. From a Kleinian perspective, the oscillation between ideal and persecutory object relations is further enhanced during the depressive position. As paranoid anxiety gradually devolves into (yet remains subsumed within) depressive anxiety, the ego is besmirched by fears of destruction and loss of love. This is very much in keeping with Lacan's position: the ego's ambitendent, aggressive–erotic structure is the narcissistic foundation for *jouissance* – the realm of excess – desire's pleasures in death.[4]

For Lacan, death plays a pivotal role in the organization of the psyche: 'aggressivity gnaws away, undermines, disintegrates; it castrates; it leads to death' (1948, p. 10). Schneiderman (1983) suggests that desire itself is the desire for death, one that is 'cultivated to the extend that death is kept at a distance' (p. 74). The pleasure of death is not to be experienced as a real death, rather as the euphoria of *jouissance*, the pleasure of its sublimation. This sublimation, however, is not bound to the homeostatic (economic) laws that govern the pleasure principle, rather it exceeds it. We might say that death satisfies desire, but only if it is sustained, prolonged. Death is only satisfying if it is protracted. The pleasure of death, hence the process of death, makes the experience of satisfaction satisfying.

Boothby (1991) cogently shows that Lacan's treatment of the death drive is pivotal in his theoretical innovations that intimately link death with the functions of speech, language and desire. As Lacan (1954–1955b) states, 'the death instinct is only the mask of the symbolic order' (p. 326). Thus, the death drive hides behind the veil of speech. Language castrates *jouissance*, it alienates desire from satisfaction and thus introduces a division within the subject, leaving a palpable void (Ragland, 1995). Lacan's repositioning of death provides us with a hermeneutics of unconscious desire. With reference to Freud, Lacan (1958) suggests that 'life . . . has only one meaning, that in which desire is borne by death'(p. 277). Desire is the spawn of intrusion, violation, and laceration from the Other – speech and language are by nature aggressive; they *cut*.

The *de*-structure of language

As we have seen, Lacan's developmental picture of the ego is clearly imbued with a negative dialectic: imagoes are alien and threatening, identification is formed in relation to lack, object relations are primarily aggressive and rivalrous, and desire is always imposed. From this account, the ego is vigilant and suspicious; hence it takes a paranoid relation toward the world at large which becomes unconsciously fortified. But when the ego acquires language, paranoia takes a symbolic turn signified through the demands of speech. The notion of the symbolic order of mental functioning came to the fore during the Rome Report.[5] Developed by Saussure and Jakobson, and taken over by Lévi-Strauss' formalization of the elementary structure of kinship with its reliance on Jakobson's binarism, Lacan's emphasis on symbols refers not to icons or stylized figurations, but rather to signifiers that he extends into a general definition with differential elements; in themselves without meaning, signifiers acquire value only in their mutual relations, which form a closed order (*E* 1977, p. ix). Language lends structure to the psyche, thus it is the symbolic that gives order to the subject. In fact, for Lacan, the subject is ultimately *determined* by the symbolic function of signifiers, speech and language. The relationship between the imaginary and the symbolic is contrasted by the experiences of the ego and its images on the one hand, and the fortification of linguistic attributions on the other. We are thrown into the realm of the symbolic: language is already constituted *a priori* within a pre-existing social ontology, predefined, predetermined. Lacan (1957) tells us: 'language and its structure exist prior to the moment at which each subject at a certain point in his mental development makes his entry into it' (p. 148). Symbolization attempts to give desire structure and order. Submitted to its systemic facticity, desire is moulded by linguistic ontological pressures.

The introduction of the symbolic category marks a radical departure from Freud's metapsychology, indeed a rewriting of the structure of the psyche. Borne out in 'The Agency of the Letter in the Unconscious or Reason since Freud', Lacan (1957) deliberately refigures Saussurian linguistics, insinuating the radical claim that not only is the unconscious structured like a language, but the unconscious *is* language (also see, 1955–1956a, pp. 11, 1955–1956c, 119, 1955–1956d, 166). For Lacan, the unconscious is not just conceived metaphorically as language, it is literally the Letter, thus the signifier. He states: 'But how are we to take this "letter" here? Quite simply, literally . . . the unconscious is the whole structure of language' (1957, p. 147). More specifically, letters (words) function as an infinite deferral within the signifying chain. This infinity in the link of signifiers shares affinities with Freud's concept of primary process thinking: signifiers break through obstacles, they know no limits, there is merely a constant flow. The agency (*instance, Instanz*) of the letter suggests that there is an authority to language, indeed an 'insistence'. Furthermore, Lacan's reference to 'reason since Freud' refers to what reason has become since Freud due to his insistence on the agency of the unconscious; hence the unconscious is our reason why the illusory is our consciousness.

The symbolic order was important to Lacan precisely because it was inclusive and versatile, capable of referring to an entire range of signifying practices (Bowie, 1991; Fink, 1995; Marcelle, 1992). Due to its coherence and malleability, the symbolic category links the world of the unconscious to the structures of speech, and thus even more broadly to a social linguistic ontology. While repression is the prototype of the unconscious for Freud (1923, p. 15), language is the *sine qua non* of Lacan's new symbolic science.

Lacan's admiration of the symbolic is clearly contrasted to his derisive view of the imaginary.[6] The symbolic is the seat of motion and heterogeneity, thus transcending the field of illusory similarity: opposition and difference are firmly retained. The symbolic gives rise to the subject distinct from the imaginary ego as an order of being that is always intermittent and disjoined (Bowie, 1991). Thus the symbolic is characterized by the ontology of absence, negativity and nothingness. The relation between absence and presence, vacuity and abundance, accents the power of signification. Lack has as much signifying potency as excess and none may operate alone without evoking antithesis. For Lacan (1953, 1957, 1960), the signification of lack parallels castration, as the 'Name-of-the-Father' is the symbol for an authority that is both punitive and legislative. As the 'paternal metaphor' that inheres in symbolization, lack is given significance in relation to otherness structured in symbolic opposition to the subject. Without such dialectical positionality, desire would succumb to a psychotic universe imprisoned within an absence of signification.

The imaginary is determined by signifiers, thus language is crucial in the construction of identity (Sarup, 1992). For Lacan, words are interpreted and given meaning retroactively; the behaviour and verbal communication of another is always in need of interpretation, refracted through language. Lacan (1960) emphasizes the interpersonal demand for recognition that operates within the dialectic of desire. Within contemporary psychoanalysis, Kohut (1971, 1977, 1984) has made the need for validation and recognition the pinnacled motive force of desire: the subject craves attunement and mirroring from its selfobject milieu. While Lacan's (1953, 1958) mature period deifies the symbolic at the expense of decentring the subject, his approach nevertheless underscores the 'lack of being' that characterizes desire, the 'want-to-be' (*manque-à-être*) that characterizes the dialectic of recognition (pp. 259, 274).

While Lacan (1964c, d) says that 'the unconscious is structured like a language' (pp. 149, 203), language itself can be dialectically destructive: the symbolic has the capacity to *de-structure* as it imposes order and meaning. The symbolic is an imposition, it places a demand on the subject. Language by its very nature is assaultive: through distinctions, disjunctives and classifications it makes exclusions and omissions, thus dividing particulars from universals as it discriminates, separates and categorizes. The order and structure of the letter as an insistence is only possible in the wake of disorder and destruction that is determined by its dialectical relation. The metonymy of what *is*, is defined by what it is *not*. Language breaks up meaning and fractures it through negation, an act of de-structuring based on engagement with opposition. While the symbolic order frames, composes and constructs, it can conversely displace one meaning for another.

The very structure and imposition of the symbolic can geld and dismember. Words take on signifying functions that activate cognitive, affective and fantasy systems, which rip through the very core of our being. Speech – the spoken word – is the medium of caustic oral aggression that can be so acerbic and devaluing that it may scar one's self-concept and inner representational world. Negation – 'No!' – by its very definition and execution introduces lack, absence and deprivation. This is why so often we see conflicted individuals fixate on what was said or unsaid by others, thus assuming obsessional forms and repetitions. The perseveration of thought affixed to lack can be a living hell. Speech creates psychic pain through the affliction of desire and lack, as does silence – a poignant withholding. This may be why we all have 'paranoid affinities' in relation to how the other uses language and speech: we fear evaluation and judgment – the other's desire, hence the unknown.

The desire not to know

We have shown that the paranoiac process of acquiring knowledge has its genesis in the imaginary, first as the subject's misidentification with its alienated image in the reflection of the other, and second as the fundamental distortion and miscognition of external objects (also see Muller and Richardson, 1982). Human knowledge is paranoiac because the subject projects its imaginary ego-properties into objects, which become distorted and perceived as fixed entities that terrorize the subject with persecutory anxiety in the form of the other's desire. While the terrifying part-object experiences of the dislocated body arise in the imaginary, the symbolic register introduces another form of fragmentation. Desire and speech by their very nature impose a command. Knowledge is saturated with paranoia because it threatens to invade the subject, and it is precisely this knowledge that must be defended against as the desire not to know.

Interpreting Lacan, Bruce Fink (1997) tells us that just as patients do not possess a genuine desire for change, they further lack a genuine desire for self-knowledge. While people may show interest in knowing why their lives and interpersonal relationships are unsatisfactory, and specifically what keeps interfering with their adjustment and happiness, Lacan (1955–1956a) suggests that there is a more fundamental unconscious wish not to know any of those things. 'The subject's entire subsequent development shows that he wants to know nothing about it' (p. 12). In *Encore*, Lacan (1972–1973) further adds that 'the unconscious is the fact that being, by speaking, enjoys, and . . . wants to know nothing more about it' – that is, 'know nothing about it at all' (pp. 104–105). This is why patients often resist therapy and avoid the process of self-examination and change. They have no desire to know the root of their symptoms or neurotic mechanisms, what functions their defences serve, and why they are instituted in the first place. This is why Lacan says that patients do not want to give up their symptoms because they provide familiarity and meaning: we enjoy our symptoms too much! (Žižek, 1992). This is the insidious structure of *jouissance*, namely, pleasure in pain, or the satisfaction individuals find in dissatisfaction to the point that they wish not to give it up. As Ragland (1995) asserts, 'the inertia of *jouissance* . . . makes a person's love of his or her symptoms greater than any desire to change them' (p. 85). From this standpoint, the unconscious is first and foremost sadomasochistic: it inflicts a perverse pleasure through suffering at its own hands.

There is a self-destructive element to the enjoyment of symptoms, a revelry in the realm of excess to the point that truth or knowledge must be suspended, disavowed, or denied. This is why Lacan thinks that all knowledge of objects as such become tainted with paranoia: they threaten the subject's *jouissance*, and thus must be defended against as the desire not to know. So we may see how Lacan's theoretical insights have clinical applicability, let us now turn our attention to a case of paranoia.

The case of Mrs Z

The patient is a 48-year-old white female with a presenting clinical picture of paranoid agitation, domestic violence and suicidal gestures in response to her suspicion that her husband was having an extramarital affair. She was voluntarily admitted to an inpatient psychiatry unit of a general hospital after she was found intoxicated standing in the rain naked for approximately two hours. Upon confronting her husband about the alleged affair, Mrs Z had reportedly slapped and hit him and then set a blanket on fire in the upstairs bedroom of their house before running outside in the cold with no clothes on, refusing to come back inside, saying she would rather die. She deliberately tried to hide from a small neighbourhood search party but was eventually located and brought to Emergency by the police. This was the patient's first hospitalization and she had no previous psychiatric history.

Mrs Z has been married to her husband for 23 years and has a 20-year-old daughter who recently got married and moved out of the home. Following her daughter's marriage, the patient was removing something from her husband's car when she noticed that there was a crack in the upholstery of the driver's seat. Apparently the seat was splitting at the seam in the upper right-hand corner, yet she paid it little attention. A week had passed when she noticed that the rip in the seam had widened and with panic she immediately fantasized that her husband was having vigorous sexual relations with another woman in the car, thus causing damage to the seat. Upon having this fantasy, Mrs Z reported that she recalled an event that took place approximately four months prior to her daughter's wedding when she thought she smelled perfume on her husband's shirt while doing the laundry, something she dismissed at the time. This recollection further revived a painful 20-year-old memory of when her husband blurted out another woman's name during intercourse, leaving an unabated narcissistic injury; yet he assured her at the time his slip was only a fantasy and that he had never been unfaithful, an explanation which she believed.

After discovering the torn seat for the second time, Mrs Z's suspicions started to assume more paranoid qualities, thereby producing obsessional preoccupations that her husband was cheating on her each day as he went to work. She started checking and cleaning the car every night as he returned home, hoping *not* to find evidence to corroborate her intuitions. One evening, however, she found a small piece of wire fencing underneath the front passenger seat and concluded that someone had been in the car. When she asked her husband to explain how it got there, he could not, only suggesting that she must have overlooked the object when she previously vacuumed the car.

The patient now started to record the car's mileage each day as her husband drove to and from work. She had already driven the same route he normally took and recorded the mileage so she could have a baseline for comparison. When the mileage on the odometer proved to be significantly higher than expected on his next return from work, she confronted her husband on the discrepancy and accused him of having an affair. He vociferously denied any such thing and told the patient that she was paranoid. Mrs Z admitted that while she had little proof at the time, she thought her husband was lying because he could not look her directly in the eye.

Convinced of her husband's infidelity, Mrs Z purchased a voice-activated tape recorder and secretly concealed it in her husband's car. Upon returning from work that evening, the patient retrieved the tape recorder from the car and listened to the tape in its entirety. Initially the tape played back familiar sounds of a moving car on the road, conveying common traffic noises and music from the radio. After approximately 20 minutes of listening to the tape, Mrs Z reported that she began to feel foolish that she had mistrusted her husband. But just as she was ready to turn off the tape, she reportedly began to hear her husband converse with another woman. The conversation soon led to passion as she heard the couple engage in the act of sexual relations.

Mrs Z immediately confronted her husband on the affair to which he point-blankly denied. When she then produced the tape recorder and explained how she had hidden it in the car, recording his entire drive to work, he supposedly became frantic and disoriented. But when she played the section of the tape of the man conversing with the woman, he emphatically stated, 'That's not my voice!' Steadfastly denying that he was the one on the tape, the husband conjectured that someone from work must be stealing his car during the day, driving to some undisclosed location to have sex with some woman, and then returning the car before he gets off from work. At first Mrs Z could not believe his story, but he assured her that he was not the man on the tape. Because the sound of the recording was crude, she had reason to doubt her previous assessment. Furthermore, he informed the patient that someone could have had access to his car unbeknownst to him because he routinely leaves his keys on a hook at the office so not to lose them before he takes the company truck to the construction site each morning. However, he could not explain why two strangers would do such a thing or what possible motives they could have. He could think of no one at work with whom he had conflict or who would be inclined to take his car.

Wanting to believe her husband, Mrs Z accepted his story and tried to convince herself that someone was playing a prank on them. It was during this time that she began abusing alcohol on a daily basis in order to cope. A few days had passed before she secretly resumed planting the tape recorder in the car. When she listened to the tape the second time, however, she suspected that the tape had been tampered with or changed. Over the days that followed, the patient was convinced that someone was removing the tape recorder, changing the tape from side A to side B, and replacing it in its original position with an altered recording. In desperation, she confided in her daughter and other family members that her husband was having an affair, but he had convinced them that she was mistaken. Mrs Z had continued to hide the tape recorder in the car for sometime and reportedly recorded another discussion between a man and a woman. Maintaining his innocence, the husband speculated that the strangers must have made a duplicate set of keys to the car since he no longer left his keys hanging publicly on a hook in the office for people to take at their leisure.

The couple maintained this charade for a few more weeks, first getting an anti-theft device – 'The Club' – and securing it to the wheel when away from his car at work, and then installing an elaborate car-alarm system. These protective devices were to no avail, because the alleged 'strangers' were still apparently taking the car.

When Mrs Z heard once more what she perceived to be her husband's voice on the tape conversing with another woman, she became increasingly more accusatory, volatile and inebriated on a regular basis. The patient began to secretly follow her husband to work to spy, watching to see if he would deviate from his route or if she could catch the culprits. After a few days of observing nothing unusual, she began to suspect that her husband knew that he was being followed and the car observed. Around this time, the patient reported that she started noticing objects in the house missing, and that dish towels were being removed from the kitchen drawer but returned days later folded incorrectly. Her family was convinced that she was 'crazy'. Her paranoia was either due to an overly active imagination or alcohol, and her drunkenness was simply a means of 'getting attention'.

Although the complexities of this case are by no means exhausted in this short description, we may nevertheless see how the patient's discovery of her husband's transgressions was tinged with paranoia. Even during her hospitalization, the patient was struggling with accepting the realization of his infidelity which persecuted her as paranoiac knowledge. She did not wish to know, and the desire not to know marked by a disavowal of the evidence at hand was experienced as a persecutory assault on her psychic integrity. Lurking in the shadows, this knowledge stalked her, prowling in the recesses of her mind in the form of fixed repetitions and fantasies, thus leading to obsessional cycles of fear, dread, anxiety and rage – violating her self-cohesion.

In discussing a case of hysteria, Freud (1893–1895) referred to the 'blindness of the seeing eye' as not wanting to know (p. 117, fn. 1). But Mrs Z's desire not to know was not merely a desire to remain ignorant of her husband's deeds, it was a desire not to know *his* desire. As Lacan (1959–1960a) puts it, 'the moving force of paranoia is essentially the rejection of a certain support in the symbolic order' (p. 54) – she could not accept his desire, hence his demand. The need to mobilize specific defensive manoeuvres designed to deny the possibility of the truth in the service of self-deception was exacerbated by the acute nature of her paranoiac intrusions: she was painfully exposed to the other's desire. In his lecture, 'The See-Saw of Desire', Lacan (1953–1954) writes:

> What is ignorance? Certainly it is a dialectical notion, since it is within the perspective of truth that it is constituted as such. If the subject does not refer himself to the truth, there is no ignorance. If the subject doesn't begin to ask himself the question what is and what is not, there is no reason for there to be a true and a false, nor even, beyond that, reality and appearance.
>
> (p. 167)

The structure of human knowledge is paranoid for the simple reason that it is constituted in dialectical relation to truth: To know or not to know? – that is the question. In either instance, there is an apprehension to knowing because of the possibility of being subjected to a painful realization: in this case, the other's desire. She *sees*, she *saw* – hence 'See-Saw', and this must be negated. Having knowledge or not is in relation to presence and lack. Paranoia is a reaction to anxiety generated in response to desire as demand and/or in relation to absence.

Mrs Z knew the truth but it had to be disavowed; she so desperately wanted to remain ignorant of the affair that she inverted and displaced the truth through the mechanism of misrecognition. In the most general sense, she became lost in the imaginary and could not see the real for what it was. Lacan (1953–1954) asserts:

> Misrecognition represents a certain organization of affirmations and negations, to which the subject is attached. Hence it cannot not be conceived without correlative knowledge. If the subject is capable of misrecognizing something, he surely must know what this function has operated upon. There must be, behind his misrecognition, a kind of knowledge of what there is to misrecognize.
>
> (p. 167)

The patient's misrecognition is a function of her desire not to know what she knows. She is 'attached' to her own wish. What she wishes to know is a symptom of her misrecognition, namely that her husband could not be guilty of desiring another woman. In fact, her self-deception was so entrenched that she had reportedly taken the tapes to a private investigator for a voice-analysis, the results of which were still pending during her hospitalization. Because her husband denied that the voice on the tape was his, yet had no explanation to account for the alleged incidents, the patient felt this was the only way to reconcile the situation. Lacan (1953–1954) adds, '[s]he misrecognizes, or refuses to recognize . . . but everything in the way [s]he behaves indicates that [s]he knows that there is something that [s]he doesn't want to recognize' (p. 167). What Mrs Z refused to recognize was her husband's desire. 'The delusional intuition is a full phenomenon that has an overflowing, inundating character for the subject' (1955–1956b, p. 33). She so badly wanted to believe the untruth that she set out to prove him innocent: 'The voice-analysis will exonerate him!' she exclaimed. During her hospitalization she had still hoped that the voice match would come back negative, which would prove in her mind that unidentified strangers were the offenders, yet as Lacan informs us, deep down she had already recognized the truth which she so despairingly wanted not to believe. But as Lacan (1959–1960b) says elsewhere: 'nothing is more ambiguous than belief' (p. 171). He further states: 'At the basis of paranoia itself, which nevertheless seems to be animated by belief, there reigns the phenomenon of the *Unglauben* [disbelief]' (1964c, p. 238). If the voice-analysis exonerated her husband, her paranoia would be confirmed only on the condition that it was not him, a wishful expression of her desire not to know. But if the results were inconclusive, she would continue to be plagued by suspicion, mistrust and doubt.

Mrs Z's misrecognition was maintained through periods of 'transitivism', what Lacan refers to as moments of 'see-sawing' in which the subject takes the other's actions (or thoughts) to be equivalent with her own. The patient's husband did not want her to know and he deliberately and calculatingly lied to cover up his deed and desire. Through projective identification, she identified with his desire, which she introjected and made her own. 'He would not do such a thing because he loves only me. He would not hurt me!' Wanting to accept his story – his lie, she misrecognized his original desire for his counter-intention, namely his reparatory, secondary wish for her not to know the truth. But all his reassurances and pleading could not stave off what she had already affirmed yet negated. She recognized his desire for what it was – 'this other negates [me], literally kills [me]' (1955–1956d, p. 209): it gnawed on her as a slow emotional torture. Forced on her as a savage assault, violence and self-abuse was her only recourse – the destructive affliction of the other's desire.

The subject of the other

Whether paranoiac acquisitions arise in the fragmented images and dissociated impulses that characterize the experience of the incipient ego, in the imaginary relations governing fantasy, wish, conflict and defence, or in our confrontation with the Other, the epistemic–phenomenological process of knowing is dynamically informed by unconscious paranoiac pressures. This is most evident when we confront the other's desire. As Hegel articulated over 200 years ago, the desire for recognition produces a primordial confrontation leading to 'the desire for the disappearance of the other' (Lacan, 1953–1954, p. 170). When we encounter impasse from the affliction of others, we simply wish for them to vanish. Desire is a demand to which we yield or oppose. Language imposes itself on us as demand to which we are enslaved, thus explaining in part why we fear knowing anything beyond our immediate control. Whether constructed or discovered, the process of examining what *is* and what is *not* – being and nothingness – is driven by paranoia – itself the dialectic of being in relation to lack.

But paranoiac knowledge is not merely a fear of the unknown, it is a trepidation of knowing a particular truth that the subject may find horrific. Whether knowing elicits revulsion, shame, envy or hate, it is the other's desire that is revealed in relation to our own. The juxtaposition of what is known to what is concealed always evokes the affirmation–negation contrast. As Lacan (1955–1956b) says, 'paranoid knowledge is knowledge founded on the rivalry of jealousy' (p. 39) due to the subject's realization of lack in relation to the object of the other's desire. 'This defines, within the speech relationship, something that originates somewhere else – this is exactly the distinction between the imaginary and the real' (p. 39). The object of otherness is a primitive alienation that we wish to possess, and is therefore the object of a primary identification. For Lacan, desire originates from the outside – *it* speaks. This is why he says that when the other talks about himself, he speaks to us about something that has spoken to him.

But we may ask: What part of the subject speaks from within? Analysis tells us the unconscious – the realm beyond conceptualization, namely, the real. In the imaginary and symbolic domains, we are bombarded by alienation, opposition and demand, but *the unconscious is the house of being*, and our relation to the real is a self-relation we know very little about. 'The unconscious is something that speaks within the subject, beyond the subject, and even when the subject doesn't know it, and that says more about him than he believes' (1955–1956b, p. 41). Here we may say that the unconscious is even more alienating than the imaginary, because we are ultimately estranged from ourselves – from our own inner world. Lacan's underworld is a disembodied subject constituted by the Other yet shrouded in an ineffable residue of persecution that can never be known in itself as such. Elsewhere Lacan (1964b) says: 'In the unconscious there is a corpus of knowledge [*un savoir*], which must in no way be conceived as knowledge to be completed, to be closed' (p. 134). Therefore, the goal of psychoanalysis may be said to be the creative discovery of *aletheia* (ἀλήθεια). Truth is a process of disclosedness or unconcealment, a process which may never be completely actualized.

We have an ambivalent relation to the unconscious – the desire to know is opposed by the desire to remain oblivious. For Lacan, the real is that place of limit – that which is lacking in the symbolic order: it is truly most horrific by the mere fact that it can never be known in itself. There is ultimately no safety in the unknown, and that is why the phenomenology of the lived experience carries with it the paranoiac residue of the uncertainty of the life within. The imaginary and symbolic orders interpenetrate the real, which in turn inform how the unconscious interpenetrates consciousness. Consciousness becomes an appearance, an illusory articulation of what cannot be rightfully articulated. This is why consciousness can only reveal through images and symbolization the differentiated and modified forms of unconscious reality. For Lacan (1954–1955a), objects that terrify us, such as:

> the anxiety-provoking apparition of an image . . . summarize what we can call the revelation of that which is least penetrable in the real, of the real lacking any possible mediation, of the ultimate real, of the essential object which isn't an object any longer, but this something faced with which all words cease and all categories fail, the object of anxiety *par excellence*.
>
> (p. 164)

The real resists articulation because it is simply 'the impossible', thus subjecting consciousness to the paranoid abyss of the ineffable. Freud (1900) was the first to insist on the primacy of the underworld: 'The unconscious is the true psychical reality; *in its innermost nature it is as much unknown to us as the reality of the external world*' (p. 613). And just as the nature of symptoms have a sense (Freud, 1916–1917), Lacan emphasizes the primal communication of the real as that indescribable language, that which is *paranoos*, thus beyond mind (νόος). It is not *I* who speaks; rather, *It* speaks in me.

Notes

1 From his *Seminar* on the psychoses, Lacan (1955–1956d) says,

> I'm not surprised that my discourse may have created a certain margin of misun-
> derstanding. . . . I would say that it is with a deliberate, if not entirely deliberated,
> intention that I pursue this discourse in such a way as to offer you the opportunity
> to not quite understand.

> (p. 164)

2 The implication of this position carries with it certain philosophical problematics. Lacan
assumes that just because externality temporally predates the birth of the human subject,
that the human being is strictly determined by environmental forces. Contra Hegel and
Freud, who believe that a certain internally derived intrapsychic activity apprehends the
external world of givens and modifies its self-structure through its own self-determinations;
or Heidegger and Sartre, who believe that Dasein can transcend its thrownness, Lacan commits himself to a hard determinism that leaves little wiggle-room for the notions of human
agency, freedom, choice and self-determinate action.

3 This view must be contrasted to the pleasant, soothing presence of the imago, and particularly the maternal imago, that is gradually internalized by the child, thus becoming
a stabilizing and cohesive function informing psychic structure (cf. the various developmental models of Bowlby, 1980; Klein, 1946, 1957; Kohut, 1978; Mahler et al., 1975;
Stern, 1985).

4 Eros has many faces, even in death. There is a perverse pleasure in death; for Freud, the
fusion of libido within self-destruction, for Lacan, the experience of *jouissance*. Unfortunately there is no adequate translation of this word in English. 'Enjoyment' is suffused
in its meaning but does not convey the sexual connotations retained in French. In one
sense, *jouissance* denotes the intense pleasure of orgasm; *Jouir* is slang for 'to come'.
However, pleasure does not quite capture its precise meaning for the residues of death
are encrusted in its essence. Therefore, we may say that *jouissance* is pleasure in the
realm of excess: '[it] is the essence or quality that gives one's life its value' (Ragland,
1995, p. 87).

5 'The Function and Field of Speech and Language in Psychoanalysis' was delivered to
the Rome Congress held at the Istituto di Psicologia della Università di Roma, 1953.

6 For Lacan, the implications of the imaginary are often pejorative, suggesting that the
subject seeks to remove itself from the flux of becoming by reducing itself to the stagnant aura of illusion. Although Lacan introduced some positive valence to the imaginary
in later theoretical postulations, it largely remains a negative construct. It may be argued,
however, that we can never escape the captivating presence of the imaginary. After all,
it is the world of perception and fantasy, of wish and defence. We can never transcend
the illusory.

5

JUNG'S METAPHYSICS

C.G. Jung is one of the most controversial figures in the history of psychoanalysis. He was a brilliant scholar tenaciously engaged in the human sciences, comparative religion, philosophy, cultural anthropology, mythology, theosophy, and the mystical traditions of East and West. He was also purported to suffer from mental illness, engaged in sexual transgressions with patients, and lived an unorthodox lifestyle for his era. Despite having achieved notable world fame in his lifetime for his novel theories and clinical method, including receiving eight honorary doctorates, his most radical metaphysical theses on the nature of the transpersonal psyche still remain murky and unsystematized.

Despite being the focal point of his theoretical system, I argue that Jung's notion of the archetypes is one of his least understood concepts because it was nebulous to Jung himself. Vacillating between viewing archetypes as analogous to primordial images and ideas inherited from our ancestral past, as well as instincts, formal *a priori* categories of mind, cosmic projections, emotional and valuational agencies, and numinous mystical experience, the question remains whether a 'suprapersonal' or 'transubjective' psyche exists. Here I will be preoccupied with tracing the theoretical development of Jung's thesis on the collective unconscious, with a special emphasis on the archetypes, and hence pointing out the metaphysical implications of his thought. It is not possible to critique his entire body of work in the context of this abbreviated chapter; therefore, the reader should be aware that I am limiting myself to a narrow scope of interest in explicating and analysing the philosophical viability of his major concepts. The greater question is whether the archetypes adequately answer to the question of origins, of an omnipresent and eternal dimension to the nature and structure of psychic reality.

Throughout the scope of this chapter, I attempt to clarify the main theoretical postulates that constitute Jung's metaphysics and address to what degree they are philosophically plausible. In doing so, I shall forgo the typical academic custom of reviewing all the secondary literature on the subject matter and instead remain focused on what Jung actually said in his primary texts. In this way, I will spare the reader the redundancy of offering a banal literature review and approach Jung's texts in a fresh manner unencumbered by the imposition of previous interpretations that may colour my analysis of his thought.

At the heart of his metaphysical system of inquiry lies the premise that all psychological processes are necessarily conditioned on innate universal structures of subjectivity that allow for human experience to transpire, and that these processes participate of a greater cosmic organizing principle that transcends all levels of particularity or individuality. This is not necessarily an illegitimate claim, for many philosophical schools have attempted to achieve coherence and explanatory breadth in forming a conceptual unity between religion, science and cosmology. What makes Jung peculiar in the history of metaphysical thought is that he elevates this nexus or *coniunctio* to a psychological factor that conditions all metaphysical speculations on the nature of the universe. For Jung, the nature of reality is psychic process constituted as an impersonal animating force that is superimposed on human experience and transgenerationally transmitted throughout the ages. This is the doctrine of archetypes.

Implicit throughout Jung's theoretical corpus is the notion that there is another dimension to reality that structures and colours our internal experiences and perception of the world. There is something very appealing yet eerie to this view, at once accommodating but uncanny, sublime yet horrific. Perhaps this annulling duality signifies the dialectical tension of opposites Jung himself emphasizes in his quest for wholeness, a *mysterium tremendum* that becomes intuitively problematic when examined under the microscope of reason. But intuition is also recalcitrant to reason, hence revealing a deeply felt gnosis that resonates within the interiority of our being. Can we remain on a rational plane when discussing inner felt experience that speaks to us personally, and with bona fide self-certainty, while at the same time being neutered by the inhospitable hands of logos?

Jung champions a metaphysics of experience that is guided by an internalized yet originally inherited collective consciousness, which has been unconsciously transmuted and memorialized within spacetime, and laid down within the structural configurations of human imagination. The question becomes whether this imagination emanates from an equiprimordial wellspring that conditions the production of all contents of imagination, or whether images and psychic artefacts can be sufficiently explained without appealing to earlier archaic elements that predate the birth of the concretely existing human subject. In other words, do we need to appeal to an ancestral past in order to explain present experience? Do we currently occupy a spirit(ual) world emanating from a central ubiquitous Source that is responsible for the collective development of the human race? In order to broach these questions respectfully, we must understand what Jung meant by the collective unconscious.

The collective unconscious as a metaphysical category

The collective unconscious is a term Jung uses almost interchangeably and synonymously with the archetypes and is in essence a spacing, container, or receptacle that symbolizes world human experience. Despite the fact that the collective unconscious may symbolize universal culture, namely, the anthropological images, practices, mores, edicts and values that embody a particular society and its *mythos*, which become the structural invariants of subjectivity, it may be argued that Jung assigns a certain ontology to the collective unconscious, for anything that has being or presence is professed to exist. Whether or not the ontology of the collective unconscious is a hypostatization or anthropomorphism is another issue, one that will be explored later on. For the time being, however, Jung certainly did not mean to imply that the collective unconscious was merely a metaphor, social construction, or linguistic signifier determined by grammatical relativism. On the contrary, he wanted to delineate its presence as real and elevate it to the proper stature of a metaphysical category that was operative within all human beings regardless of history, gender, race, geography, or time. In this sense, Jung was first and foremost an ontologist interested in defending a universal theory of mind.[1]

The collective unconscious, what Jung also refers to as the *'transpersonal unconscious'* or 'objective psyche' (*CW* 7: p. 66, fn4), lies 'beyond everyday reality', yet we are simultaneously 'in touch with that other reality' at all times (Kirsh, 2000, p. 256). Joseph Henderson (1964), one of Jung's early 'patrons' of the C.G. Jung Institute in Zurich, describes the collective unconscious as 'the part of the psyche that retains and transmits the common psychological inheritance of mankind' (p. 107). In his translation of Jung's 'Psychological Commentary' on the *Bardo Thödol*, or *The Tibetan Book of the Dead*, R.F.C. Hull (in Jung, 1957) characterizes the collective unconscious as 'the matrix of everything' (p. xxxvi), hence lending a cosmic animating principle to the collective psyche, what we may even compare to Plato's *chora* – the womb of all becoming. For Jung, the collective unconscious is the Encompassing, the condition and ground of existence, World Soul (*anima mundi*).[2]

Jung's philosophy of the collective unconscious presupposes a psychologism at the heart of all metaphysical processes, for in Jung's (1957) words, 'metaphysical assertions . . . *are statements of the psyche*' (p. xxxvii) ultimately rooted in the soul's (*Seele*) projections. For Jung, psychic reality and metaphysical reality are identical:

> It is the soul which, by the divine creative power inherent in it, makes the metaphysical assertion; it posits the distinctions between metaphysical enti-
> ties. Not only is it the condition of all metaphysical reality, it *is* that reality.
> (Jung, 1957, p. xxxviii)

Here Jung joins the ranks of the great German Idealists who view reality as the product of mind. But he could also be accused of espousing a crass idealism, where the psyche is believed to think the world into existence. I do not believe Jung makes this explicit statement anywhere in his *Collected Works*; however, he does not want to bifurcate nature from psyche, namely, that which is given, thrown, or predetermined, and hence psyche and reality are ontologically conjoined.

Throughout his body of writings, Jung refers to the collective unconscious as comprising both the drives or instincts (*Triebe*) and the archetypes or primordial images (*CW* 8: pp. 133–134, 138) that he equates with a 'supra-individual psychic activity' (*CW* 8: p. 148) conditioned by our ancestral heritage belonging to 'a timeless and universal psyche' (*CW* 8: p. 152). Jung goes so far to say that 'the whole of mythology could be taken as a sort of projection of the collective unconscious' (*CW* 8: p. 152), raising the question and problematic of whether it is an agency in its own right, what the editors of his *Collected Works* attribute to an 'unconscious entity' (*CW* 8: p. 133, fn7). This conclusion imports many philosophical conundrums including: how could separate agencies interact; how could different psychic organizations and productions participate of one another when by definition they would have incompatible essences; and what or who is the agent or process responsible for orchestrating psychic activity to begin with? Jung's whole thesis could be easily (mis)interpreted to mean that there is an absolute mind, primary source, principle of the ultimate, or cosmic deity underlying all facets of the universe.

Although Jung's implicit supernaturalism has been a major criticism of his theory, it becomes less problematic once viewed from the standpoint of evolution. He uses the example of how early man would have been exposed to the daily physical occurrences of nature, such as the cycle of day and night, which were imprinted on the primitive psyche as primordial images and preserved unconsciously, which we still reproduce today in some transmuted yet similar fashion. This is why all cultures have a symbolism of the sun that evokes a form of natural divinity as Life (e.g. 'Mother Nature'). What this logically means is that such early primordial experiences would have been laid down within the nucleotide sequence of DNA and evolutionarily undergone genetic transmogrifications over the millennia that now predispose and influence our dreams, fantasies, imagination, and the specific imagos each individual produces within their specific familial and cultural contexts.

In much of his early writings, when he is first introducing the notions of the collective unconscious and the archetypes, he wants to impress upon us that his theories are based on empirical facts, when he also relies on speculative metaphysics. Extending a natural explananda to the collective, he postulates a dynamic imaginal life prefaced on previous archaic experiences genetically encoded and memorialized within the human psyche, only then to be transmitted transgenerationally and transculturally; hence explaining why such universal images are reproduced and why the human mind is attracted to seek these experiences and imbue them with emotional meaning. Is it far-fetched to assume that the psychic apparatus is drawn to various colours, forms and images over others because they serve an evolutionary purpose of providing symbolic meaning imbued with aesthetic and spiritual properties?

Jung is very clear when he tells us that the collective psyche is 'impersonal' (*CW* 7: p. 66; 8: p. 204) and 'identical' in all people (*CW* 8: p. 436). Here, any notion that the collective is a personal agency is displaced by a generic universality that comprises the psychological processes operative within human experience. However, Jung complicates matters when he says this unconscious universality 'constitutes a common psychic substrate of a suprapersonal nature which is present in every one of us' (*CW* 9: p. 4). Is he implying that the collective unconscious is earlier than, hence merely beyond, the personal, viz. that it cannot be reduced to individual experience simply because these are universal structures of mind? Or is he suggesting that such a 'suprapersonal' element is indeed simultaneously above, over, greater than, and transcendent (Lat. *supra*, above, beyond, earlier)? Jung's imposition of multiple meanings is also compounded by the fact that he changes his mind about the essential characteristics of the collective psyche over time. Here is a passage from his later writings:

> I must content myself with the hypothesis of an omnipresent, but differentiated, psychic structure which is inherited and which necessarily gives a certain form and direction to all experience . . . The archetypes, as organs of the psyche, are dynamic, instinctual complexes which determine psychic life to an extraordinary degree. That is why I also call them *dominants* of the unconscious. The layer of unconscious psyche which is made up of these universal dynamic forms I have termed the *collective unconscious*.
>
> (Jung, 1957, p. xlv)

Jung returns to equating the collective unconscious with a ubiquitous container or psychic spacing that houses the archetypes. Here he emphasizes their dominion over psychic life, and their dynamism implies that they are alive, powerful and causal. This emphasis on psychic determinism further resonates throughout his thought from the first time he introduces the term:

> The collective unconscious comprises in itself the psychic life of our ancestors right back to the earliest beginnings. It is the matrix of all conscious psychic occurrences, and hence it exerts an influence that compromises the freedom of consciousness in the highest degree.
>
> (*CW* 8: p. 112)

Jung reiterates the notion that the collective psyche is 'the deposit of all human experience right back to its remotest beginnings . . . a living system of reactions and aptitudes that determine the individual's life in invisible ways' (*CW* 8: p. 157). Here the collective unconscious is not just confined to primordial images, which are 'involuntary spontaneous manifestations' (Jung, 1964, p. 55), rather it is a 'living system' that animates mind. He continues to say that it is not merely the product of our ancestral history, but is a 'creative impulse' that 'contains the whole spiritual heritage of mankind's evolution, born anew in the brain structure of every individual' (*CW* 8: p. 158). Once again, this statement could avail itself of an evolutionary explanation. Our capacity to experience life in any manner is conditioned on our animal past and our embodied neurobiological facticity.

Despite the fact that Jung attributes many aspects to the archaic mind, where various emendations, redirecting shifts in emphasis and conceptual modifications make their way into his mature theorizing, we can conclude that the collective unconscious has the following characteristics. It may be viewed as a:

(a) metaphysical orienting principle underlying all aspects of mental life;
(b) a process system instituting its own dynamic determinants, thus lending structure and ontological order to human experience;
(c) an innate receptacle, repository, or psychic spacing where the archaic past is inherited, retained and preserved;
(d) the sum total amalgamation of ancestral forms of human experience that date back to the prehistory of humankind;
(e) a highly adaptive organic, biological system subject to the natural laws of evolution; and
(f) a cosmic template, matrix, or unifying web where all psychic experiences emanate from, intermingle with, and ultimately return to, for no human experience may be said to exist independent of the collective source.

This assessment is not without inherent difficulty, for it leads to several corollary problems. For one, we need to explain how these processes or mechanisms actually operate. Even if we come to an agreement about what constitutes human experience, we need to explicate how primordial phenomena were originally retained within the primitive mind and why they manifest now. How is archaic experience memorialized? How is it transmitted? It is not enough to simply offer a hypothesis that these things just happened that way and are currently operative on our present day psyches, for we need to theoretically work out all the details in order to avoid an unsophisticated folk psychology. Perhaps we can justify in some rudimentary fashion how the earliest experiences of primitive man were genetically encoded and modified through biological transmutations over time, as this would apply to any organic developmental, evolutionary process effective within other species. Along these lines, do we wish to equate prehistoric experience with phylogenetic memories? If predispositions or proclivities toward experiential occurrences are conditioned on the primordial past, including images, thoughts, feelings, behavioural patterns, aptitudes, fantasies and ideation, then the penumbra and assortment of these collective experiences would have to be memorialized within the psyche and transferred (as information) over our maturation as a human species. Jung would not likely approve of the notion that *représentations collectives* are memories, because this implies specific experiential content within a subjective context; yet, with qualifications, he does refer to the archetypes as inherited ideas, although he prefers to emphasize the imagistic. But toward the end of his life he does specifically refer to 'archetypal memory' from the 'prehistoric past' that 'we have entirely forgotten' (1961, p. 246). This seems more than just suggestive of phylogenetic memories populating the deep substratum of the unconscious. Regardless of the conventional meaning of memory or recollection, the term 'memorialization' signifies the preservative element of retaining certain psychic events,[3] here extended to a collective psyche.

For Jung, there is a causal efficacy to the past that attempts to pull the present back to the *archē*, a metaphysical principle that is salient throughout his entire philosophy. I have explained this phenomena under the rubric of what I refer to as the 'principle of archaic primacy' (Mills, 2010, pp. 54–56). The past must be ontologically preserved and operative within the present, which further influences how we approach the future, a metaphysical destiny that is diachronically super-imposed on all experience. Archaic primacy holds a privileged causal status in the psyche, for mind presupposes a historicity that informs its present operations and is conditioned on all previous shapes of unconscious experience. This means that every mental form and its derivatives draws on the internalized and dialectically preserved past ensconced within an unconscious abyss, for psychic processes and their contents cannot simply pop up *ex nihilo*. Following the principle of sufficient reason, there must be a ground or origin to every mental event that stands in rela-tion to every mental object. In principle, this is not incompatible with a collective unconscious insofar as these generic processes are universal *a priori* dynamic structures that compose the substratum of mind.

What becomes a most vociferous yet vexing question is the question of a transpersonal or suprapersonal mind. What do we mean by this exactly? If we are merely saying that mind transcends or reaches beyond the actual limits of our subjective elements through imagination, fantasy, or phenomenal experiences, then that is not controversial (Lat. *trans*, beyond, through). If the transpersonal is merely universal, formal, and not subject to personal life events, then Jung can readily defend his theoretical position. If we mean mind is transcendental (Lat. *transcendere*: *trans*, over + *scandere*, to climb), that is, to surpass itself in vari-ous forms, this is also philosophically defensible given that the a priorists devised very elaborate justifications for postulating faculties of mind that do not merely rely on sense experience for knowledge claims. Even mystical experience may (in principle) be metaphysically and psychoanalytically justified, especially when emotional, intuitive and aesthetic supplements complement the spiritual dimen-sion of personal experience that reason is quick to prejudicially disregard. Yet, if we import a transcendent realm independent of the material universe, where space and time are suspended for an unembodied supernatural or cosmic paranormal order, then we must be prepared to leave the language of metaphysics and adopt another discourse. For example, Dan Merkur (1999) argues for a relocation of mysticism from supernatural ontology to natural psychology in order to obviate these problematics. Whether or not Jung falls within this categorical realignment is not transparent. He certainly oscillates in his thinking, and the metaphysical reverberations of his ambivalence are felt.

How could there be a Cosmic Mind, a suprapersonal agency or entity that exists 'out there', as if it is a Creator force or Source of everything we typically call God? If there is an independent agency, power, energy, or entity operating in the extant world outside of the living subject, which *a fortiori* animates the universe, then are we not treading into religiosity, panpsychism, anthroposophy, or some form of shamanistic folklore? Although the collective unconscious may have a certain appeal to theologians, theosophists, and mystics of all types – and perhaps even for process philosophers, cosmologists and physicists – we must readily admit the difficulty that lies before us when positing a suprapersonal entity or Cosmic Being responsible for all aspects of our mental life.

Here I am concerned with delineating the problem. Of course I cannot offer a definitive answer of my own, for I am unable to resolve it. But we must attempt to offer some modicum of an explanation despite it being inherently delinquent or unsatisfactory. Can we escape the intrinsic mystery of these paradoxes? Can we broach a plausible hypothesis that lends some sensibility to our dilemma? I am doubtful, but with a trickle of hope.

If the *via mystica* leads us to the conclusion that there is a suprapersonal cosmic mind underlying all productions of psychic life, then Jung's theories will always generate incredulity. However, if we ground the transpersonal within a model of natural psychology, the metaphysical quandaries I am highlighting become less problematic because they are relegated to the domain of phenomenology rather than ontology.[4] Jung concedes to the limits of reason alone, and hence must resort to the life of experience, and particularly affect. If the collective unconscious answers to spiritual questions based on unitive thinking, then they have metaphorical and phenomenal value. But if mystical moments lead to ontological claims independent of scientific evidence or logical reason, then they open themselves up to being judged as based on wish-fulfilment, emotional prejudice, or subjective intuition imbued with idiosyncratic meaning. While subjective and objective elements of lived psychic reality exist simultaneously, we cannot escape the indubitable psychologism that ultimately grounds Jung's metaphysics. Whether this psychologism can be extrapolated to a supernatural metaphysical entity that governs the psyche of all living individuals is yet another issue.

The mystical nature of archetypes

Jung's theory of archetypes is the fulcrum of his entire metaphysics and is modelled after two tensions in his thinking. The first involves his predilection for the spiritual, while the second involves his pursuit of scientific rationalism. This tension can be observed in his choice of adopting the term archetype, which derives from the ancients, particularly Plato, is echoed in the medievalists, and is further taken up by Kant in attempting to close the divide between appearance and reality. In fact, Jung frequently makes reference to these philosophers respectively for their attempts to describe the 'universal dispositions of the mind' that characterize the archetype, which he describes should:

> be understood as analogous to Plato's forms (*eidola*), in accordance with which the mind organizes its contents. One could also describe these forms as *categories* analogous to the logical categories which are always and everywhere present as the basic postulates of reason. Only in the case of our 'forms', we are not dealing with categories of reason but with

categories of *imagination*. As the products of imagination are always in essence visual, their forms must, from the outset, have the character of images and moreover of typical *images*, which is why, following St. Augustine, I call them 'archetypes'.

(Jung, 1957, p. xliv)

Here Jung emphasizes imagination and imago, and with his reference to Augustine, relocates the image within the original form in which it emanates. His life-long preoccupation with the medievalists also finds its origin in Plato, where spirit and imago participate. Jung was attracted to Plato's notion of forms and Kant's logical categories, which condition our experiences of both the sensible world and our conceptual capacity for understanding, because each model serves as a conceptual scheme on which all experience is based and constructed. In other words, the forms and the categories become the a priori ground that conditions all experience. Therefore, *form* becomes the basic constituent of an archetype.

Jung's first usage of the term archetype (*Archetypus*) appears in 'Instinct and the Unconscious' (1919). His previous references to the 'primordial image' (*Urbild*) are now used almost interchangeably with the word archetype, which the editors of his *Collected Works* refer to as 'an essentially unconscious entity' (see *CW* 8: p. 133, fn7). But Jung does not make this claim here explicitly, so it is misleading to refer to the archetypes as entities, because this implies they have an ontological status apart from the experiential person. What Jung does say is the following:

We also find in the unconscious qualities that are not individually acquired but are inherited, e.g., instincts as impulses to carry out actions from necessity, without conscious motivation. In this 'deeper' stratum we also find the *a priori*, inborn forms of 'intuition', namely the *archetypes* of perception and apprehension, which are the necessary *a priori* determinants of all psychic processes.

(*CW* 8: p. 133)

Here Jung refers almost verbatim to Kant's (1781) intuitive forms of sensibility (that inform the perceptual apparatus) and the categories for understanding the sensible world as outlined in his *Critique of Pure Reason*.[5] Jung says they are necessary, universal, and underlie *all* psychic activity of the mind. Furthermore, the archetypes 'force' themselves on human perception 'into specifically human patterns'. He continues to delineate that the instincts and archetypes are *distinct*, but together they form the content of the collective unconscious.

Drawing on his historical precursors, from the ancients to scholasticism, modern philosophy, and German idealism, Jung emphasizes how archetypes are 'natural images engraved' on the human psyche that took the form of 'ideas' in a Platonic sense (*CW* 8: p. 136). He also equates them with the most ancient of universal '"thought-forms" of humanity' that have their own 'independent life' (*CW* 7: p. 66). These primordial images are essentially autonomous mental templates that 'determine the form and direction of instinct' (*CW* 8: p. 137). Here Jung introduces a causal impetus as archetype determines how drives will be enacted. He furthermore implies in this original essay that archetypes are a type of perceiving agency, like an ego. In his words: '*Archetypes are typical modes of apprehension, and whenever we meet with uniform and regularly recurring modes of apprehension we are dealing with an archetype*' (*CW* 8: pp. 137–138, italics in original). This suggests that archetypes have an organizational and agentic structure all to their own. I will return to this notion shortly, but for now, let us continue to examine the chronological nature of Jung's thought.

From image and form to affect and fantasy

The instincts and archetypes, Jung explains, are universal and common collective phenomena, yet he tends to equivocate on their relation to each other, which he states 'determine one another' (*CW* 8: p. 134). Yet the two are not the same. A primordial image is not an impersonal biological drive. As Jung's thinking matures, he goes into other developmental directions, whereby the properties of an archetype evolve in definitional character.

By 1927 Jung's views on the archetype have expanded. Here the archetypes generate 'myth-motifs' that arise from 'affect-laden fantasies' (*CW* 8: p. 155). Here fantasy becomes the experiential link to ancient imagos. Now the collective unconscious is described as 'a kind of supra-individual psychic activity' distinct from personal experience (*CW* 8: p. 148), yet it harbours 'the ancestral heritage of possibilities of representation', which become 'the true basis of the individual psyche' (*CW* 8: p. 152). Here Jung may be accused of confounding universal forms or faculties that make cognition possible with the collective unconscious, which is a category mistake. Drives, for example, are not faculties of cognition; they are psychophysical urges that impel a sentient organism to act. Faculties as *a priori* forms of cognition allow for experience to arise and be presented to consciousness, just as perception requires the *re-presentation* of objects to be retrieved from memory, which necessarily mediates experience. Although Jung does not directly say so here that images are recovered representations from the collective, he certainly does so elsewhere when he refers to archetypical figures, dream symbols and mythological motifs as *représentations collectives* (*CW* 8: p. 122; 9: p. 41).

While the collective unconscious is the cosmic receptacle and issuance of form, the archetypes are the content of the collective without themselves having content. Yet Jung introduces content into this formless archetype when he claims that image, affect, fantasy, motifs and patterns constitute this formless property of the collective. He furthermore equivocates drive with archetype when he says that 'the archetypes are simply the forms which the instincts assume' (*CW* 8: p. 157). Here instincts transmogrify into archetypes, what Jung says is 'the very source of the creative pulse'. Presumably Jung wants to locate the creative wellspring within instinct, while creative expression flows through the archetype. But this is not clear. He does speak of the 'creative instinct' as a psychical impulse, but he does not want to make them identical (see *CW* 7: p. 118). Elsewhere

128

he locates creativity within fantasy as a unifying function, which he makes the 'creative matrix of everything' (*CW* 7: p. 290) ultimately having its source within the archetypal collective. But it may be argued, as does Freud, that fantasy is the modification of drive. Jung concludes that the collective is the 'source' of 'instinctual forces', while the forms or categories 'that regulate them' are the archetypes (*CW* 8: p. 158). Here Jung defers to his earlier position that the archetypes are merely formal.

He also affirms this position in *Memories, Dreams, Reflections*, when he tells us unambiguously that:

> the archetypes, which are pre-existent to consciousness and condition it, appear in the part they actually play in reality . . . As an attribute of instinct they partake of its dynamic nature, and consequently possess a specific energy which causes or compels definite modes of behaviour or impulses.
>
> (1961, p. 347)

Notice that Jung posits the archetypes to be 'pre-existent to consciousness'. This is an ontological commitment to realism. They predate the existence of the living human subject and causally condition how the individual experiences and acts. But once again Jung interjects a contradictory statement by making the archetype 'an attribute of instinct'. It is important to raise this issue, because if the archetype emanates from instinct, such as by acquiring modified attributes and properties, then drive or instinct would be the ground of all psychic activity. What would follow is that archetypes would become differentiated mental productions that appear as psychic objects derived from an original natural drive. But this is not what Jung ultimately postulates, which, I suggest, needs this added corrective. Archetypes are the ontological ground of all psychic productions since they pro-create images, fantasies, and so forth that dominate mental life. We may say they are instinctually innate, but they are not instincts in themselves. Here it would be more correct to preserve the distinction between instinct as embodied drive that belongs to the corporeality of the living subject, while archetypes retain their special status and consistent character as the 'primordial' ground of the psyche, which is the hallmark of Jung's philosophy.

What this implies is that, emanating from within the collective, there is a particular form of unconscious recognition with an image that we are drawn to as a numinous phenomenon, presumably having its origins in the minds of primitive humankind, such as certain shapes or colours associated with sense impressions, which are genetically encoded and transmitted over the ages. Problems arise, however, when Jung attributes 'emotional fantasies' (*CW* 8: p. 154) to archetypes in addition to powers for the 'possibilities of representations'. Here he moves from formal properties of universality to contents that have specific images and fantasies that are thematic or generic in form. Jung delineates them as patterns or motifs, therefore they still maintain their formal structure, but the pattern or motif itself conveys a specific content (e.g. the *anima mundi*), which may be revealed in countless ways in the personal unconscious. But Jung advances his thesis to include additional properties: form and image now acquire affect and fantasy.

The 'possibilities' to represent the innumerable archetypes are unbounded. However, representations do not necessarily mean the retrieval of an idea or image that once belonged to a caveman. Although Jungians are sensitive to this issue, and are quick to defend Jung, as he did himself, it does not mean that this inference cannot be implied. Jung would say that it is not the specific image or idea itself, but the formalism that allows for these ideas and images to emerge in the subjective mind. Here he is no different than Kant. But Kant counts on conscious presentations of sense impressions to occur, what he calls the manifold world of sensible objects presented to 'intuition', before the unconscious mind can represent those images to subjective consciousness. Jung inverts this process. He requires the collective unconscious to supply the form and the properties which the conscious mind takes up. Here we cannot separate the two domains because instinct, imago, affect, fantasy and form are interdependent.

To summarize this progression, archetypes are originally devoid of content, hence they are merely formal. Despite having a specific content that varies from person to person, the theme or motif represented in the subject's consciousness still reveals a basic pattern. Jung refers to them as aboriginal shapes or patterns of mind that are both biological and transpersonal, belonging to the 'prehistoric and unconscious development of the mind in archaic man, whose psyche was still close to that of the animal . . . This immensely old psyche forms the basis of our mind' (Jung, 1964, p. 67). This is an ontological assertion, but he draws on an evolutionary argument to support the primacy of archetypes by claiming they are instinctive processes analogous to birds, which are hard-wired to build nests. Put laconically, we have evolutionarily developed our minds in this fashion, and have a mental apparatus that perceives phenomena and structures our personal experience of reality in this manner.

Patterns of behaviour

If instinct, form, image, affect and fantasy are not enough defining attributes, Jung includes 'patterns of behaviour' as another characteristic inhering in an archetype. Here instinct and archetype are conjoined, hence deviating from his original conception that the collective contained both the instincts and the archetypes. He states:

> There are, in fact, no amorphous instincts, as every instinct bears in itself the pattern of its situation. Always it fulfills an image, and the image has fixed qualities: . . . it cannot exist without its total pattern, without its image. Such an image is an *a priori* type . . . We may say that the image represents the *meaning* of the instinct.
>
> (*CW* 8: p. 201)

Jung speaks from a position of *ex cathedra*; however, his arguments are convoluted. Here he deviates radically from Freud's (1915a) definition of *Trieb*. Jung makes instinct formless (viz. 'amorphous') yet patterned – itself a contradiction – and furthermore with the properties of images with 'fixed qualities' that are given a priori, namely, as innate or inborn. This is a radical proposition. Archetypes now have fixed qualities of images that are instinctually reproduced through patterned forms of thought, feeling, fantasy and behaviour. What this logically entails is that we are programmed to reproduce images and behavioural acts that were originally conditioned by early man and inherited through gradual evolution. That claim is not necessarily controversial in itself; but what is controversial is the notion that 'images' are reproduced from a fund of archaic *re-presentations* belonging to the 'collective'. This intimates a Lamarckian view of a fount of inherent phylogenetic memories within mind. Moreover, they are 'fixed' not malleable; hence they are predetermined rather than determinate. Here the collective is portrayed as more of a supernatural *mysterium*.

Jung furthermore says that images convey 'the *meaning* of the instincts'. This statement can be interpreted as though drives have intentional states expressed through imagos, but I believe Jung is referring to the notion that they have a purpose or function to the psyche. He equivocates in separating instinct from archetype, equating behaviour to instinct and image to archetype, yet he also says that the archetypes 'act like the instincts'; and he would not 'refute this possibility' of their 'identical' nature (*CW* 8: p. 205).

Jung is attempting to use the hypothesis of archetypes as a heuristic connection to explain and mediate all aspects of psychic life. By incorporating instinct within archetypal structure, he seeks a unitive synthesis. All aspects of human psychology must be accounted for in his theoretical system in order to have a monistic theory of mind, what Jung refers to as the *unus mundus* – one unitary order that structures the universe. The doctrine of archetypes fulfils this mediating role. And behaviour is no exception. The archetype postulate serves a unitary function of binding thought, image, affect and behaviour within the instinctual substrate that conditions human psychology. But we may not inappropriately ask: Why do we need the archetype concept when the notion of drive may potentially explain the same thing?

Human behaviour cannot be divorced from the archetypal world because primitive imagos form the basis of human motivation that drives human action. Jung tells us: 'Archetypes are typical forms of behaviour which, once they become conscious, naturally present themselves *as ideas and images*' (*CW* 8: p. 227). Like Freudian drive theory, in principle, the archetype cannot be directly known, for it appears as modified content and is 'irrepresentable' in itself (*CW* 8: p. 214). In this case, only images, ideas, and so forth are known or experienced as the transmogrification of its emanating source. But Jung goes on to refute this identity thesis between instinct and archetype, for he says that: 'Archetype and instinct are the most polar opposites imaginable', because archetype is tantamount to 'spirit' or the psychical, while instinct is tantamount to bodily urge or impulse; yet they have 'so close a bond' they are dialectically inseparable (*CW* 8: p. 206). This is Jung's attempt to explain the mind/body problem, yet it reveals the pole of his tacit dualism. Archetype becomes the ontological bridge to mind and body. But as we will shortly see, he ultimately makes that bridge a purely psychic process.

Now that Jung has captured the breadth of human psychology within his metaphysical system, he seeks to offer an integrative paradigm that amplifies his previous emphasis on imago, fantasy and affect. He does this by evoking the spiritual within the aesthetic and emotional life of the collective human subject. Here enters the numinous.

Archetype as numinosity

By the time Jung wrote 'On the Nature of the Psyche' (1947), the concept of the archetype had undergone more emendations. This is when Jung introduces the notion of the archetype as *numen*. Drawing on medieval astrology and the alchemists, particularly Paracelsus, he compares the collective archetypes 'in all their luminosity and numinosity' to 'cosmic projection' (*CW* 8: p. 195) reflective of a World Soul: 'The world-soul is a natural force which is responsible for all the phenomena of life and the psyche' (*CW* 8: p. 196). Although Jung is only making comparisons, he is suggestive that his notion of the archetypes signifies the same phenomena.

Merkur (1996), interpreting Rudolf Otto (1932), describes the *sensus numinous* as a category of values that inspires majestic awe and splendour, which at the same time is clouded in mystery imbued with an emotional sense of urgency. This phenomenological amalgamation of psychic experience nicely captures Jung's notion of an archetype. But Jung also takes some supernatural leaps of faith in attributing spiritual and magical properties to the archetypes:

> The archetypes have, when they appear, a distinctly numinous character which can only be described as 'spiritual', if 'magical' is too strong a word . . . It not infrequently happens that the archetype appears in the form of a spirit in dreams or fantasy-products, or even comports itself like a ghost. There is a mystical aura about its numinosity, and it has a corresponding effect upon the emotions.

> (*CW* 8: pp. 205–206)

Although Jung is not technically making a metaphysical assertion about a supernatural world, instead focusing on the phenomenal appearances that appeal to the emotional and valuational processes of the experiential subject, he is nevertheless presupposing that archetypes 'appear' from behind the Kantian veil of the noumena, what we may attribute to the transcendent world of things in themselves as something supersensible. There is little doubt that the term numinosity is derived from this historical philosophical context, and particularly given that Kant's (1790) major work on aesthetics, *Critique of Judgment*, was preoccupied with the question of the sublime and the teleology of nature.

Jung wants to capture the qualitative unitive sense of emotional experience that is simultaneously wondrous, affectively intense and spiritually meaningful yet shrouded in a transcendent ontology. This is why he emphasizes the '*feeling-value* of the archetype' that 'determines' how it will experientially unfold (*CW* 8: p. 209). This probably has a certain eschatological significance for Jung, but it should be pointed out that this is the same language Whitehead (1929) uses, himself an atheist, when he describes the emotional and value-laden aspects of the unitive processes involved in 'prehension' and 'concrescence', which he argues are the building blocks of all cosmological reality. The archetype could be viewed almost synonymously with 'actual entities', or in Jung's language, 'psychic entities' (*CW* 8: p. 231). For Jung, the numinous element of an archetypal image produces a dynamism and *fascinans* to lived experience that resonates as unconscious qualia.

Jung elevates the numinous character of an archetype to a 'psychoid factor that belongs, as it were, to the invisible, ultraviolet end of the psychic spectrum. It does not appear, in itself, to be capable of reaching consciousness' (*CW* 8: p. 213). What does Jung exactly mean by 'psychoid?' This is the same term posed by his first mentor and supervisor, Eugen Bleuler, at the Burghölzli psychiatric clinic in Jung's early days, when he was a staff psychiatrist, before his relationship with Freud commenced (see *CW* 8: pp. 176–177). And parenthetically, it also might be useful to point out that the psychoid factor Jung refers to is no different *in function* than Freud's notion of *Trieb*: a drive can never be known directly, only through its derivative manifestations.[6]

Jung adopts this term *psychoid* to designate a purely unconscious process as 'elements' incapable of being represented in consciousness (*CW* 8: p. 184), but it is not to be equated with the unconscious itself, which is composed of many different elements, processes, contents, and so forth. However, like the archetype, he equates psychoid processes with the 'transcendent' (*CW* 8: p. 213). The psychoid function is the liaison between mind and body, yet it is unclear *how* this function operates, let alone the specifics, and whether the psychoid is independent from the archetype or inheres within it. We must assume it is an organizing principle operative within the archetype because Jung locates the archetype 'beyond the psychic sphere'; and 'with its psychoid nature, forms the bridge to matter in general' (*CW* 8: p. 216). But Jung is also inconsistent in his usage and at times equates 'the psychoid' with 'factors I call archetypes' (*CW* 8: p. 515). In *Memories, Dreams, Reflections*, he states that archetypal configurations 'may be founded upon a *psychoid* base, that is, upon an only partially psychic and possibly altogether different form of being' (1961, p. 351). Notice his tentative language here, as well as his allusion to an ethereal realm. Yet it is only poetically suggestive. But when Jung uses language such as 'beyond the psychic sphere', he is clearly evoking transpersonalism. More specifically, he is referring to the Transcendent, that which lies beyond the faculties of mind.

The psychoid function is also intimately connected to Jung's thesis on synchronicity, which is a highly transpersonal phenomenon. Synchronized moments suspend the phenomenology of spacetime, hence producing numinous affects that raise the conscious experience of objects to a 'supernormal degree of luminosity' (*CW* 8: p. 436) due to the intervening elements of the psychoid function. The synchronicity principle allows for the experiential relativity of 'causeless order' that is marked by simultaneity and meaningful correspondence of events, what Jung concludes is 'transcendental' (*CW* 8: p. 506). If synchronicity is diachronic, relative to personal perspective, and displaces natural causal laws for an acausal orderliness or connecting principle that transcends our current understanding of natural science, then not only is this numinous, it arouses the uncanny mystique of imagination, fear and wonder.

Jung's mature hypothesis

In his mature theory, Jung reiterates his earlier views on the archetypal collective in an integrative but somewhat less pedantic manner. Recall that in *Symbols of Transformation*, he privileges collective images as inborn ideas, while later in his works he articulates the instinctual, behavioural and numinous character of the archetypes that express themselves as affects and fantasies. Late in his life, Jung (1957) defined the archetypes as 'eternally inherited forms and ideas which have at first no specific content. Their specific content only appears in the course of the individual's life, when personal experience is taken up in precisely these forms' (p. xliv). Here he emphasizes forms *and* ideas. But notice that form and idea are the Greek equivalent of ἰδέα, as 'to form in', taken from *idein*, to see. This is why Jung equates form with image as an idea.

In his final writing project, *Man and his Symbols*, Jung (1964) defines the archetypes in the following fashion:

> They are, at the same time, as both images and emotions. One can speak of an archetype only when these two aspects are simultaneous. When there is merely the image, then there is simply a word-picture of little consequence. But by being charged with emotion, the image gains numinosity (or psychic energy); it becomes dynamic, and consequences of some kind must flow from it.
>
> (p. 96)

Here Jung emphasizes a synthetic relation or trinity between imago, emotionality and numinosity that lead to an interactive dynamism. This represents Jung's final word on the matter given that it was completed ten days before he died. The archetype is composed of imagos and emotion that have 'a special feeling tone' or affective–energetic structure; hence they give a certain subjective phenomenal intensity and personal meaning to experience. As he continues to state, 'it is essential to insist that they are not mere [linguistic] names, or even philosophical concepts. They are pieces of life itself – images that are integrally connected to the living individual by the bridge of the emotions' (p. 97). Here affect is emphasized over imago as both a mediating factor producing a numinous quality and a unitive psychological (transcendent) function; yet it is more accurate to say that image, affect and thought form a dynamic synthetic unity. The numinous becomes the sacred symbolic that unites the emotional, aesthetic and spiritual dimension within the qualia of the concretely lived experience. This unitive experience further loses its distinctive clarity in its declension to this felt union or fusion, which may be properly attributed to the *mysterium tremendum*.

Jung also confesses to the nebulous nature of the archetypes because words cannot adequately capture their true essence. In Jung's words, he is attempting 'to describe something whose very nature makes it incapable of precise definition' (p. 97). This preserves the *via mystica* of an archetype, which also makes it incapable of being either proven or refuted. Just like the psychoid factor, which lacks explication or definitional precision in how it is structured or actually works on a functional, mechanical, or operational level, the epistemological problem of the archetype becomes displaced by the inherent valuation attributed to lived phenomenology. Is it sufficient for Jung to claim that any experience the subject has *is* reality – in other words, a psychic fact – and that is all that matters? This Gnostic opaqueness is what leads to charges of mysticism, folk psychology lacking scientific verity, and that the so-called archetypes are merely personal mythologies, illusions, or fantasies one wishes to believe in.

Integration and critique

Jung was a deeply spiritual man captivated by the marvel of the universal. The ancients called it wonder. The numinous nature of the archetype signifies that marvel united in a concrete symbolic function where all fundamental psychological characteristics and qualitative facets of human experience can participate in some semblance of harmony, even if this symbolic factor devolves into mystical abstraction. Even though he would not classify his theories this way, instead insisting they are scientific and empirical, Jung wants to capture and potentially explain all aspects of human psychology under the rubric of his metaphysics, which ultimately rests on the doctrine of archetypes. In the end, what are we to make of his major theoretical contributions and the philosophical implications of his analytical psychology?

The archetypal collective may be viewed as residues of archaic mind grafted onto our present-day psyche with psychophysical correlates that fuse mind and body, yet the numinous nature of the archetypes ultimately commits Jung to a transcendentalism that is non-corporeal. Jung is first and foremost concerned with the quest for explicating universality, which he attributes to an a priorism of form. Idea, image, emotionality and behavioural manifestations coalesce into a single psychological category that serves as the ontological fabric of all mental structures. Archetypes are formal but they are comprised of inherited imagos *as* ideation, hence they are purported to be primordial perceptual content that is mediated by psychic faculties responsible for conceptual reason, affect and behavioural propensities. Although archetypes are irrepresentable in themselves, because they are only 'basic form', they nevertheless appear as images, motifs, mythologems and the like (*CW* 8: p. 213). Jung seems to be teetering on a fine line between universal form (*a priori* categories) and content (images as inborn ideas) on the one hand, and past (collective unconscious) and present (personal experience) on the other.

Although there is a fair amount of debate among Jungians and post-Jungians, we do not see many critiques of Jung by Jungians because, I suggest, it offends a group identification, which is taboo within that professional culture. However, I wish to open a permissible space to question Jung's major concepts not as a polemic, but as a genuine search for meaning in his philosophy and with respect for his textual word. When Jung speaks of the 'suprapersonal nature' of the collective unconscious (*CW* 9: p. 4), is this merely metaphor or ontology? Is Jung making claims about ultimate reality, or are his 'hypotheses' of the collective psyche and the archetypes simply chalked up to poetic literary aesthetics? If the latter is the case, would this not cheapen the unique value of his philosophical contributions to human psychology and the pursuit of the spiritual? Jungian apologists may warn us not to read Jung through Jungian lenses that translate the language of psychology into ontology; however, we must take him at face value. Jung makes psychic processes the foundation of all human experience, possessing a transpersonal character, and this by definition is a metaphysical treatise of mind. It is untenable to separate phenomenological psychology from metaphysics because any inquiries or assertions about experience and reality are ontologically conjoined and mutually infer each other. Drawing on what he actually says in his written texts, my conclusion is Jung believed that the Collective Psyche is *real* and exists independently of any individual. This is an ontological claim that surpasses any methodological agnosticism, phenomenology, or naturalized psychology.

Jung makes contradictory statements throughout his theoretical corpus, at times averring scientific empiricism, philosophical rationalism and dialectical logic, yet at the same time he differentiates mind from matter, only then to suggest that matter is an emergent property of spirit, thus pointing toward a transubjective reality. Vacillating between viewing an archetype as an inborn idea versus the possibility or potentiality for ideation wed to personal experience, his obscurantism is further evinced when he says on the one hand that the archetype is 'pure, unvitiated nature', (*CW* 8: p. 210), but on the other that it is also suprapersonal, transcendent and beyond the sensible world. By envisioning the collective psyche as a reservoir of abstract objects inherent to cosmic process, Jung theoretically evokes a supernaturalism and aligns with disciplines sympathetic to mysticism, shamanism and theology.

Jung is very clear in stating that archetypes have a 'nonpsychic aspect' or counterpart to the cosmos connected through synchronicity, or the transcendent 'psychoid' function that supposedly mediates the 'space-time continuum'. Here he implies that the collective unconscious is a 'supernatural faculty' (*CW* 8: p. 231) full of psychic dispositions. But how can this be? How does such a faculty exist? How are psychic forms and contents dispersed into the singular minds of individuals? Why do they materialize to begin with? How could they be omnipresent and eternal if they are only capable of being apprehended by finite subjectivity?

Are these *aporiai* adequately resolved if we translate Jung's language into the modern day equivalent of biological heredity, like genetic attributes inscribed within DNA? Yet how could images and ideas be encoded and transmitted genetically when you need to have conscious experience and perception in order to internalize, memorialize and re-*present* those images in the mind? Jung wants to fall back on *a priori* formalism to explain this conundrum, and in this sense he is no different from the idealists to certain linguists who endeavour to delineate the formal structural origins of subjectivity that make conscious experience possible. But when he evokes the spectre of transpersonalism, he is getting away from the evolutionary implications of his earlier commitments and is hinting toward supernatural emanationism. And given Jung's affinity for Plotinus and the medievalists, it is no wonder he generates contradiction and paradox. This is particularly evident when he says that the archetypes have the 'functional significance of a world-constituting factor' (*CW* 8: p. 515). If archetypes constitute the world, then we are espousing a form of creationism. And Jung is not apologetic about this speculation since he posits that synchronicity flows from '*creative acts*, as the continuous creation of a pattern that exists from all eternity'. This statement is followed by a reference to God (*CW* 8: p. 518, fn17). Although Jung was enamoured with universals and makes repeated metaphysical claims that they have existed from all eternity, we are now headed toward some form of panpsychism or cosmic theosophy.

James Hillman (1975) and the archetypal school emphasize the centrality of the phenomenology of imagos and fantasy images as the main locus of analytic work, and for this reason they largely jettison many of the metaphysical presuppositions that burden the classical Jungian corpus, including rejecting the Kantian noumena (Adams, 1997). Although further divergences exist between the classical school, archetypalists and the developmentalists, giving rise to an often polemical and competitive exchange of ideas in Jungian circles (Samuels, 1997), the textual fact remains that Jung was committed to many transpersonal hypotheses that carried metaphysical ramifications.

Sherry Salman (1997) alerts us to Jung's monism derived from the medieval concept of a *unus mundus* or 'one world', which is the original undifferentiated unity that binds everything – from matter to psychic energy – within the universe. It should be noted this philosophy derives from Plotinus's emanationism, and his neo-Platonism became quite attractive to Christianity, later forming the bedrock of more sophisticated theosophies during the Middle Ages. In his work on alchemy culminating in his *Mysterium Coniunctionis*, Jung shows such breadth of scholarship that most classicists would likely applaud his synthetic ambition. In this work, Jung seeks to integrate his views on the collective unconscious and archetypal psychology with the medieval tradition. He specifically champions a process view of the many within the one, and diversity within unity, yet he draws on a creationism argument extrapolated from Plotinus:

> In the beginning God created one world (*unus mundus*), . . . the original non-differentiated unity of the world or of Being, . . . the primordial unconsciousness. While the concept of the *unus mundus* is a metaphysical speculation, the unconscious can be indirectly experienced via its manifestations.
>
> (*CW* 14: p. 462)

Jung goes on to support a monistic ontological view where everything is interconnected; and although this generates paradoxes, despite the fact that there is a multitude of manifestations, 'they are at bottom a unity'. If Jung is to be criticized for espousing this view, then he would be in good company with many philosophers over the centuries up to contemporary modes of process thought. Criticisms of metaphysical monism where diversity, plurality and differentiation are still dialectically tied to an interpenetrating unification system or principle of unity should not be directed at Jung *per se*, for this thesis preoccupies many diverse philosophical systems from East to West, criticisms I will not entertain here. What Jung is more concerned with is how his psychology fits within the mysterious conjunctions that are generated from this form of philosophy. For example, the mandala symbolizes the One, which he attributes to 'the ultimate unity of all archetypes as well as of the multiplicity of the phenomenal world, and is therefore the empirical equivalent of the metaphysical concept of a *unus mundus*' (*CW* 14: p. 463), with synchronicity being its 'parapsychological equivalent'.

What I believe Jung wants to secure is an empirical basis for a justified psychoanalytic metaphysics grounded through phenomenological psychology. For example, Jung (1961) explains: 'insofar as the archetypes act upon me, they are real and actual to me, even though I do not know what their real nature is' (p. 352). Here he uses his subjective felt experience to avouch an ontological commitment despite conceding to the epistemological limits of his capacities to know. By focusing on the phenomenology of experience, he attempts to sidestep the pitfalls associated with speculative metaphysics; yet no matter how phenomenology is positioned, one can never escape the implicit ontological assumptions that underlie our experience of experience. This is why Jung ultimately proffers a metaphysics of experience that is conditioned by the archetypal collective. For Jung, the archetypes are a necessary condition of experience, without which the human mind would not exist as we presently understand it. This archaic cosmic or suprastructural condition of the collective psyche must have an origin or source, and this is justified by the metaphysical argument for one unitary world. All actual and possible experience must be accounted for within the psychic universe Jung calls the transpersonal unconscious, which is the original union or latent unity of the world. This theoretical conviction clearly mirrors Jung's quest for holism.

The 'contemplation of the transcendental *unus mundus*, the potential world out-side time' (*CW* 14: p. 505), was clearly a pivotal notion underlying Jung's meta-physics of the archetype. What creates more scepticism is his scattered references to the archetype as a 'transcendental entity' in which the empirical world emerges from this 'transcendental psychophysical background' (*CW* 14: pp. 536–538). The word 'entity' is used here not to denote a thing or object in the empirical world, but rather, I suggest, an agent or subject. Earlier conceived as 'psychic enti-ties' (*CW* 8: p. 231), archetypes are now viewed as supernatural or transpersonal, hence they are not merely psychic; or in Jung's words, they 'have a nature that *cannot with certainty be designated as psychic*' (*CW* 8: p. 230, italics in original). Between his caveats, discursive qualifications, and scholarly elucidations of oth-ers' points of view, with interspersed slippery slopes, it is hard to pin him down on the theoretical minutia of his philosophical commitments. But we must pursue our line of inquiry further. This brings us to the nature and question of agency.

Jung tells us that archetypes 'manifest themselves only through their ability to *organize* images and ideas' (*CW* 8: p. 231). This implies agency. Elsewhere he says that it is not the individual person organizing such activity, rather it is the archetype itself 'speaking through him' as a transcendental agent (1961, p. 352). Who or what is organizing these experiences? Here Jung does not speak of the ego, self, or subject, rather he refers to the *archetypes themselves* organizing the subject's expe-rience as if they are autonomous agents within the mind. In fact, earlier he says that 'they are experienced as spontaneous agencies'; their very 'nature' is derived from 'spirit' (*CW* 8: p. 216). Although he says they are 'experienced' as independent 'forces' or 'energies', hence invoking phenomenology, he attributes their essence to an ontological substrate, 'a solidity underlying all existence' (1961, p. 358). This is a very Hegelian idea, yet Jung surprisingly held Hegel in contempt for sup-posedly espousing a grandiose theory of mind similar to that of a megalomaniac or schizophrenic (see *CW* 8: pp. 170, 320). But spirit (*Geist*) and psyche are con-ceivably two interchangeable constructs that refer to a 'psychic category' (*CW* 8: p. 120) as well as the coming into being of the collective unconscious.[7]

In contrast, Jung describes how an archetype 'can break with shattering force into an individual human life and into the life of a nation. It is therefore not sur-prising that it is called "God"' (*CW* 14: p. 552). Jung is not equating the archetype with God, only its corresponding linking-experience of the numinous that it semi-otically and affectively evokes, which *appears* as an autonomous presence that takes possession of the mind. However, Jung may be said to covertly espouse his own grandiosity by elevating the archetype to that of a deified agency responsible for numinous phenomena that the experiential subject encounters. He furthermore attributes this numinosity to the 'psychoid aura that surrounds consciousness', a concept that remains nebulous and ill defined, something of a *mysterium coni-unctionis* in itself. But what Jung is clear about is 'when we talk of God or gods we are speaking of debatable images from the psychoid realm. The existence of a transcendental reality is indeed evident in itself' (*CW* 14: p. 551). Here I interpret Jung as first acknowledging the agnosticism of the origin of the image, which is dubious, yet it is mediated through some unarticulated transcendental faculty that gives it organizational clarity, order and meaning. At best we can attribute this function to fantasy. But Jung makes this a 'transcendental reality'. He goes on to say:

> That the world inside and outside ourselves rests on a transcendental background is as certain as our own existence, but it is equally certain that the direct perception of the archetypal world inside us is just as doubtfully correct as that of the physical world outside us.
>
> (*CW* 14: p. 551)

Is it so certain that a 'transcendental background' is needed to explain these phenomena, let alone that it exists in the first place? And would not the explanation of *fantasy* answer to the psychological need to posit *certainty* to begin with?

My interpretation of these statements is that Jung has officially abandoned the notion that the archetypal collective is only formal, hence comprised of universal structures of subjectivity that condition our conscious experience of the world; but rather they are now extant suprapersonal realms of cosmic process responsible for all psychic productions the human mind manufactures. Therefore, they are causally determined by this transcendent reality, for, following this logic, there would be no mental productions without the archetypal world. This makes human experience necessarily dependent on the transpersonal netherworld, what could be easily equated with some form of supernatural intelligence that orbits and/or suffuses the natural world. We must question whether it is legitimate to attribute agency to archetypes. How could they pre-exist as entirely extra-psychic agencies in the mind? How could they have any agency at all? Just exactly, how could such agentic processes function? How could they have ego-functions of processing and unifying information or performing synthetic activity, let alone possess meaning-making signifying powers and properties?

If we sustain this line of thinking further, the concept of the collective unconscious collapses into a macroanthropos. Here archetypes take on a hypostatized quality, to the point that they may be viewed as supernatural structures inherent in the cosmos rather than a psychic faculty that allows for experience to materialize, such as Kant's categories, Fichte's principles (*Grundsät*) as transcendental acts of mind, or Hegel's dialectic (*Aufhebung*). In this way, Jung deviates from primordial form and gives archetypes a transpersonal organizational ontology that conditions the quality of experience for individuals and cultures, and hence he elevates an archetype to a majestic or divine provenance.

Is Jung committing a genetic fallacy? Does he presuppose that all internal experiences and contents can be traced back to their most basal roots, which are held to be the causal determinants of all present experiences that furthermore retain their original attributes and properties constituted long ago? Is he drawing an inappropriate conclusion that the reconstructed trace or path back to origins presumes that the present experience contains the same properties as it may have held at one time in the archaic past? When Jung says that psychic energy 'follows its own gradient down into the depths of the unconscious, and there activates what has lain slumbering from the beginning' (*CW* 7: pp. 66–67), he is presumptive that prehistoric mind would be preserved in its original manner. This assumes that psychic contents would not undergo transmogrification and, like an artefact, can be unearthed and discovered as they once existed. But this notion is highly suspicious. Because we do not have direct access to things in themselves, especially the mental contents of primitive man, we can only speculate, interpret and creatively construct meaning based on our plausible inferences. We make reasonable comparisons between particulars and universals, but are we philosophically justified to equate the concrete present with the abstract past as being identical in composition? To assume that these ancient forces and contents would be perfectly preserved within an archaic transpersonal psyche and transmitted in any form seems to beg the question that everything is a reproduction from an antecedent stage in the history of the human race rather than the cognitive modification of one's own personal life history that is mistaken for prehistory.

Critics pose the question: Do we need the collective unconscious hypothesis to explain archetypal phenomena? For example, it may be argued that human experience becomes memorialized as communal knowledge that gives rise to social practices, symbols, rituals and linguistic order that inform cultural anthropology; and that these historical remembrances become transgenerationally and transculturally transmitted over the millennia. You do not need to appeal to a collective transcendent psyche to explain these universal phenomena, save only in the formal sense that there must be a collection of individual subjects that form the greater collective consciousness that is part of our objective social existence. Appealing to a supernatural entity that becomes the ontological ground for human experience is unnecessary and introduces a whole host of philosophical conundrums.

As Dan Merkur points out,[8] one could object to the use of my term 'supernatural' because this presupposes an inherent duality between nature and spirit or psyche. Jung's unique brand of *Naturphilosophie* is indeed an attempt to dialectically bridge that dichotomy; however, he does not conceptualize the natural as metaphysical. Rather, he makes the archetypal collective something that stands above or beyond the mere natural as Transcendent, and hence he reinstates oppositionality and difference despite their underlying monistic order. Although psyche is naturalized, it is Something More than its corporeal embodiment. When Jung introduces the notion of synchronicity, the archetype now fully acquires the status of an independent being that simultaneously is experienced within the psyche, but it still lies beyond individual agency. Although archetypes are the *locus classicus*, synchronicty becomes the *causus belli*. For example, Jung wants to reclaim the spiritual function of what religion has typically addressed under the guise of the supernatural by making it an aspect of the psyche. Here religion itself becomes transformed into ontological psychology as a naturalized psychic system, but this system is ultimately informed by a suprapersonal netherworld.

Jung would likely challenge this by replying that although images, symbols, ritualistic behaviours, and so forth developed throughout the slow progression of human civilization, they could not have been simply transmitted cross-generationally or transculturally because they happen everywhere in every society. When cultures that were geographically and temporally segregated from one another, and hence had no communication with each other whatsoever on the human history timeline, they nevertheless experienced psychic phenomena that was universal to all people at all times and places personified by primordial images. But images are ubiquitous and empirical. There is nothing supernatural or mystical about them in themselves, for they are common to all of us. This is part of our natural thrownness, namely, that which is given. There is no magic to them, because this is how we perceive and think as human beings. They are simply part of our *a priori* nature, not a supernatural agency. Common experiences happen throughout the world regardless of culture, time and history. An emotion is a specific affective experience regardless of who is having it, or when and where. Could it be plausible that instead of summoning a magical sea of transcendent objects derived from an anthropic psyche, we may more humbly conceive of archetypes as psychic contents derived from internalized personal experience of images embedded within our culture and the environs that penetrate our minds from birth onward?

Jung's doctrine of the archetypes becomes an all encompassing psychic category that potentially explains every facet of human psychology. Whether Jung is successful in achieving this goal is disputable. Jung has been accused of espousing and living his life based on a psychomythology as a substitute for religion (Wehr, 1985). Is the belief in an archetypal collective merely a fiction or illusion, an exalted anthropomorphic projection, or perhaps a deposit from omnipotent infantile fantasies still clamouring for wish-fulfilment? We have good reason to suspect that Jung's longing for wholeness is the passion behind his philosophy, and that the sober logic of reason or antiseptic science could not answer or fulfil the greater metaphysical questions and spiritual quandaries we perennially face. Jung found some consolation in the *via mystica*. This is his answer to the question of complexification. I think a more generous reading of Jung, and in the spirit of his life project, is that the pursuit of the *numinosum* is what brings a qualitative exuberance and existential purpose to life that grounds our own personally created metaphysics of experience. Whether this applies to an objectivist epistemology or to social or scientific consensus is not the issue. We define our reality through our experience of the world mediated through mind. In this way, Jung's metaphysics share intimate affinities with the Idealist tradition of philosophy.[9]

One conundrum Jung perpetually faces is that he is begging the question of human spirituality as a transcendent eternity, when it can be persuasively argued that one does not need a transpersonal psyche or metaphysical divinity to explain the numinous. This conclusion, of course, meets with little emotional satisfaction, for man is a wishing animal. It is all too human to attempt to find a rational system that fulfils our wishes, but in the end, we cannot simply dismiss our fundamental desires as illegitimate or conclude that psychological dynamics are irrelevant to metaphysical speculations or theological hope. Our appetition, longing, or spiritual pining does not eradicate the fact that it originally comes from somewhere. Whether we call this archetype, instinct, evolution, intuition, mysticism or faith, it may very well sufficiently justify a belief in the transcendental. Whether such belief is an illusion reflective of a complex psychological dynamic is yet another issue. The point is we experience its call. The human spirit knows no negation.

The conclusion that we cannot help but draw is that Jung, like most of us, is chasing after God[10] – that we all want the comfort of a divine provenance where our anxieties are ameliorated and we can finally participate of solace and deep peace free of suffering, where bountiful pleasure, contentment, ultimate meaning, or any descriptor we call bliss is guaranteed to be our granting salvation. And for Jung, God is synonymous with the unconscious.[11] The truth of our *pathos* is that we can never know what lies beyond.[12] But what we do know is that we are all headed for a pine box. Here our Being-toward-death becomes the primal ground (*Bythos*) underlying our spiritual anxieties, perhaps even the impetus fuelling our unitive wish to return to a collective origin, what we might call home.

Notes

1 Because the term 'metaphysics' was such an explosive issue for Jung, and remains so today for his apologists, it becomes important to offer an adumbrated explanation of its philosophical usage. Metaphysics signifies Being, existence and reality, that which *is*. It is often contrasted to empiricism as a scientific endeavour and phenomenology as an experiential factor, when metaphysics subsumes these categories within a unifying perspective that accounts for all facets of human subjectivity including the nature of the psychological or spiritual, as well as religion as a naturalized human inquiry. Therefore, when we speak of metaphysics, we do not need to bifurcate the empirical from the phenomenological, for speculative propositions about psychic reality are simultaneously metaphysical phenomena.

2 In many ways the collective unconscious is anticipated by Hegel's conception of Absolute Spirit as the sum totality or self-articulated complex holism that defines psychic process (see Kelly, 1993; Mills 2002a). Specifically, refer to Hegel's (1807) discussion of 'unconscious universality' within the context of collective spirit in the *Phenomenology* (*PS* §§ 460–462, 474).

3 See my thesis on memorialization versus memory in *Origins: On the Genesis of Psychic Reality* (Mills, 2010, pp. 244–249).

4 Although ontologists from Heidegger to Sartre wish to make phenomenology the ground of Being, here I wish to retain their categorical distinction, for Jung was attempting to highlight lived experience while privileging the greater metaphysical conditions that make experience possible.

5 Particularly see I, part 1, §§ 1–2; part 2, book 1, § 3.

6 Freud's notion of *Trieb* is usually interpreted as a 'borderline concept' between the somatic and the psychical which, it could be argued, Jung substituted with archetype, with the psychoid further being an intervening animating principle that straddles the two spheres and institutes a unifying function. This is particularly relevant to the nature of synchronicity, where the psychoid function gathers the material world into the psychic domain and forms a meaningful unity.

7 As we had seen in Chapter 1, Hegel is concerned not only about explaining individual psychology, but also about providing a universal, anthropological account of humankind.

For Hegel, individuality is ultimately subordinated to higher social orders constituted in society by participating in the ethical life (*Sittlichkeit*) of a collective community. This participation rests on the development of a continuous psychosocial matrix of relations that has its origin in the family. The communal spirit and the ethical law embodied within the family of communal consciousness arises from 'the power of the nether world' (*PS* § 462) – what one might not inappropriately call the collective unconscious. For Hegel, collective spirit 'binds all into one, solely in the mute unconscious substance of all' (*PS* § 474). This 'unconscious universality' contains the ethical order as divine law as well as the 'pathos' of humanity, the 'darkness' of the 'underworld' (*PS* § 474).

8 Personal communication (2010).
9 In his memoirs, Jung (1961) expresses the idealist pole of his thinking this way: 'Human consciousness created objective existence and meaning, and man found his indispensable place in the great process of being' (p. 256).
10 John Freeman, the BBC reporter and deputy editor of the *New Statesman*, recorded an interview with Jung in March 1959 that was first broadcast on the radio later that year and afterwards as a television film. Jung's biographer, Gerhard Wehr (1985), tells us:

> The interview contained the remarkable passage in which the reporter swung from Jung's childhood experiences and religious upbringing in the Jung's family parsonage to the present, posing the direct question whether he believed in God now. 'Now?' Jung replied, and paused for a moment like a subject in one of his association experiments on the hot seat. Then he admitted that it was really quite a difficult question. And to the surprise of his listeners he added very definitely: 'I *know*. I don't need to believe. I know'.
>
> (p. 440)

This sentiment echoes Jung's (1926) earlier view in 'Spirit and Life' where he says that 'God is a psychic fact of immediate experience, otherwise there would never have been any talk of God' (*CW* 8: p. 328).
11 'I prefer the term "the unconscious", knowing that I might equally well speak of "God" or "daimon" if I wished to express myself in mythic language. When I do use such mythic language, I am aware that "mana", "daimon", and "God" are synonyms for the unconscious' (Jung, 1961, pp. 336–337).
12 Contra Kant, who believed that there was always a firm epistemological limit to pure reason or absolute knowing, Hegel believed that mind readily grasps the *Ding an sich* by virtue of the fact that we posit it. In the act of positing, we have already breached the limit. Here he employs an argument similar to Anselm's ontological proof of the existence of God; however, just because we can conceive of an idea does not mean that we can think something into existence.

6

WHITEHEAD'S UNCONSCIOUS COSMOLOGY

Our exploration of the philosophy of the unconscious from diverse theoretic traditions has taken us through many different glimpses of psychical underworlds, each exposing us to various facets of psychic reality. From the general dialectical features of mind, to the dynamic composition of the soul, the existential disclosure of worldhood, linguistic causal structures, and the numinous character of the archetypes as a supernatural faculty, we have traversed the odyssey of human spirit. In all of these theoretical systems, the unconscious is conferred the ontological status of being or presence, which underlies the universal processes that condition human subjectivity. Hegel first celebrated the mind as a burgeoning process of becoming, and this is echoed in various psychoanalytic and existential disciplines in many compatible ways. It may be said that Hegel, Freud and Jung articulate a dialectic that endures conflict and is at odds with itself, but one that is oriented toward higher unitive experiences of progressive growth and psychic wholeness. Hegel emphasizes sublation, Freud sublimation, and Jung transcendence. This is further complemented by the transcendental philosophies of Heidegger and Sartre who place ultimate value in human freedom and agency. It is only with Lacan that we see a purely negative dialectic at play, where the three registers of mental life combat and pressurize one another in an endless impasse, and where the unconscious is both caused by its environs and is the cause of perpetual suffering.

In all the philosophical systems we have examined so far, there is an attempt to lend a synthetic function or unity to the complexities and dynamic systems that constitute mental phenomena, albeit with varying degrees of success. The powers of negation, conflict, anxiety and death are vital processes in every philosophic tradition, ones that permeate the essence of the human condition. Each system privileges a certain hybrid form of determinism, whether it is internally driven and expressive, such as in Hegel's teleology, Freud's developmental ontology and Sartre's transcendental freedom, or externally imposed and/or simply given, such as in Heidegger's world thrownness, Lacan's causal orders, and Jung's transpersonal cosmos. We began this inquiry with metaphysics and we will conclude with metaphysics, although the various theories of the unconscious examined throughout this project are ultimately an ontological enterprise. One common thread that connects them all is the unequivocal avowal of the unconscious as a dynamic process.

This brings us to the metaphysical nature of process illuminated in the cosmology of Alfred North Whitehead.

The field of psychology, let alone psychoanalysis, is largely unaware of the magnitude of Whitehead's contributions to philosophical psychology. But surprisingly, so is the field of philosophy. Unless you are a fervent Whiteheadian immersed in the minutia of process studies, Whitehead's contributions to human psychology largely remain eclipsed by his other bodies of work that have left their mark in the fields of mathematics, logic, the philosophy of science, religion, education, and most notably, metaphysics. Having said this, one of the most under-emphasized aspects of Whitehead's metaphysics is that it embodies an unconscious ontology.[1] The fundamental activity that comprises and underlies the cosmology of actual entities is the eternal process of unconscious experience. The cosmos is alive insofar as it is active,[2] constituted through a dynamic flux of microcosmic orderly events, much of which are non-conscious organizations as 'drops of experience, complex and interdependent' (*PR*, p. 18). Whitehead specifically refers to the realm of unconscious process as the basis for human consciousness, yet the broader treatment of unconscious occasions that underlie his metaphysical system remains only peripherally addressed. What is of greater significance is that his process reality is governed by unconscious forces which form the *a priori* foundation for all modes of human experience to manifest. Despite the fact that Whitehead did not articulate a formal theory of unconscious ontology, it is embedded in the most basic fabric of his philosophy.

Whitehead's system rests on an unconscious ontology of actual entities exemplified through the activity of *prehension*, thus constituting the experiential process of becoming. Not only does unconscious activity undergird the most basal operations of actual occasions, but unconscious processes are responsible for higher modes of self-conscious life. Therefore Whitehead's entire cosmology rests on an appeal to unconscious activity, what today's physicists would attribute to the hidden universe of quantum mechanics. This has significant implications for appreciating Whitehead's general metaphysical scheme as well as specifically contributing to our understanding of his philosophical psychology, a topic that brings him into dialogue with Freud. In what follows, I will explicitly examine Whitehead's rather terse treatment of psychological physiology in relation to the question of embodiment, and thus show how he answers to the mind/body problem. We will further see how he complements psychoanalytic thought. Through our understanding of the role of unconscious processes in Whitehead's system, we may hope to gain greater appreciation of the dynamic ontological configurations that constitute human psychology.

Nature as mind

Although it was Hegel who first argued systematically that reality is a process of becoming, it is Whitehead who is most commonly referred to as the founder of process philosophy. For those readers not familiar with the nuances of Whitehead's system, a brief account is in order. Having a long accomplished career as a mathematician, logician, philosopher of science, and metaphysician, Whitehead is probably best known for his speculative metaphysics.[3] Discontented with materialism and the physical paradigms of his day, he reconceptualized the notion of experience and thereby attempted to integrate various disciplines as diverse as the natural sciences, logic, theology and anthropology within a revisionist framework of evolutionary cosmology. Whitehead argued that the fundamental activity that comprises and underlies the cosmos is the eternal process of experience organized through an ongoing and interactive trajectory of dynamic patterns instantiated in all aspects of the universe. In other words, everything that exists is comprised of active units of experiential complexity, from the robust psychological processes of human cognition, to the elementary particles inherent in a stone. Whitehead's system emphasizes the creative and novel advance of nature as a continuously transforming and progressive series of events that are purposeful, directional and unifying. Like Heraclitus and Hegel before him, Whitehead stresses the dialectical exchange of oppositions that advance the process of becoming.

Whitehead's invented technical language is tedious and at times inaccessible to the non-specialist, therefore it will become important to understand some basic concepts before addressing the more intricate aspects of his psychology. For Whitehead, the cosmos is composed of what he refers to as 'actual entities' or 'actual occasions', which are 'the final real things of which the world is made up' (*PR*, p. 18). Actual entities constitute the flux of energy continuous throughout nature and are the fundamental building blocks of the universe: they are ontologically undifferentiated in essence, distinguished only in form or by the mode in which they appear. This is why Whitehead (1933) says there is only one genus of actual entities. In essence, 'each actual occasion is in truth a process of activity' (*AI*, p. 254).

In *The Concept of Nature* (1920), Whitehead was concerned with addressing the place of mind in nature. This led to their initial reconciliation in *Science and the Modern World* (1925), which was resolved in his Gifford Lectures (1927–1928), the subject matter of *Process and Reality* (1929). Whitehead's solution to the question of mind and nature is a philosophy of organism, what he calls the doctrine of 'prehensions'. Although lacking articulation and development, the primacy of unconscious process is already prepared in his most elementary treatment of prehension. For Whitehead, prehending is pure activity: it may be understood as a process of seizing, absorbing, and synthesizing the elements of the surround into an internal unity or organized emotional pattern. Prehending is equivalent to feeling: it is a purposeful, valuative, self-determined act. In Whitehead's (1927) words, 'To be an actual entity is to have self-interest. This self-interest is a feeling of self-valuation; it is an emotional tone' (*RM*, p. 97). Thus feeling becomes the expression of an actual entity's subjectivity. 'Concrescence', a similarly related concept, is a higher-order event or process of unification that underlies the internal constitution of an actual entity, a subject that feels and unifies its relation to experience through the act of prehending.

An actual entity is tantamount to an occasion because it is an instance – an 'event', 'stream', or 'throb' of experience arising out of data (*PR*, pp. 40, 190), subsequently appropriating elements from its environment and making it part of its internal structure. In fact, Whitehead views the world as composed of endless 'societies' of actual entities that are constantly in flux and interpenetrate one another at any given time, thereby leading to vast transmogrifications and evolutionary developments. The infinite societies of occasions that comprise the universe embody every mode of electrodynamic energy explained through quantum mechanics to the highest instantiations of human consciousness. Through the philosophy of organism, Whitehead is able to show that nature is not inert or static substance, but rather a dynamic array of transactions constituted as actual agencies that respond to and express themselves in the flow of interrelational activity that constitutes all reality.

Whitehead cognizes nature: namely, he lends cognition to microcosmic events and hence attributes mentation to all actual occasions. 'Mental activity is one of the modes of feeling belonging to all actual entities' (*PR*, p. 56). In this sense, nature is mental or psychic process that is differentiated only in its level of manifest complexity, creativity and qualitative novelty. Elsewhere he states, 'I am using the term "mind" to mean the complex of mental operations involved in the constitution of an actual entity' (*PR*, p. 85). From Whitehead's account, nature *is* mind; what Catherine Keller (1989) refers to as a '*psychocosmic*' process (p. 134). Thus the human mind and consciousness are higher modified complexifications that have derived and evolved from the more primitive mental activity that constitutes the natural world.

I shall forego the temptation to dismiss Whitehead's system outright, as some of his critics do, by claiming he is an animist or panpsychist. Although his cosmology describes the animate nature of the universe, he would deny assertions that he attributes a soul or supernatural spiritual force to natural order. Although he grants actual entities mental features, he would resist being associated with panpsychism, which is the belief that all matter is sentient and conscious, or pantheism, where God is said to permeate everything. In his metaphysical system, Whitehead makes God an abstract unifying principle – the non-temporal concrescence of all eternal objects, but here God is more of a logical (impersonal) category rather than a personal supreme being. It is certainly true that Whitehead's philosophy could be seen as a form of panexperientialism, in that all of reality is constituted as experience, and perhaps even hylopathism, where all matter is viewed as being sentient (insofar as it experiences) and gives rise to higher-order subjective experiences, although he would negate any transpersonal attributions of spiritual animation or supernatural transcendence. He defends his animistic language as a deposit of our linguistic anthropomorphism as modes of human communication, which is an imperfect attempt to describe the basic processes of the cosmos through naturalized psychology. Because we have no other way of communicating or expressing ourselves other than through human language, it is natural to describe natural events in terms that are reflective of mental processes, for all human experience is mediated by mind.

With the exception of animate life possessing the capacities of consciousness, the pulsation of events that lends order to the process of prehension is an unconscious operation. Yet even with entities that possess consciousness, unconscious processes maintain ontological primacy. Whitehead specifically says that 'consciousness is not the order of metaphysical priority' (*PR*, p. 162). Unconscious events constitute the formal structure of actual entities even when they possess consciousness. In other words, conscious acts involve unconscious prehensions. As Whitehead tells us, 'consciousness presupposes experience, and not experience consciousness. . . . Thus an actual entity may, or may not, be conscious of some part of its experience' (*PR*, p. 53). Prehensive activity is first and foremost organized unconscious experience. Therefore, the fundamental processes that comprise the nature of reality have an unconscious ontology.

Whitehead uses the word 'unconscious' in a few limited contexts, in which it carries different meanings. While not formally distinguished by him, we can say that there are five distinct usages of unconsciousness: (1) That which lacks consciousness, or is aconscious, such as most of the natural universe; (2) A state or condition of non- or *un*self-consciousness; (3) A realm other-than or dialectically opposed to consciousness; (4) That which is beyond or outside an occasion in its current constitution or moment, which we may either attribute to (a) the realm of pure potentiality not yet actualized by an entity, that is, a non-prehended eternal object (which could apply to the second definition), or (b) that which is negativity itself and thus a central feature in the creative development of an occasion; and (5) A prerational, emotive unconscious ground that serves as the foundation for higher forms of consciousness to materialize. For Whitehead, consciousness emerges from and is the logical completion of an unconscious ontology.

The ontological principle

The doctrine of prehensions rests on what Whitehead calls 'the ontological principle'. For Whitehead, this is the definition of actuality (*PR*, p. 80). By this he means that 'actual entities are the only *reasons*; so that to search for a *reason* is to search for one or more actual entities' (*PR*, p. 24). He further says that 'the reasons for things are always to be found in the composite nature of definite actual entities: . . . no actual entity, then no reason' (*PR*, p. 19). There is a rational nature to the universe and it is located in brute fact. Whitehead is a realist: the universe is a presupposed given actuality comprised of objective data.[4] For Whitehead, the reason for an actual entity is simply expressed in the nature of its being: whatever exists is actual and 'in potency everywhere' (*PR*, p. 40). There is nothing behind the veil of appearance: whatever appears must be actual.[5]

Utilizing the ontological principle, Whitehead is attempting to address the question of original ground. The reason or ground of an actual entity is construed by its determinate character as an actively constituted agency. It is from this primordial ground composing the basic constituent activity of all actual entities that other forms of complexity and novelty emerge and derive. Whitehead is clear: 'actual occasions form the ground from which all other types of existence are derivative and abstracted' (*PR*, p. 75). Because actual occasions are largely unconscious organized feeling states expressed as unifying acts, the ontological principle points toward an unconscious ontology or experiential ground that makes higher forms of prehension and concrescence possible. The ontology of an entity is pure unrest that takes subjective form and instantiates itself as objective fact. It is from this original ground of unconscious subjectivity that the nuances of prehension are realized.

If activity and experience underlie all actual events, then the essence of an actual entity may be said to be its transformative 'power' (*PR*, p. 19), a process of becoming. The ontological principle assumes the objective actuality or bare fact of the universe as a 'solidarity of many actual entities', each arising out of data as complex orders of experience (*PR*, p. 40). Whitehead explains that prehending or feeling is the elementary operation of emerging from objective data into subjective form. Thus an actual occasion comes into being as feeling subjectivity out of the field of actual objects. 'Feelings are variously specialized operations, effecting a transition into subjectivity' (*PR*, pp. 40–41). On the most generic level, this is a process of unconscious mentation: an entity is alive by virtue of the fact that it feels and is felt by other actual entities. Moreover, the universe may be said to be a composite of collective unconscious entities insofar as it is a system composed of the plurality of actual feeling entities as a unified totality whereby each entity enters into the internal constitution of all others (*PR*, p. 41). Thus Whitehead is able to blur the distinction between universals and particulars by dissolving their bifurcation and making them interpenetrating instances of a unified system – a composite unity.

Unconscious teleology

Not only does Whitehead assign mind to nature but he rescues it from the bane of reductive materialism: nature is not unintentional mechanism, but rather teleological self-expression. The prehensive activity constitutive of a concrescing occasion is a telic, purposeful, self-creative process. *Telos* (τέλος) underlies cosmic order and is largely the product of unconscious intension. Telos is not aberration, nor is it a preformed design: the universe flourishes as a self-determined, self-disclosed act. Each actual entity is an epigenetic achievement; it comes into being as feeling subjectivity from objective data and evolves into a dynamic self-articulated complex unity within the universe itself as a complex whole. Prehension is a basic unconscious teleological operation: 'it involves emotion, and purpose, and valuation, and causation' (*PR*, p. 19). For Whitehead, the life of each actual entity is a self-chosen path which 'functions in respect to its own determination' (*PR*, p. 25).

Unconscious teleology is intimately linked with the ontological principle, which Whitehead equates with efficient and final causality (*PR*, pp. 24, 47). In fact, efficient causal forces are in the service of final teleological aims. Yet the final cause of an actual entity is not a fixed, predetermined course of action; it is an internal process by which the entity becomes itself, while efficient causation effects the transition of one actual entity to another. The final end, purpose, or goal of an actual occasion is to seek 'satisfaction' in a novel fashion of self-creation, which is the impetus behind its force or drive as intentional self-determination. The aim of each individual act becomes fully actual when it evokes a response in other acts. As the final phase of concrescence, satisfaction leads to a process of 'perishing' whereby the subjective occasion becomes a transposed objective entity. Whitehead says that in the final phase of concrescence, an actual entity 'is *fully determinate* (a) as to its genesis, (b) as to its objective character for the trans-cendent creativity, and (c) as to its prehension – positive or negative – of every item in the universe' (*PR*, p. 26, italics added). The prehensive act is *affirmative* in that it feels and seizes upon particular elements in its milieu and negates other elements that are not essential to its satisfaction.

A conscrescing occasion is selective in what it chooses, absorbing and retaining certain data in its internal constitution while rejecting other elements in its milieu that become 'valued down'. Each decisive prehensive act enjoys a degree of voli-tional choice. As such, an actual entity is free to define its internal structure and its specific advance into novelty. Whitehead reinforces the point that entities are self-determined experiences: 'Actual occasions in their "formal" constitutions are devoid of all indetermination' (*PR*, p. 29). The more elaborate and inventive the hier-archies of societies become, the more freedom they acquire in their internal organ-ization, nexūs, self-expression and choice.

An actual entity is a teleological agent by virtue of the fact that it *decides* a course of action to take that brings about an intended event; although the effects of what may be intended are subject to external contingencies. Whitehead is un-equivocally specific when he says that an actual entity 'asserts the relativity of decision' (*PR*, p. 43). Moreover, the act of deciding 'constitutes the very meaning of actuality'. Once again, this process is expressed through the ontological prin-ciple: the very essence of an actual occasion is its drive to choose. Furthermore, it may choose what it sees fit to choose within the parameters of its subjective form and objective environment, despite that its choice may be 'blind'.[6] In effect, it chooses the ground for the sake of which to behave. As Whitehead informs us, it does so out of 'self-interest' and 'self-valuation' (*RM*, p. 97). From this stand-point, an actual entity is *desirous* – it wants, it seeks, it finds.

It is somewhat surprising that Whitehead himself did not depict an actual occa-sion as a desirous entity despite the fact that he canonized feeling as its principle mode of expression. This may be in part due to Whitehead's need to defend meta-physical realism despite the cryptic idealism that saturates his system. As I have argued at length elsewhere (Mills, 2002b), an entity is desirous in that it feels – it longs, it craves satisfaction. Self-interest and self-value presuppose desire as does the very *need* for satisfaction itself. If an entity did not desire, it would not seek – it would not experience, hence it would exhibit no activity at all; it simply would not be. The experience of an actual entity is pure activity that desires insofar as the expression of such activity – its emotions, decisions, valuation and appreciations – is desire. Since desire cannot emerge *ex nihilo* – out of a lack of desire, desire is an ontologically preconditioned craving. An occasion is satisfied when it perishes into objectivity: it becomes data which gives rise to new subjective forms. Before it becomes an object – an eternal return – it lacks the unity and self-expression it so craves. Therefore, before the unifying threads of concrescence transmute the feeling subject into a new entity, an actual occasion is being in relation to *lack*.

Whitehead uses this language gingerly, careful not to over-animize nature – presumably because he wishes to avoid further criticism that he anthropomorphizes nature; yet he nevertheless supports my claim that the basic ontological foundation of a prehending entity is unconscious desire. It is not enough to say that the universe is composed of active events that experience without speculating as to why. Whitehead gives us a clue; it is to be found in the nature of 'appetition'. For Whitehead, appetition involves 'unrest' – the 'realization of what is not and may be' (*PR*, p. 32). This unrest is an entity's being in relation to what it is *not* – what it lacks – and hence what it wants to become. Whitehead also refers to this desire as a 'subjective passion' and 'urge', what he further calls an 'impulse' or drive. He states that 'the urge towards the future [is] based upon an appetite in the present': the immediate goal is to 'procure' (*PR*, p. 32). Whitehead argues that all physical experience is governed by the 'appetite for, or against, its continuance': an example of this is the desire for 'self-preservation'.

Whitehead's attributions of 'appetite', 'urge' and 'passion' as motives of an occasion's internal constitution clearly show the Platonic pole of his thought. By evoking the Greek notion of appetition or desire (*eros*), he is able to stress the complex holism that an entity strives to achieve, first emanating from within the unconscious subjective contours of its prehending nature and then laboriously progressing to higher shapes of developmental achievement. In fact, Whitehead himself specifically uses this language when discussing an actual entity's yearning for God as 'the eternal urge of *desire*' (*PR*, p. 344, italics added). He himself acknowledges the danger associated with the use of the technical term 'appetition', which he even extends to Freud's psychology; yet he consistently refers to the enjoyments and novelty of desire belonging to the teleological motives and feeling intensities of actual entities. In fact, Whitehead says, 'the primary meaning of "life" is the origination of conceptual novelty – novelty of appetition' (*PR*, p. 102).[7] The qualia of appetite affecting choice may take a special form, what Whitehead calls a 'propositional prehension' (*PR*, p. 184). Feeling propositions are 'theories' that provide immediate enjoyment and purpose to a conscrescing occasion: they direct the telos of decision and guide object choice. Prehensive propositions are not to be construed as conscious judgments, which belong to intelligent self-conscious life: they are largely physical purposes belonging to the internal constitution of an entity, such as heat is to fire. On this level, propositional feeling entities don't think; they are 'unconscious elements in the aesthetic supplement of an actual occasion' (Kraus, 1998, p. 95). Hence, propositional feelings are largely unconscious purposes that serve as the sediment for higher forms of societies to emerge. This is exemplified in the phenomena of conscious and self-conscious life. As Whitehead avouches, unconscious propositions provide the *a priori* conditions for consciousness to arise.

Consciousness and the unconscious

Up until now, we have been largely concerned with delineating the ground and telic functions of non-conscious subjective experience that constitute the inner structure and activity of an actual occasion. It is important to show, however, how these unconscious processes become fertile soil for more sophisticated forms of complexity to transpire. Whitehead attributes higher phases of experience to human consciousness exemplified as perception, thought and rational judgment. Yet he is clear to show that the achievement of consciousness is rooted in an unconscious ontology:

> Consciousness flickers; and even at its brightest, there is a small focal region of clear illumination, and a large penumbral region of experience which tells of intense experience in dim apprehension. The simplicity of clear consciousness is no measure of the complexity of complete experience. Also this character of our existence suggests that consciousness is the crown of experience, only occasionally attained, not its necessary base.
> *(PR*, p. 267)

Whitehead is saying that unconscious experience is the ground of consciousness; therefore, the unconscious is a necessary presupposition. Recall that for Whitehead, consciousness presupposes experience (*PR*, p. 53); thus consciousness is the differentiated evolutionary outgrowth of unconscious structure that is realized through intricate matrices and unified strands of complex social integration. As Whitehead puts it, consciousness is a developmental achievement that 'illuminates the more primitive types of prehension' (*PR*, p. 162). This is why he says consciousness is not the order of metaphysical priority: 'the philosophy of organism . . . relegates consciousness to a subordinate metaphysical position' (*PR*, p. 139).

Unconscious processes not only developmentally precede conscious organizations, but they command ontological primacy. Whitehead attempts to show that every aspect of the universe participates in the same underlying essence differentiated only by form. Actual occasions are architectonic: they build on their most primitive enactments and gain richer complexity and dynamic integrity as they advance toward higher tiers of creative self-expression and synthetic integration. Consciousness is only a late derivative phase of unconscious subjectivity: 'Those elements of our experience which stand out clearly and distinctly in our consciousness are not its basic facts; they are the derivative modifications which arise in the process' (*PR*, p. 162). These derivative modifications are the structures, operations, properties and attributes assigned to conscious perception, attention, thought, understanding, and so on that only a few entities are able to enjoy among the vast sea of occasions that remain within the turbid recesses of unconscious void. But as Whitehead continues to explain, unconscious elements 'remain components in the higher phase'; they are absorbed, preserved and incorporated as the lower relation passes over into the higher relation. Occasions have the capacity to surpass their previous shapes while retaining the nuances of their previous morphology. This is not unlike Hegel's notion of *Aufhebung*, with one noted addition: an actual entity has the capacity to *choose* what elements it wishes to retain and which it wishes to reject. In effect, consciousness is the coming into being of unconscious choice, yet the unique configurations inherent in each conscious entity vary with respect to content and qualitative self-determination.

Whitehead mainly uses the word 'unconscious' to signify unawareness or non-conscious process, but he alludes to a realm or agency that we may properly call 'the unconscious'. Whitehead patently states that feeling propositions take place at the physical level of 'unconsciousness'. It is within the pit or abyss of this original subjective ground where we can locate the 'source for the origination of feeling' (*PR*, p. 186). Not only is the source unconscious, the source is an organized unconscious agency – an aggregate of complex societies – affecting transitions into conscious awareness. The complex hierarchy of societies constituting conscious life is the product of a systemic unconscious infrastructure that is formed out of previous 'structured' and/or 'subordinate' societies (*PR*, p. 99). As hierarchies gain in complexity, supported by structured subordinate societies that lend order to the interdependent environment, more sophisticated societies may emerge, what Whitehead calls 'regnant' societies (*PR*, p. 103).

Regnant societies are sophisticated organizations that may belong to unconscious, conscious and self-conscious organisms. The confluence of many sophisticated societies gives rise to even higher regnant societies, each effecting their own autonomy within the interpenetrating ocean of actual entities. Within the unconscious human mind, for example, regnant societies may be delicate and transitory or well formed, enduring fantasy systems that seek fulfilment via displacement into conscious reality. While they are themselves sophisticated modes of orderly activity seeking creative self-utterance, they are also subordinate to higher constellations of mental activity; yet they still make their presence felt as they too are feeling entities. Whitehead even tacitly refers to the realm of fantasy and our tendency to project unconscious wishes:

> Anyone who at bedtime consciously reviews the events of the day is subconsciously projecting them against the penumbral welter of alternatives. He is also unconsciously deciding feelings so as to maximize his primary feeling, and to secure its propagation beyond his immediate present occasion.
>
> (*PR*, p. 187)

An occasion is concerned with maximizing its primary pleasure feeling – its enjoyment – as well as sustaining its continuance by procuring a future state of satisfaction. This is not at all incongruous with psychoanalytic doctrine: the ego must secure boundaries for the fulfilment of unconscious wishes governed by the pleasure principle.[8] But Whitehead most vividly acknowledges the reality of unconscious agency when he remarks on conscious recognition: 'Whenever there is consciousness there is some element of recognition. It recalls earlier phases from the dim recesses of the unconscious' (*PR*, p. 242). Note the use of the demonstrative word '*the*'. Here, Whitehead is reminded of Plato's theory of reminiscence, but his insight could as easily be applied to Freud's doctrine of repression – 'the prototype of the unconscious' (*SE* 19:15). There can be no doubt that Whitehead purports an ontology of unconscious agency that he attributes to both the characteristic activity of an actual entity as well as a concealed province within the domain of the human mind.

For Whitehead, 'consciousness is how we feel the affirmation-negation contrast' (*PR*, p. 243), or in other words, the dialectic of being and nothingness within the realm of perceptual judgment. But the dialectic of affirmation and denial also transpires on the unconscious level: preliminary grades of affirmation and negation (e.g. what Whitehead calls positive prehension, valuing-up, and adversion vs. negative prehension, valuing-down, and aversion) occur on the most elemental level of decision making for an actual entity. By situating a preliminary, archetypal affirmation–negation dialectic in the most basic movements constituting the internal process of an unconscious occasion, Whitehead is able to extend this ontological model to the development of consciousness. Thus the unconscious is the template for consciousness. Consciousness is a more elaborate and sophisticated dialectic – 'the crown of experience', but as Whitehead concludes, unconscious experience is its 'necessary base' (*PR*, p. 267). The epigenesis of consciousness out of unconscious structure will become more lucid once we turn our attention to how Whitehead describes the developmental process of perception.

Whitehead's theory of consciousness is illuminated in his treatment of three modes of perception: (1) the mode of causal efficacy, (2) the mode of presentational immediacy, and (3) the mixed mode of symbolic reference.[9] Perception in the mode of causal efficacy is a very 'crude', pervasive feature of reality that comprises the earliest phase of concrescence known as conformal feeling. Prehensions are one-way internal relations; thus prehensive relations must take account of something. In this crude form of perception, prehensions take account of data that are inherited from their past. The past pours itself into the present, which is felt as the efficaciousness of past feelings; yet the feelings it transmits are ill-defined, massive and inarticulate. Whitehead (1929) states:

> [When] we descend the scale, it seems that we find . . . a dim unconscious drowse, of undiscriminated feeling. . . . Experience loses its illustration of forms, and its illumination by consciousness, and its discrimination of purpose. It seems finally to end in a massive unconscious urge derived from undiscriminated feeling, this feeling being itself a derivation from the immediate past.
>
> (*FR*, pp. 63–64)

Perception in the mode of presentational immediacy, on the other hand, is the clear and distinct apprehension of the extensive relations of the manifold of objects presented in the contemporary world. They lack the power and massiveness of causal efficacy but provide sharp qualities and definition to objects perceived in space and time. It is not until the final stage of perception in the mode of symbolic reference that the previous two modes are combined to lend clarity, structure and meaning to objects typical of our perceptive awareness.

What is important to emphasize here is how the unconscious past informs the present conscious modes of presentational immediacy and symbolic reference. As Whitehead states: 'There is nothing there apart from the real agency of the actual past, exercising its function of objective immortality' (*AI*, p. 243). Because perception and conceptual meaning evolve out of earlier movements and become supplemental phases of experience, the past imports its causal inheritance into an occasion's present relation. We may view this as a form of unconscious projection of a repressed piece of psychic constitution from the life-history of an actual occasion that another entity identifies with, selects as a feeling value, and incorporates into its being. An occasion directly inherits from those occasions in its immediate past, as do they *ad infinitum*. As the past is projected into the present moment, the entity's subjective emotional pattern transmutes in response to the appropriated data. Each occasion puts its stamp of subjectivity on whatever it appropriates from its past, which may be as trivial as a simple reiteration or as complex as the most sophisticated self-created novelty. This is the aspect of perception that becomes transposed in the objectification of data in that contemporary region for that particular percipient occasion. This is why an occasion is internally related to its past and externally related to its future.

One way this operates in the unconscious mind is that whenever an occasion encounters a new contemporary relation, it must look to its past modes, which inform its present state. In sense perception, this would entail being confronted with the immediacy of sense certainty directing consciousness to fix attention on the manifold, and thus retrieve images and impressions from the depths of the unconscious that are recollected, brought forth as representations and attached to the sensory objects being experienced. This mediated dynamic gains fuller force in the mode of symbolic reference when objects are imbued with signification and conceptual meaning.[10] Perceptual experiences in presentational immediacy are prereflective acts of consciousness: the subject is not self-consciously aware of the perceptive process in that moment. Because images and associations are brought up from the bowels of the mind, thus feeling the presence of the causal efficacy of the past, it would follow that an unconscious agent must be performing these synthesizing operations that effect the transition to symbolic reference and finally self-conscious awareness. This is why Whitehead says that unconscious 'prehensions are still elements in the products of [conscious] integration . . . consciousness only dimly illuminates the prehensions in the mode of causal efficacy, because these prehensions are primitive elements in our experience' (*PR*, p. 162).

Whitehead's (1927) expatiation of perception is first advanced in *Symbolism*, where the two primary modes of experience are called perceptive and the final symbolic phase called the mode of conceptual analysis (*S*, pp. 17–19). The primitiveness of causal efficacy has greater implications for understanding the most primordial regions of the unconscious mind, namely, that of instinct (*Trieb*). Whitehead tells us that during this primitive phase of experience, the subject conforms to the realities of its environment and the demands of its 'bodily organs imposing their characters on the experience in question' (*S*, p. 50). While perception in presentational immediacy is definite, crisp and ready at hand, the previous type of experience is 'vague, haunting, unmanageable' (*S*, p. 43). Whitehead clarifies the ubiquity of unconscious causal efficacy:

> Those periods in our lives – when the perception of the pressure from a world of things with characters in their own right, characters mysteriously moulding our own natures, become strongest – those periods are the product of a reversion to some primitive state. . . . Anger, hatred, fear, terror, attraction, love, hunger, eagerness, massive enjoyment, are feelings and emotions closely entwined with the primitive functioning of 'retreat from' and of 'expansion towards'. They arise in the higher organism as states due to a vivid apprehension that some such primitive mode of functioning is dominating the organism.
>
> (*S*, pp. 44–45)

We are justified to interpret this passage as a direct allusion to the most primitive and intensified features of our unconscious instinctual life that we may regress to during times of 'pressure', fuelled by the libidinal and aggressive inclinations 'moulding our own natures', those 'dominating the organism'. The tempestuous nature of our primitive processes that inform consciousness leads Whitehead to conclude: 'The present fact is luminously the outcome from its predecessors . . . Unsuspected factors may have intervened; dynamite may have exploded' (*S*, p. 46).

There can be no doubt that the unconscious inheritance of our previous primitive experiences may lead to disarray and chaos. As Whitehead puts it, 'the deep significance disclosed by Causal Efficacy is at the root of the pathos which haunts the world' (*S*, p. 47). In other words, unconscious conflict is the germ of mental disease and collective psychopathology. Elsewhere, Whitehead tells us that the creative element of process can be deflected by an 'impulse' which, if not properly managed by the self-preservative reactions of a society, can lead the society into the 'province of pathology' (*PR*, p. 102). The priority of unconscious energies operative within causal efficacy is given further voice when juxtaposed to Whitehead's notion of the soul. It becomes important for us to now turn our attention to the broader dimensions of psychic experience that Whitehead attributes to the human animal.

Psychological physiology

As one of the great Cambridge Platonists, Whitehead was interested in the human soul. In *Adventures of Ideas*, he nicely summarizes the cardinal features of the psyche:

> The primary factors in experience are first the animal passions such as love, sympathy, ferocity, together with analogous appetitions and satisfactions; and secondly, the more distinctly human experiences of beauty, and of intellectual fineness, consciously enjoyed.
>
> (*AI*, p. 19)

Whitehead further tells us that 'the moral element is derivative from the other factors in experience'. Compare this to Plato. From the *Republic*, Plato informs us that the soul is the locus of our inner world 'whereby it reckons and reasons the rational, and that with which it loves, hungers, thirsts, and feels the flutter and titillation of other desires, the irrational and appetitive – companion of various repletions and pleasures' (*Republic*, 4:439d; also see *Laws*, ib. 9:863b sq.; ib. 5:727c). Plato also ascribes to the soul the cause of our moral qualities (*Laws*, 10:896d), ends and virtues (*Republic*, ib. I:353d sq.), and the influence over our character and habit (*Laws*, 10:904c sq.), as well as mental sickness (*Gorgias*, 479b). It is rather remarkable that over 2,000 years later, Whitehead's, as well as Freud's, vision of the psyche mirrors the Platonic view. Perhaps the best allusion to Plato's conception of the soul by Freud is his analogy of the ego (*Ich*) and the id (*Es*) as a rider on horseback (*SE* 19:25), whereas Plato refers to the soul as a charioteer with a pair of steeds (*Phaedrus*, 246 sq.). It seems rather prophetic that our understanding of human psychology would become, in Freud's own words, 'the science of the life of the soul' (*SE* 22:6).[11]

A proper appreciation of Whitehead's psychology of the soul entails an understanding of what he termed 'psychological physiology'. This concept may be extended to his philosophy of organism as a whole – the psycho-physical doctrine of prehensions,[12] but Whitehead uses it in a particular context. Whitehead's discussion of psychological physiology hinges on the question and meaning of *embodiment*. His psychological physiology may be said to be an abbreviated solution to the mind/body problem, a doctrine 'still in the process of incubation' (*PR*, p. 103), much of which remains cryptic and undeveloped. Elsewhere Whitehead suggests that his conception of psychological physiology 'answers to the Platonic notion of the soul'.

> 'Psychological Physiology' seeks to deal with 'entirely living' nexūs, partly in abstraction from the inorganic apparatus, and partly in respect to their response to the inorganic apparatus, and partly in regard to their response to each other.
>
> (*PR*, p. 103)

Nexūs are typically thought of as macrocosmic entities composed of subordinate occasions held together formally, usually referred to as societies that enjoy social order (*PR*, p. 34). Structured societies are complex patterned societies with structural interrelations that include subordinate societies and/or nexūs (*PR*, pp. 99–102). According to Whitehead, an 'entirely living' nexus addresses 'the theory of the animal body' (*PR*, p. 103), which involves nexūs that are inorganic. When Whitehead refers to the inorganic apparatus, he is referring to an animal body such as a single living cell or a composite of such. An 'entirely living' nexus is subordinate; it requires protection from the whole society in order to survive. As such, it is not composed of enduring objects that are personally ordered in which its past efficaciously informs its existence. While entirely living nexūs are affected by their immediate complex environment – hence, from animal bodies, they do not inherit from their immediate past generations in temporal succession. Thus an entirely living nexus is *non-social* and purely spatial, what Whitehead says 'answers to the notion of "chaos"' (*PR*, p. 72).

Whitehead's psychological physiology attempts to explain the relationship between non-social nexūs and their animal bodies both in isolated abstraction and in their interaction. Because an entirely living nexus cannot independently support itself apart from the environment constituted by the structured society that sustains it (*PR*, p. 99), it is dependent on the material bodies in its immediate surround. The non-social nexus can enjoy intense physical experience derived from the complex order of its material body 'without the shackle of reiteration from the past' (*PR*, p. 105). Thus a non-social nexus enjoys a degree of freedom that a personally ordered nexus does not: it is the locus of 'spontaneity'. And for Whitehead, 'spontaneity is of the essence of soul' (*AI*, p. 66). But how does this answer to the notion of the soul? For Whitehead, this depends on the significance, meaning, and nature of 'life'.

In *Symbolism*, Whitehead states: 'The emergence of life is better conceived as a bid for freedom on the part of organisms, a bid for a certain independence of individuality with self-interests and activities not to be construed purely in terms of environmental obligations' (*S*, p. 65). Recall that a non-social nexus depends on its material body for survival, but it is free from the temporal inheritance of past generations; thus 'life' must not be confined or 'shackled' to its mere determined corporeality. While a non-social nexus relies on its greater regnant society, it also has influence over how that society is to be mentally realized in a novel fashion. As Whitehead says, an organism seeks autonomy and 'individuality' apart from its material embodiment. Here we have a partial solution to the question of soul: 'The essence of life is the teleological introduction of novelty' (*AI*, p. 241).

For Whitehead, the fundamental question of the soul is not whether it can exist as an independent agent apart from its material counterpart, but whether or not it can freely introduce novelty into the holistic process that constitutes the human being.

> Life is a bid for freedom: an enduring entity binds any one of its occasions to the line of its ancestry. The doctrine of the enduring soul with its permanent characteristics is exactly the irrelevant answer to the problem which life presents. That problem is, How can there be originality? And the answer explains how the soul need be no more original than a stone.
>
> (*PR*, p. 104)

Remember, for Whitehead, '"life" means novelty' (*PR*, p. 104); it need not be necessarily bound to its physical ancestry. As Donald Sherburne (1969, p. 403) cogently points out, this argument has force against a substance view of the soul; but it also militates against a view of the soul as an enduring, personally ordered regnant society. This is further complicated by the fact that elsewhere Whitehead equates the soul with an enduring, personally ordered society:

> Each animal body is an organ of sensation. It is a living society which may include in itself a dominant 'personal' society of occasions. This 'personal' society is composed of occasions enjoying the individual experiences of the animals. It is the soul of man.
>
> (*AI*, p. 245)

Originality needs a body; as Whitehead says, 'it is the organ of novelty'. As such, life is the introduction of novelty that depends on a body; yet it also permeates non-social nexūs, which stand free from the serially ordered, personally antecedent past that constitutes the burgeoning process of a structured society. This is not to say that a non-social nexus is not embodied; yet it is free from the chains that bind prehensive novelty to its serially ordered ancestry. Then what about the nature of the soul's embodiment? Whitehead speculates that a non-social nexus wanders through empty space in the brain connected by some 'thread of happenings' which it inherits from its biological environment (*PR*, p. 339). So a second partial solution to the riddle of soul emerges. Not only is novelty wed to life, but the life of a non-social nexus sustains the material bodies in a structured society. It appears that in that space that constitutes the non-social nexus lies the necessary interrelation between mind and body. Thus, non-social nexūs mediate between body and soul.

The central issue is not whether there is an ontological difference between mind and body, but rather the degree of the *qualitative* power of freedom that each enjoy as part of a unified system. For Whitehead, 'the difference between a living organism and the inorganic environment is only a question of degree; but it is a difference of degree which makes all the difference – in effect, it is a difference of quality' (*PR*, p. 179). Therefore, Whitehead's introduction of a non-social nexus that enjoys the freedom of novelty allows for both causal and qualitative differences to permeate the interaction between entirely living nexūs and their inorganic components. While the production of novelty constitutes the prehending activity of all actual entities on some crude level, the qualitative degree of freedom makes all the difference between the soul and a stone.

Recall that Whitehead is concerned with *how* there can be originality. While a non-social nexus derives experience from the complex order of its material body, such as the sensory organs penetrating the 'interstices of the brain', thus producing feeling intensities, it nevertheless has the telic freedom to produce its own brand of novelty independent from the succession of its own prior generations. This is the condition for spontaneity – how originality occurs. But what of the enduring personally ordered society Whitehead equates with the human soul? Because a non-social nexus derives from its complex environment – its regnant society, but is sheltered from the constrictions of the past, it has the liberty to generate its own creative novelty in its own purely determinate moment. This process allows the entirely living nexus to have a relational effect on the personal enduring society of occasions that pour into and through the subordinate non-social nexus. In effect, the non-social nexus is the medium that allows the personally ordered society to endure, flourish and evolve into a more complex social structure. This is why Whitehead says that an 'entirely living' nexus 'may support a thread of personal order along some historical route of its members. Such an enduring entity is a "living person". It is not of the essence of life to be a living person. Indeed a living person requires that its immediate environment be a living, non-social nexus' (*PR*, p. 107).

Non-social nexūs are those purely spatial entities that support the existence of the enduring personally ordered human soul. Thus the question of the soul's embodiment is explained through the 'entirely living' nexus's relation to its material corporeality and the spontaneity of life it generates within its immediate environment. This is why Whitehead is justified in saying:

In a man, the living body is permeated by living societies of low-grade occasions so far as mentality is concerned. But the whole is co-ordinated so far as to support a personal living society of high grade occasions. This personal society is the man defined as a person. It is the soul of which Plato spoke.

(*AI*, pp. 241–242)

It would be more accurate to say that the soul is the unification of the physical and mental polarities that constitute a personal society of actual occasions: 'the succession of my occasions of experience, extending from birth to the present moment . . . a complete person embodying all these occasions' (*MT*, p. 163). This is why Whitehead includes within the soul the animal passions and bodily impulses residing within the deepest regions of the unconscious mind – 'the animal body ministering to the soul' (*AI*, p. 335). These primitive features of the psyche are primary processes from which the human mind emerges, only to evolve into a more refined and sophisticated regnant society. Whereas the non-social nexus meanders through parts of the brain registering and emitting physical activity, the soul is the unified personality that reigns over the entire complex structured society we know as the human being. In effect, Whitehead's solution to mind/brain dependence is to (a) make the soul a freely determinant activity *within* its own corporeality that is (b) qualitatively differentiated and enhanced from its material counterpart, and which (c) furthermore enjoys greater degrees of novelty and self-expression.

Whitehead's concept of the non-social nexus becomes the bridge linking the divide between the mind and the body. Sherburne (1969) interprets this connection in the following manner:

> The regnant nexus answers to the notion of the conscious ego while the supporting non-social nexus answers to the dimly conscious regions of the 'depth' dimension of the psyche, flittingly illuminated by the movements of the ego . . . probing . . . in the largely obscure psychic depths.
>
> (p. 406)

The regnant nexus is the organized sentient agency supported by unconscious processes, what Freud also equates with the ego, for 'the ego is first and foremost a bodily ego' (*SE* 19:26). The ego is derived from bodily sensations, which both Whitehead and Freud would emphatically confirm. As Whitehead says, 'The body is mine, and the antecedent experience is mine. Still more, there is only one ego, to claim the body and to claim the stream of experience' (*MT*, p. 161). But we must not conclude that the non-social nexus is the only unconscious entity, because as Freud tells us, 'the ego is also unconscious' (*SE* 19:23). Yet the non-social nexus answers to a specific aspect of unconscious mentation, that of alienated mind which Freud equates with the It. In fact, the It, like the non-social nexus, is non-temporal, enduring, impersonal, and immortal. Freud (1933a) asserts:

> There is nothing in the it that corresponds to the idea of time; there is no recognition of the passage of time, and – a thing that is most remarkable and awaits consideration in philosophical thought – no alternation in its mental processes is produced by the passage of time. Wishful impulses which have never passed beyond the it, but impressions, too, which have been sunk into the it by repression, are virtually immortal.
>
> (*SE* 22:74)

Here Freud and Whitehead are on the same page; the primitive forces of desire appear alienated from the conscious ego where they enjoy adventures of change and novelty within their own underworld. The ego may illuminate these primitive features but they remain largely unconscious, which further serve to fuel and sustain conscious life. Even Whitehead gives primacy to these primordial drives that support the sustenance of the psyche, for 'Eros urges the soul' (*AI*, p. 317). But just as Whitehead equates a non-social nexus with 'the notion of "chaos"' (*PR*, p. 72), Freud too views the It as 'the dark, inaccessible part of our personality; . . . we call it chaos, a cauldron full of seething excitations' (*SE* 22:73).

For Freud, the soul is the unification of the structural and temporal processes that comprise and nourish human experience; namely, the trinity of the It, ego, and superego. Like Plato's conception of the psyche, the soul derives from the interplay between passion, rationality and moral judgment. The dual drives – libido, falling under the principle of Eros, and aggression, the expression of the death drive (*Todestrieb*) – comprise the basic dialectical force behind mental process originating in the It. This dialectic is generally captured in Whitehead's depiction of the positive and negative valuation of prehension, but also in the greater dimensions of Harmony and Discord that govern cosmic process. It is rather remarkable that Whitehead himself would portray the dialectical nature of harmonious and destructive forces that emanate from the unconscious It to characterize the soul.

> The key to the explanation [of Harmony and Discord] is the understanding of the prehension of individuality. This is the feeling of each objective factor as an individual '*It*' with its own significance. The emotional significance of an object as '*It*', divorced from its qualitative aspects at the moment presented, is one of the strongest forces in human nature. It is at the base of family affection, and of the love of particular possessions. . . . But the original *It* commands a poignancy of feeling.
>
> (*AI*, pp. 301–302)

The unconscious *It* becomes the objective actual occasion for the subjective prehending ego leaving an emotional residue of intense magnitude. As Whitehead continues to describe, the *It* resonates through the soul in 'successive immanence' and produces generalized emotional qualities of love, hate, admiration, worth, horror, and so forth that are 'intertwined within one's own existence' (*AI*, p. 302). This process underscores the significance of the immediate press of instinctual forces as well as the causal efficacy of the past that saturates the life of the enduring soul. The *It* is prehended as an individual entity despite the fact that it is an impersonal thrust – a pulsation of experience. And it is precisely this unconscious thrust that sustains 'a thread of personal order' which we identify as the human soul.

If Freud read Whitehead

We do not know if Freud ever read Whitehead, but he would have likely frowned upon the cosmological vision of *Process and Reality*. Both men had much in common as empiricists and scientists, yet Freud distrusted metaphysics and particularly loathed speculative philosophy. While Whitehead saw the value of religion, Freud looked down with contempt, dismissing it as an infantile wish ensconced in the futility of repetition compulsion. Yet if Freud had taken care to read Whitehead devoid of personal bias, he might have appreciated the fact that Whitehead's system encompasses an unconscious ontology.

At first glance, Freud's and Whitehead's systems may seem as far apart as one could imagine, but both fundamentally rely on the primacy of unconscious process that conditions all subsequent development of the organism. While I have no intention of stressing a complete convergence of their respective thoughts, which is neither possible nor desirable, there are many interesting points of connection between Freud and Whitehead, a full account of which is beyond the scope of this immediate project. Nevertheless, I wish to highlight a few theoretical compatibilities between their respective systems that may have some relevance for the contemporary reader. Freud frequently refers to the tripartite structures of the soul (*Seele*) as psychical 'agencies', 'provinces', 'regions', 'realms', 'instances', 'systems', and 'powers' (*SE* 5:537; 22:72; 23:146). This is not unlike Whitehead's use of the terms 'entities' and 'occasions'. Both Freud and Whitehead conceive of the internal activity, events and psychic experiences that belong to these agencies to be self-constitutive and self-determinate in nature. Hence, they are not static, inert, or antiseptic substances, but rather burgeoning telic processes of becoming.

For Freud, the tripartite agencies of the soul comprise the necessary features of personality as the ontological fabric of mind. It is important to note that these provinces are frequently interpreted as three (ontologically) distinct psychical agents, hence separate entities, when, as we saw in a previous chapter, they are in fact epigenetic achievements that derive from the same monistic ontology. While Freud himself was ambiguous through much of his early writings with regards to psychic ontology, in his mature theory he is, like Whitehead, very clear that the ego develops out of its natural unconscious immediacy. Recall that in *Inhibitions, Symptoms and Anxiety*, Freud (1926a) states:

> We were justified, I think, in dividing the ego from the it, for there are certain considerations which necessitate that step. On the other hand *the ego is identical with the it, and is merely a specially differentiated part of it*. If we think of this part by itself in contradistinction to the whole, or if a real split has occurred between the two, the weakness of the ego becomes apparent. But if the ego remains bound up with the it and indistinguishable from it, then it displays its strength. The same is true of the relation between the ego and the super-ego. In many situations the two are merged; and as a rule we can only distinguish one from the other when there is a tension or conflict between them. . . . [T]he ego is an *organization* and the it is not. *The ego is, indeed, the organized portion of the it.*
>
> (*SE* 20:97, italics added)

Freud clearly explains that the ego is a modally differentiated aspect of the It that becomes the mental organization of its prior shape – in Whitehead's terms, a regnant society. As too for Whitehead, conscious organizations are 'derivative modifications' (*PR*, p. 162) of unconscious subjectivity which is its 'necessary base' (*PR*, p. 267). Elsewhere Freud (1933a) says: 'the ego is that portion of the it that was modified . . . tak[ing] on the task of representing the external world to the it' (*SE* 22:75). This may be said to correspond to Whitehead's notion of perception where the sensuous material encountered in presentational immediacy and symbolic reference is mediated, stored and retrieved from the inner depths of the mind, those regions imbued with the lingering affects of causal efficacy. Furthermore, Freud (1923) says that 'the ego is not sharply separated from the it; its lower portion merges into it' (*SE* 19:24). This answers to the relation between a regnant society – the ego – and its non-social nexus, the former merging into the latter, which supports its existence. The two interpenetrate each other, undifferentiated in essence, yet modally differentiated in form.

Like the basic prehending activity of an actual entity, the ego's main feature is that it is a mediatory synthesizing agent: 'what distinguishes the ego from the it quite especially is a tendency to *synthesis* in its contents, to a *combination* and *unification* in its mental processes' (*SE* 22:76, italics added). This activity corresponds to the sophisticated operations of the soul whereby lower-grade occasions devolve into higher-grade societies unified within the complex totality of the living person (*AI*, pp. 241–242). But the acts of synthesis and unification also belong to the most elementary constituent experiences of a prehending occasion whereby the purpose is to achieve a 'synthesis in the final unity of one actual entity' (*PR*, p. 44).

Both Whitehead and Freud adhere to a developmental ontology: the mind acquires increased dynamic complexity and organization as modally differentiated shapes of earlier processes assume new forms. Freud's recognition that organized psychic processes develop from unorganized hence undifferentiated natural determinations insulates him from criticism that his theory of mind purports three ontologically distinct agents that participate in mutual causal relations. Here, Freud, like Whitehead, is a monist: all higher-level mental organizations derive from the same genus. Because the trinity of the three provinces is modally differentiated forms or shapes from its original undifferentiated being, each participates in the same essence and thus none are independent nominal agents. Rather they are interdependent forces that *appear* as separate entities, when they in fact together form the unification of the dynamic temporal processes that govern mental life.

Not only do Freud and Whitehead share a developmental monistic ontology, but Whitehead's characterization of prehending may be compared to Freud's profile of a drive. Recall that in 'Instincts and Their Vicissitudes', Freud (1915a) describes four principle features of a *Trieb*, namely, its (a) pressure, (b) aim, (c) object, and (d) source. The pressure or force (*Drang*) corresponds to its urge or wish which Freud identifies as its 'very essence' (*Wesen*). 'Every drive is a piece of activity'(*SE* 14:122). Compare to Whitehead: 'each actual occasion is . . . a process of activity' (*AI*, p. 254). Recall earlier that Whitehead also refers to such activity as an 'impulse' and 'urge'. The aim (*Ziel*) of a drive is unwaveringly to achieve 'satisfaction', the fulfilment of which results in a reduction in the amount of tension it experiences. Here, too, Whitehead delineates that the telos of an actual entity is to seek 'satisfaction'. The object (*Objekt*) is anything that is capable of being used through which its aim may be achieved, and it is the most fluid or variable aspect to a drive. The source (*Quelle*) of a drive is somatic processes or any 'part of the body and whose stimulus is represented in mental life by a drive'

(*SE* 14:123). Freud is very careful to note that the exact nature of a drive's source may not be fully known by material reductive explanations such as those that refer to chemical or mechanical forces; rather in mental life we can know them only by their aims. Furthermore, 'sometimes its source may be inferred from its aim', which is the 'need' itself.

Freud's depiction of a drive captures the very process by which an actual occasion operates. An actual entity is pure activity – an impulse to express itself as determinate being. Indeed, an actual entity is a constant force or pressure as essence that prehends objects in its surround, the aim of which is to fulfil itself, hence achieve self-completion, a primordial need for 'satisfaction'. For Whitehead, the locus of such unrest is 'appetition'. An actual entity is a continuous dynamic force that experiences: it values, desires, seeks and decides. Furthermore, it chooses and seizes specific objects for its pleasure, negating others that are not essential to its aim. Like Freud, who explains that drive discharge brings pleasure as tension reduction, Whitehead also informs us that 'termination is the "satisfaction" of the actual entity' (*PR*, p. 44). Its will to procure satisfaction is the manifestation of desire. Whitehead, like Freud, cannot deny the body – our natural foundation – which may be taken as its source but only known as its aim, its own stimulus as need. Indeed, for Whitehead, 'nature in general and the body in particular provide the stuff for the personal endurance of the soul' (*MT*, p. 162).

On a few occasions, Whitehead discusses the role of instinct in personality and in the process of human civilization, a subject matter Freud revolutionized. Whitehead's explication of instinct rests on his emphasis on the primacy of the past, 'the response of an organism to pure causal efficacy' (*S*, p. 78). Elsewhere Whitehead refers to instinct as 'the mode of experience directly arising out of the urge of inheritance, individual and environmental' (*AI*, p. 61). Here Freud would agree that the significance of the past, the unabated striving of desire springing forth from the drives, from the lair of repression, from the return of conflict – repetition – is a steady causal influence on the functioning of the organism. 'Pure instinct is the most primitive type of response which is yielded by organisms to the stimulus of their environment' (*S*, p. 78). But both Whitehead and Freud would contend that such instinct is not a fixed or rigid predetermined path of behaviour, but rather is a malleable, flexible and dynamic impetus that is purely telic, responding to its milieu with determinate choice no matter how primitive its aim. This is why Whitehead says that instinct is the 'function of directing action for the purposes of the living organism' (*S*, p. 79).

Freud tells us (1920) of two competing forces in human nature: the will toward life and the will toward death manifested as Eros or libido, the sexual force responsible for erotic life, and its antithetical companion conceived under the drive toward destruction. This dual class of innate drives comprises those which seek to preserve and unite and those which seek to kill and destroy. 'Neither of these drives are any less essential than the other; the phenomena of life arise from the concurrent or mutually opposing action of both' (*SE* 22:209). Furthermore, they scarcely operate in isolation, both borrowing from the resources of the other as an accompanied or alloyed counterpart, drawing a certain quota from the other side, which in turn modifies its aim or is even used to achieve its aim.[13]

This union between life and death is the ontological fabric of the human mind to which all other dialectical polarities arise, including the universality of love and hate. Self-preservation is clearly an erotic impulse but it must have aggression at its disposal in order to accomplish its task; just as in love, the aggressive drive is utilized in order to gain mastery and possession over an object in which the attachment to it brings about. While the self-preservative drives stand in stark opposition to the destructive ones, the two are dialectical complementarities that effect their confluence.

Yet this poses a problem. If instinct is not checked or transformed, it may lead to atrophy, decay and annihilation, thus leading to the ruin of society. This is the proper subject matter of *Civilization and Its Discontents*, where Freud (1930) declares that 'civilization is built upon a renunciation of instinct, how much it presupposes precisely the non-satisfaction (by suppression, repression or some other means?) of powerful instincts', or else it will destroy itself (*SE* 21:97). Whitehead seems to be in agreement with Freud when he affirms that:

> a social system is kept together by the blind force of instinctive actions, and of instinctive emotions clustered around habits and prejudices. It is therefore not true that any advance in the scale of culture inevitably tends to the preservation of society.
>
> (*S*, pp. 68–69)

In history and in nature, decay is the language of life. But discord and destruction also bring the positive significance of the negative: civilization could hardly advance without the negation of its previous modes of existence, 'processes which all but wreck the societies in which they occur' (*S*, p. 88).

For both Freud and Whitehead, civilization is a *process*, a process of becoming.[14] It requires destruction in order to build, consensus in order to behave, and temperance in order to survive. For Freud, social advance is scarcely possible without a redirection of our libidinal investments through the transformative powers of *sublimation*.

> Sublimation of instinct is an especially conspicuous feature of cultural development; it is what makes it possible for higher psychical activities, scientific, artistic, or ideological, to play such an important part in civilized life . . . sublimation is a vicissitude which has been forced upon the instincts entirely by civilization.
>
> (*SE* 21:97)

Whitehead would aptly agree: it is through our advanced capacities of symbolization that transfigure our more primitive mental states into rational, political, aesthetic and moral affiliations that constitute cultured life. For Whitehead, the social reverence of symbols with the 'freedom of revision' leads to a creative advance into novelty, the sublimation of instinct. Through symbolization, 'pure instinct is superseded' (*S*, pp. 80–81).

Freud's somewhat pessimistic attitude about the fate of civilization hinges on our capacity to sublimate our nature through the commandments of reason. 'Our best hope for the future is that intellect – the scientific spirit, reason – may in process of time establish a dictatorship in the mental life of man' (*SE* 22:171). Whitehead extends this process to include *wisdom*, the 'modifying agency' that unites instinct with the intellect (*AI*, p. 61). We may venture to say that this is the proper goal of psychoanalysis: 'Where it was, there I shall become' (*Wo Es war, soll Ich werden*) (*SE* 22:80). And with the pursuit of wisdom, the purpose of the examined life is to make what is unconscious conscious. For Whitehead, 'Wisdom is [a] persistent pursuit of the deeper understanding' (*AI*, p. 62), an understanding that brings us face to face with our unconscious ontology. Whitehead recognizes the controlling and unmanageable presence of our instinctive processes lurking within the dim recesses of our minds; and like Freud, it is precisely this underworld of unconscious experience that we wish to understand.

> But for all their vagueness, for all their lack of definition, these controlling presences, these sources of power, these things with an inner life, with their own richness of content, these beings with the destiny of the world hidden in their natures, are what we want to know about.
>
> (*S*, p. 57)

Whitehead's process philosophy is a treatise on the inner life of the organism, an attempt to describe the innate power of existence, to articulate the richness of content, and to disclose the inner reality that remains hidden within nature, a desire to know. Symbolization is the externalized expression of instinct, an articulation of the inner world – the manifestation of unconscious structure. This is why Whitehead says 'the symbolic expression of instinctive forces drags them out into the open: it differentiates them and delineates them' (*S*, p. 69). Whitehead's language of prehension is itself the symbolization of that part of unconscious experience which 'we want to know about'.

Both Whitehead and Freud despised simplicity: when encountered, it was dismissed. This is typified by Whitehead's observation of the fallacy of misplaced concreteness, when high-order abstractions are mistakenly presumed to quantitatively inhere in the simply located particle (*SMW*, pp. 49, 51, 58). Freud (1900) also warns us to 'avoid the temptation to determine psychical locality in any anatomical fashion' (*SE* 5:536), insisting that the mind should not be reduced to 'anatomical, chemical or physiological' properties alone (*SE* 15:21). Whitehead extends this dictum to include all reality: nature is not inert matter, but rather a purposeful, valuative and dynamic instantiation of subjectivity. Unconscious mental activity is the base experience of all events that comprise the nature of the real.

Coda

Throughout this chapter, I have attempted to show how Whitehead's metaphysical system rests on a philosophy of unconscious experience responsible for every conceivable element in the universe, including the higher-order aspects of refined organic life. I have further tried to emphasize that the most elementary cosmic processes governing the unconscious activity of actual occasions are ubiquitous features enacted in human consciousness. In other words, the human being participates in the same essence that sustains the universe, namely, the universality of unconscious process. As I have demonstrated, this has direct implications for understanding Whitehead's philosophical psychology and its extension to psychodynamic thought.

For Whitehead, as for Hegel, Freud and Jung, consciousness arises out of the unconscious and is perennially conditioned by instinct and the presence of the past. Furthermore, all theorists stress the epigenetic and architectonic dynamic movements inherent in psychic development that evolve from more primordial unconscious configurations: human subjectivity – self-conscious rational life – is the cultivated outgrowth of actualized complexity. Their theoretical systems build on the most primitive aspects of mental organization and progress to more robust manifestations, accounting for transmutations in form and qualitative experience. This is especially evinced in Whitehead's adumbrated attempt to answer to the mind/body problem: the soul is free to choose the objects of its satisfaction without the causal constraints from the past. In other words, the soul is *not* determined by its embodiment, rather it teleologically actualizes itself within its corporeality. Whether the soul (identity) transcends the body and endures a personal immortality is not a question Whitehead would particularly entertain, because, for him, when actual occasions attain satisfaction, hence perish, they are incorporated in the cosmos as objective data that become the foundation for other actual occasions to materialize and thrive, thus ensuring the 'immortal fact' of the soul. What is most germane to both Whitehead and Freud is that the soul is a psychodynamic process of actualized freedom. Just as the goal of psychoanalysis is to make the unconscious conscious, the aim of an actual occasion is to advance in creative novelty by actualizing its possibilities. With regards to the self-conscious human soul, we may only be free through knowledge.

Throughout *Process and Reality*, Whitehead reminds us time and again that actual occasions do not necessarily require consciousness in order to function, and in fact mainly operate on unconscious levels of organization and zest. This is why he chooses the language of feeling: feeling symbolizes the more primordial dialectical activity of internal experience and its inherent inner relations, which our human language can only attempt to specify. He lends sentience to nature as a way of showing that the phenomena of consciousness are merely modifications of more primitive, less abstract orders of experiential hypostatized events. Within the world of brute fact, there is an underworld of marbled creative vision impregnating the undulating streams of energy that constitute cosmic order.

But did he go far enough? Could he not have extended the language of pre-hension to include that primordial element of inner reality that feelings signify, namely *desire*? We want to be sensitive not to over-anthropomorphize existence or animize nature in a crude fashion,[15] but as Whitehead himself says, speculative philosophy is a coherent systematic attempt to account for 'every element of our experience' (*PR*, p. 3). We have already determined that an actual occasion is a desirous, appetitive entity by virtue of the fact that it hungers and seeks satisfac-tion in order to enjoy, to complete itself, to fill the inner lack in being. Thus desire becomes the impetus behind the process of becoming. As a self-related, purpose-ful act of valuation, desire constitutes the inner essence of an actual entity whose aim is to achieve 'novelty of appetition' (*PR*, p. 102). And for Whitehead, desire is ultimately the desire for God – the 'initial "object of desire"'; for 'He is the lure for feeling, the eternal urge of desire' (*PR*, p. 344). Here he shares affinities with Jung.

However we care to verbalize that which cannot directly verbalize itself, we are abandoned to the limitation of our own language that endeavours to capture those basic elements of all experience. We are justified, I think, to extend the language of prehension to signify the adventures of unconscious desire, the most primitive process of all inner experience. Therefore, even the most low-grade occasions desire. But we must remember Whitehead's dictum that the qualitative difference of originality and self-articulation make all the difference between the human soul and a stone. Although the universe desires, its qualitative expression is merely a matter of degree.

But shall we dare to go even further? One is left with curious speculation about whether or not a non-human entity, even the inorganic, could have some form of consciousness, some crude mode of self-awareness.[16] Whitehead himself is sug-gestive: 'a pure concept does not involve consciousness, *at least in our human experience*' (*PR*, p. 243, italics added). Could it be possible that on some muffled level an actual entity has some vague or primitive sense of felt familiarity with itself, a muted type of prereflective self-realization that it is a feeling being; per-haps what might not be inappropriately called *unconscious self-consciousness*? As Whitehead says, the pure unrest or appetition of an occasion possesses the '*realization* of what is not and may be' (*PR*, p. 32, italics added). Would it not be fantastic – ineffable – that the most elemental processes of the universe desire and are aware of their desire? Perhaps this is merely a fantasy. I wonder. But with the purported discovery of the Higgs boson particle, that unseen and unob-servable entity, which according to the Standard Model of fundamental particle physics is responsible for creating mass, and hence belonging to the invisible sea of elementary particles including virtual objects that materialize into existence then disappear into the backdrop of dark energy/matter, is it so phantasmal to entertain the notion that if the quantum world is an informational process system governing all aspects of reality, that it could possibly possess some crude form of agency as well? This could lead us into the absurd, or broach a wonder beyond wonder itself.

170

Notes

1 But with a few exceptions (cf. Blyth, 1941; Hughes, 1941; Kraus, 1998; Weber, 1940), the role of unconscious processes underlying the constitution and activity of actual entities has not been sufficiently emphasized.

2 Whitehead himself says that 'the difference between living and non-living occasions is not sharp' (*PR*, p. 109); but given that 'mental activity' (*PR*, p. 56) belongs to all actual entities, we may be justified in saying that the universe is alive. In fact, Whitehead says 'a single occasion is alive when the subjective aim . . . introduce[s] a novelty' (*PR*, p. 104). Furthermore, in *The Function of Reason* (1929),Whitehead says that 'the root principles of life are, in some lowly form, exemplified in all types of physical existence' (p. 17). Also see Whitehead's seventh and eighth lecture on the status of life in *Modes of Thought* (1938).

3 Whitehead established himself early in his career as an outstanding mathematician and logician, having co-authored with Bertrand Russell their groundbreaking three volume-set *Principia Mathematica*, which literally launched the field of modern symbolic logic. While Whitehead's middle period was occupied with the question and meaning of nature and science, it was not until he was appointed professor of philosophy at Harvard that he formally initiated his metaphysical system represented in his magnum opus, *Process and Reality*.

4 Elsewhere I trace the emergence of subjectivity within nature, thus revealing the cryptic idealism that infiltrates Whitehead's realism (see Mills, 2002b).

5 William Ernest Hocking (1941) draws a similar conclusion about Whitehead's metaphysics (see p. 389). But Whitehead himself supports this claim: 'There can be no general metaphysical principles which determine how in any occasion appearance differs from the reality out of which it originates' (*AI*, p. 245). It may be observed, however, that it was originally Hegel who dissolved the bifurcation of reality and appearance. From *The Encyclopaedia Logic*, Hegel (1817a) makes this clear: 'Essence must *appear*. . . . Essence therefore is not *behind* or *beyond* appearance, but since the essence is what exists, existence is appearance' (*EL* § 131, p. 199). Also see the *Phenomenology*, § 147, p. 89.

6 Whitehead states that 'blind prehensions, physical and mental, are the ultimate bricks of the physical universe' (*PR*, p. 308).

7 This sentence may be said to be self-revealing, because it nicely summarizes Whitehead's own novel and ingenious metaphysical system.

8 See Freud's (1911) discussion of the pleasure principle (pp. 218–226).

9 Whitehead's discussion of perception is scattered throughout *Process and Reality*, but is more thematically presented in *Symbolism: Its Meaning and Effect*. Donald Sherburne also provides a useful discussion of perception in *A Key to Whitehead's Process and Reality* (1966, pp. 98–99).

10 Whitehead gives a full account of this process in *Symbolism*, especially see Chapter I.

11 Freud's concluding remarks in his Preface to *New Introductory Lectures* are more appropriately translated 'the life of the soul' (*Seeleenleben liebt*), rather than 'the science of mental life' as rendered by Strachey's translation in the *Standard Edition*.

12 Robert C. Whittemore (1961) implies this when he says that Whitehead's philosophy of organism has become 'the new psycho-physiological orthodoxy' (p. 110). Whitehead himself also suggests this when he says: 'The philosophy of organism "the soul" as it appears in Hume, and "the mind" as it appears in Locke and Hume, are replaced by the phrases "the actual entity", and "the actual occasion", these phrases being synonymous' (*PR*, p. 141).

13 Freud (1923) discusses this in his letter to Einstein, 'Why War?' (*SE* 22:209).

14 See Freud's discussion in *Civilization and Its Discontents* (*SE* 21:96–98, 139).

15 This is perhaps the single most common criticism of Whitehead's metaphysics: He animizes nature and makes the cosmos a panpsychic, all-encompassing process system.

Here he runs into the same problematics as Jung. However, Whitehead is embraced – even revered – by many physicists who adopt anthropomorphic language to describe the most elemental aspects of the quantum world (see Eastman and Keeton, 2004), which cannot be avoided in any methodological science.

16 Philosopher Janusz Polanowski (2008) discusses how all actual occasions are imbued with forms of consciousness, self and imago in Whitehead's system, and that he could not elude a model of consciousness when using the language of prehensions. Whitehead, on the other hand, was sensitive to criticisms that he animated the cosmos under an anthropic principle, and was quick to reject such attributions to his metaphysics, which he dismissed as 'misunderstandings'. We may conjecture that he needed to distance himself from a theoretical model of consciousness because it would not correspond to the so-called objective science of his day.

BIBLIOGRAPHY

Adams, M.V. (1997). The Archetypal School. In P. Young-Eisendrath and T. Dawson (eds), *The Cambridge Companion to Jung* (pp. 101–118). Cambridge: Cambridge University Press.

Aristotle. *De Anima* (On the Soul). In J. Barnes (ed.), *The Complete Works of Aristotle.* 2 vols. (The revised Oxford trans.) (pp. 641–692). Princeton, NJ: Princeton University Press, 1984.

—— *Metaphysics.* In J. Barnes (ed.), *The Complete Works of Aristotle.* 2 vols. (The revised Oxford trans.) (pp. 1552–1728). Princeton, NJ: Princeton University Press, 1984.

—— *On Memory.* In J. Barnes (ed.), *The Complete Works of Aristotle.* 2 vols. (The revised Oxford trans.) (pp. 715–720). Princeton, NJ: Princeton University Press, 1984.

Aron, L. and F.S. Anderson (eds) (1998). *Relational Perspectives on the Body.* Hillsdale, NJ: The Analytic Press.

Askay, R. and J. Farquhar (2011). *Of Philosophers and Madmen.* Amsterdam/New York: Rodopi.

Barnes, Jonathan (1979). *The PreSocratic Philosophers.* London: Routledge.

Beach, Edward Allen (1994). *The Potencies of God(s): Schelling's Philosophy of Mythology.* Albany, NY: SUNY Press.

Beiser, F.C. (ed.) (1993). *The Cambridge Companion to Hegel.* New York: Cambridge University Press.

Berthhold-Bond, Daniel (1991). Hegel, Nietzsche, and Freud on Madness and the Unconscious. *The Journal of Speculative Philosophy, V*(3), 193–213.

—— (1992). Intentionality and Madness in Hegel's Psychology of Action. *International Philosophical Quarterly, XXXII*(4), 427–441.

—— (1994). Hegel on Madness and Tragedy. *History of Philosophy Quarterly, 11*(1), 71–99.

—— (1995). *Hegel's Theory of Madness.* Albany, NY: SUNY Press.

Bettelheim, Bruno (1982). *Freud and Man's Soul.* New York: Vintage Books.

Bion, W.R. (1988) [1959]. Attacks on Linking. In E.B. Spillius (ed.), *Melanie Klein Today: Developments in Theory and Practice. Volume 1: Mainly Theory* (pp. 187–201). London: Routledge.

Blyth, John W. (1967) [1941]. *Whitehead's Theory of Knowledge.* New York: Kraus Reprint Corp.

Boehme, Jacob (1963–1966) [1730]. *Die Urschriften.* 2 vols. Werner Buddecke (ed.). Stuttgart: Frommanns Verlag.

—— (1955–1961) [1730]. *Sämtliche Schriften.* 11 vols. Will-Erich Peuckert and August Faust (eds). Stuttgart: Frommanns Verlag.

Boothby, Richard (1991). *Death and Desire: Psychoanalytic Theory in Lacan's Return to Freud*. New York: Routledge.

Boss, M. (1978–1979). *Martin Heidegger's Zollikon Seminars*. Trans. B. Kenny. *Review of Existential Psychiatry and Psychology, 16*, 1–21.

Bowie, Malcolm (1991). *Lacan*. Cambridge, MA: Harvard University Press.

Bowlby, J. (1980). *Attachment and Loss*. London: Hogarth Press.

Burbidge, John (1981). *On Hegel's Logic: Fragments of a Commentary*. Atlantic Highlands, NJ: Humanities Press.

Burnet, John (1957). *Early Greek Philosophy*. New York: Meridian Books.

Cassimatis, E.G. (1984). The 'False Self.' *International Review of Psycho-Analysis, 11*(1), 69–77.

Chescheir, M.W. (1985). Some Implications of Winnicott's Concept for Clinical Practice. *Clinical Social Work Journal, 13*(3), 218–233.

Christensen, Darrel (1968). The Theory of Mental Derangement and the Role and Function of Subjectivity in Hegel. *The Personalist, 49*, 433–453.

Craig, E. (1988). An Encounter with Medard Boss. *The Humanistic Psychologist*, 16: 34–47.

Creed, J.L. (Trans.) (1965). Psychology. In Renford Bambrough (ed.), *The Philosophy of Aristotle* (pp. 229–279). New York: Mentor.

Descartes, R. (1984) [1641]. *Meditations on First Philosophy*. In *The Philosophical Writings of Descartes: Vol. II*. Trans. J. Cottingham, R. Stoothoff and D. Murdoch. Cambridge: Cambridge University Press.

Dreyfus, Hubert L. (1991). *Being-in-the-world*. Cambridge, MA: MIT Press.

Eastman, T.E. and H. Keeton (eds) (2004). *Physics and Whitehead*. Albany, NY: SUNY Press.

Eriugena, Joannes Scotus (1976). *Periphyseon: On the Division of Nature*. Trans. and ed. Myra Uhlfelder. Summaries by Jean Potter. Indianapolis, IN: Bobbs-Merrill.

Faulkner, R.O. and O. Goelet (Trans.) (1972/1994). *The Egyptian Book of the Dead: The Book of Going Forth by Day. The Complete Papyrus of Ani*. Ed. James Wasserman. San Francisco: Chronicle Books.

Feldstein, Richard (1996). The Mirror of Manufactured Cultural Relations. In R. Feldstein, B. Fink and M. Jaanus (eds), *Reading Seminars I and II: Lacan's Return to Freud* (pp. 130–169). Albany, NY: SUNY Press.

Fichte, J.G. (1993) [1794]. *The Science of Knowledge*. Trans. and ed. P. Heath and J. Lachs. Cambridge: Cambridge University Press.

Fink, Bruce (1995). *The Lacanian Subject: Between Language and Jouissance*. Princeton, NJ: Princeton University Press.

—— (1997). *A Clinical Introduction to Lacanian Psychoanalysis*. Cambridge, MA: Harvard University Press.

Forster, Michael N. (1993). Hegel's Dialectical Method. In F.C. Beiser (ed.), *The Cambridge Companion to Hegel* (pp. 130–170). New York: Cambridge University Press.

Frank, George (2003). *Triebe* and Their Vicissitudes: Freud's Theory of Motivation Reconsidered. *Psychoanalytic Psychology, 20*(4), 691–697.

Freeman, Kathleen (1956). *Ancilla to the Pre-Socratic Philosophers*. Oxford: Basil Blackwell.

Freud, Sigmund. (1968) [1940–52]. *Gesammelte Werke, Chronologisch Geordnet*, 18 vols. Eds. Anna Freud, Edward Bibring, Willi Hoffer, Ernst Kris and Otto Isakower, in colloboration with Marie Bonaparte. London/Frankfurt am Main: Imago Publishing Co. Ltd.

—— (1966–95) [1886–1940]. *The Standard Edition of the Complete Psychological Works of Sigmund Freud*, 24 vols. Trans. and Gen. Ed. James Strachey, in collaboration with Anna Freud, assisted by Alix Strachey and Alan Tyson. London: Hogarth Press.

174

—— [1888]. Hysteria. In Freud 1966–95, 1:39–59.

—— [1888]. Hystero-Epilepsy. In Freud 1966–95, 1:41–59.

—— [1893]. Some Points for a Comparative Study of Organic and Hysterical Motor Paralyses. In Freud 1966–95, 1:160–172.

—— [1895]. *Project for a Scientific Psychology*. In Freud 1966–95, vol. 1.

—— [1893–95]. *Studies on Hysteria* (with Josef Breuer). In Freud 1966–95, vol. 2.

—— [1894]. The Neuro-Psychoses of Defence. In Freud 1966–95, 3:43–61.

——– [1896a]. Further Remarks on the Neuro-Psychoses of Defense. In Freud 1966–95, 3:159–185.

—— (1985) [1896b]. *The Complete Letters of Sigmund Freud to Wilhelm Fliess, 1887–1904*. Trans. and ed. J.M. Masson. Cambridge, MA: Harvard University Press.

—— [1898]. The Psychical Mechanism of Forgetfulness. In Freud 1966–95, 3:287–297.

—— [1900]. *The Interpretation of Dreams*. In Freud 1966–95, vols 4–5.

—— [1901]. *The Psychopathology of Everyday Life*. In Freud 1966–95, vol. 6.

—— [1905a]. *Three Essays on the Theory of Sexuality*. In Freud 1966–95, vol. 7.

—— [1905b]. Psychical (or Mental) Treatment. In Freud 1966–95, 7:283–304.

—— [1909]. *Analysis of a Phobia in a Five-Year-Old Boy*. In Freud 1966–95, vol. 10.

—— [1911]. Formulations on the Two Principles of Mental Functioning. In Freud 1966–95, 12:213–226.

—— [1912]. The Dynamics of Transference. In Freud 1966–95, 12:97–108.

—— [1914a]. *On the History of the Psycho-Analytic Movement*. In Freud 1966–95, vol. 14.

—— [1914b]. On Narcissism: An Introduction. In Freud 1966–95, 14:67–104.

—— [1914c]. Remembering, Repeating, and Working Through. In Freud 1966–95, 12:145–156.

—— [1915a]. Instincts and Their Vicissitudes. In Freud 1966–95, 14:109–140.

—— [1915b]. Repression. In Freud 1966–95, 14:141–158.

—— [1915c]. The Unconscious. In Freud 1966–95, 14:159–216.

—— [1917 (1915)]. Mourning and Melancholia. In Freud 1966–95, 14:237–260.

—— [1916–17]. *Introductory Lectures on Psycho-Analysis*. In Freud 1966–95, vols 15–16.

—— [1918 [1914]. *From the History of an Infantile Neurosis*. In Freud 1966–95, vol. 17.

—— [1919]. The 'Uncanny'. In Freud 1966–95, 17:217–252.

—— [1920]. *Beyond the Pleasure Principle*. In Freud 1966–95, vol. 18.

—— [1921]. *Group Psychology and the Analysis of the Ego*. In Freud 1966–95, vol. 18.

—— [1923]. *The Ego and the Id*. In Freud 1966–95, vol. 19.

—— [1924a (1923)]. Neurosis and Psychosis. In Freud 1966–95, 19:149–156.

—— [1924b]. The Loss of Reality in Neurosis and Psychosis. In Freud 1966–95, 19:183–190.

—— [1924c]. A Short Account of Psychoanalysis. In Freud 1966–95, 19:191–212.

—— [1924d]. The Economic Problem of Masochism. In Freud 1966–95, 19:155–170.

—— [1925a]. A Note upon the 'Mystic Writing-Pad'. In Freud 1966–95, 19:226–232.

—— [1925b]. Negation. In Freud 1966–95, 19:234–239.

—— [1925c (1924)]. The Resistances to Psycho-Analysis. In Freud 1966–95, 19:212–222.

—— [1925d]. An Autobiographical Study. In Freud 1966–95, 20:1–74.

—— [1926a]. *Inhibitions, Symptoms and Anxiety*. In Freud 1966–95, vol. 20.

—— [1926b]. The Question of Lay Analysis. In Freud 1966–95, 20:179–258.

—— [1927a]. Fetishism. In Freud 1966–95, 21:149–158.

—— [1927b]. *Future of an Illusion*. In Freud 1966–95, vol. 21.

—— [1930]. *Civilization and Its Discontents*. In Freud 1966–95, vol. 21.

——[1933a (1932)]. *New Introductory Lectures on Psycho-Analysis*. In Freud 1966–95, vol. 22.

—— [1933b (1932)]. 'Why War?' Freud's Letter to Einstein. In Freud 1966–95, 22:197–218.

—— [1940a (1938)]. *An Outline of Psycho-Analysis*. In Freud 1966–95, 23:141–208.

—— [1940b (1938)]. Splitting of the Ego in the Process of Defence. In Freud 1966–95, 23: 271–278.

Frie, Roger (1997). *Subjectivity and Intersubjectivity in Modern Philosophy and Psychoanalysis: A Study of Sartre, Binswanger, Lacan, and Habermas*. Lanham, MD: Rowman and Littlefield.

—— (2003). *Understanding Experience: Psychotherapy and Postmodernism*. London: Routledge.

Greenberg, Jay (1991). *Oedipus and Beyond: A Clinical Theory*. Cambridge, MA: Harvard University Press.

Greenberg, J. and S. Mitchell (1983). *Object Relations in Psychoanalytic Theory*. Cambridge, MA: Harvard University Press.

Grene, M. (1948). *Introduction to Existentialism*. Chicago: University of Chicago Press.

Guignon, C. (1984). Heidegger's 'Authenticity' Revisited. *Review of Metaphysics, 38*, 321–339.

—— (1993). Authenticity, Moral Values, and Psychotherapy. In C. Guignon (ed.), *The Cambridge Companion to Heidegger* (pp. 215–239). Cambridge: Cambridge University Press.

Haddad, Gérard (1981). Une Pratique [A Practice]. *L'Ane, 3*, 20 September.

Harris, Errol E. (1993). *The Spirit of Hegel*. Atlantic Highlands, NJ: Humanities Press.

Hartmann, Heinz (1939/1958). *Ego Psychology and the Problems of Adaptation*. New York: International Universities Press.

Hegel, G.F.W. (1807). *Phenomenology of Spirit*. Trans. A.V. Miller. Oxford: Oxford University Press, 1977.

—— (1812/1831). *Science of Logic*. Trans. A.V. Miller. London: George Allen and Unwin, 1969.

—— (1817a/1827/1830). *Encyclopaedia of the Philosophical Sciences*. Vol. 1: *Encyclopaedia Logic*. Trans. T.F. Geraets, W.A. Suchting, and H.S. Harris. Indianapolis: Hackett Publishing Company, Inc., 1991.

—— (1817b/1827/1830). *Encyclopaedia of the Philosophical Sciences*. Vol. 2: *Philosophy of Nature*. Trans. A.V. Miller. Oxford: Clarendon Press, 1970.

—— (1817c/1827/1830). *Encyclopaedia of the Philosophical Sciences*. Vol. 3: *Philosophy of Mind*. Trans. William Wallace and A.V. Miller. Oxford: Clarendon Press, 1971.

—— (1821). *Philosophy of Right*. Trans. T.M. Knox. Oxford: Oxford University Press, 1967.

—— (1830). *Philosophy of Spirit*. In *Hegel's Philosophy of Subjective Spirit*. Vol. 3: *Phenomenology and Psychology*. Trans. and ed. M.J. Petry. Dordrecht, The Netherlands: D. Reidel Publishing Company, 1978.

—— (1830). *Enzyklopädie der philosophischen Wissenschaften im Grundrisse*. Heidelberg: C.F. Winter. Ed. F. Nicolin and O. Pöggeler. 3rd edn. Hamburg: Felix Meiner, 1969.

—— (1833/1985). *Introduction to the Lectures on the History of Philosophy*. Trans. T.M. Knox and A.V. Miller. Oxford: Clarendon Press.

—— (1900). *Reason in History*. Introduction to the *Lectures on the Philosophy of History*. Trans. J. Sibree. New York: Willey Book Co.

—— (1968ff). *Gesammelte Werke*. Ed. Rheinisch-Westfaelischen Akademie der Wissenschaften. Hamburg: Felix Meiner.

—— (1978) *Hegel's Philosophy of Subjective Spirit* [*Hegel's Philosophie des subjektiven Geistes*]. Vol. 1: *Introductions*; Vol. 2: *Anthropology*; Vol. 3: *Phenomenology and Psychology*. Ed. M.J. Petry. Dordrecht, The Netherlands: D. Reidel Publishing Company.

Heidegger, M. (1927). *Being and Time*. Trans. J. Macquarrie and E. Robinson. San Francisco: Harper Collins, 1962.

—— (1930). On the Essence of Truth. In D.F. Krell (ed.), *Basic Writings* (pp. 113–142). New York: Harper Collins, 1977.

Henderson, J.L. (1964). Ancient Myths and Modern Man. In C. G. Jung (ed.), *Man and His Symbols* (pp. 104–157). New York: Doubleday.

Hibben, J.G. (1984). *Hegel's Logic: An Essay in Interpretation*. New York: Garland.

Hillman, J. (1975). *Loose Ends*. Dallas, TX: Spring Publications.

Hocking, William Ernest (1941). Whitehead on Mind and Nature. In P.A. Schilp (ed.), *The Philosophy of Alfred North Whitehead*. New York: Tudor Publishing, 1951.

Homer (800 BCEa). *The Odyssey*. Trans. Samuel Butler. http://classics.mit.edu/Homer/odyssey.html

—— (800 BCEb) *The Iliad*. Trans. Samuel Butler. http://classics.mit.edu/Homer/iliad.html

Hughes, Percy (1941). Is Whitehead's Psychology Adequate? In P.A. Schilp (ed.), *The Philosophy of Alfred North Whitehead*. New York: Tudor Publishing Co., 1951.

Husserl, E. (1950). *Cartesian Meditations: An Introduction to Phenomenology*. Trans. D. Cairns. Dordrecht, The Netherlands: Kluwer.

Irenaeus of Lyons (1857/1965). *Adversus Haereses*. 2 vols. Ed. W.W. Harvey. Cambridge; reprint Ridgewood, NJ, 1965.

Jonas, Hans (1958). *The Gnostic Religion*. 2nd edn. Boston: Beacon Press.

Julien, P. (1994). *Jacques Lacan's Return to Freud: The Real, the Symbolic, and the Imaginary*. New York: New York University Press.

Jung. C.G. (1953–1977). *Collected Works of C.G. Jung*. Bollingen Series, 20 vols. Ed. H. Read, M. Fordham and G. Adler. Trans. R.F.C. Hull. London: Routledge and Kegan Paul; Princeton: Princeton University Press (Hereafter referred to as CW by vol. no.).

—— (1911–12). *Symbols of Transformation*. CW, 5.

—— (1912). The Significance of Constitution and Heredity in Psychology. CW, 8, pp. 107–113.

—— (1916). *The Relations Between the Ego and the Unconscious*. CW, 7, pp. 121–241.

—— (1917). *On the Psychology of the Unconscious*. CW, 7, pp. 1–119.

—— (1919). Instinct and the Unconscious. CW, 8, pp. 129–138.

—— (1926). Spirit and Life. CW, 8, pp. 319–337.

—— (1927). The Structure of the Psyche. CW, 8, pp. 139–158.

—— (1928). The Structure of the Unconscious. CW, 7, pp. 269–304.

—— (1933). The Real and the Surreal. CW, 8, pp. 382–384.

—— (1936). The Concept of the Collective Unconscious. CW, 9, pp. 42–53.

—— (1936/1942). Psychological Factors Determining Human Behaviour. CW, 8, pp. 114–125.

—— (1936/1954). Psychological Aspects of the Mother Archetype. CW, 9, pp. 75–110.

—— (1937). Psychological Factors Determining Human Behaviour. CW, 7, pp. 114–125.

—— (1939). Conscious, Unconscious, and Individuation. CW, 9, pp. 275–289.

—— (1941). The Psychology of the Child Archetype. CW, 9, pp. 151–181.

—— (1947). On the Nature of the Psyche. CW, 8, pp. 159–234.

—— (1948). The Phenomenology of the Spirit in Fairytales. CW, 9, pp. 207–254.

—— (1952). Synchronicity: An Acausal Connecting Principle. CW, 8, pp. 417–531.

—— (1954). Archetypes of the Collective Unconscious. CW, 9, pp. 3–41.

—— (1954). Concerning the Archetypes, with Special References to the Anima Concept. CW, 9, pp. 54–72.

—— (1955). *Mysterium Coniunctionis*. CW, 14.

—— (1957). Psychological Commentary. *The Tibetan Book of the Dead*. 3rd edn (pp. xxxv–lii). Ed. W.Y. Evans-Wentz. Trans. R.F.C. Hull. Oxford: Oxford University Press.

—— (1961). *Memories, Dreams, Reflections*. New York: Vintage.

—— (1964). Approaching the Unconscious. In C.G. Jung (ed.), *Man and His Symbols* (pp. 18–103). New York: Doubleday.

Kant, I. (1781/1787). *Critique of Pure Reason*. Trans. N.K. Smith. New York: St. Martin's Press, 1965.

—— (1790). *Critique of Judgement*. Trans. W.S. Pluhar. Indianapolis, IN: Hackett Publishing Company, 1987.

Keller, Catherine (1989). Psychocosmetics and the Underworld Connection. In David Ray Griffin (ed.), *Archetypal Process: Self and Divine in Whitehead, Jung, and Hillman* (pp. 133–156). Evanston, IL: Northwestern University Press.

Kelly, S. (1993). *Individuation and the Absolute: Hegel, Jung, and the Path toward Wholeness*. New York: Paulist Press.

Khan, M.M. (1971). Infantile Neurosis as a False Self Organization. *Psychoanalytic Quarterly, 40*(2), 245–263.

Kirk, G.S., J.E. Raven, and M.Schofield (1957). *The Presocratic Philosophers*. 2nd edn. Cambridge: Cambridge University Press.

Kirsh, T.B. (2000). *The Jungians: A Comparative and Historical Perspective*. London: Routledge.

Klein, Melanie. (1932). *The Psycho-Analysis of Children*. London: Hogarth Press.

—— (1946). Notes on Some Schizoid Mechanisms. *International Journal of Psycho-Analysis, 27*, 99–110. Reprinted in Klein, *Envy and Gratitude and Other Works, 1946–1963* (pp. 1–24). London: Virago Press, 1988.

—— (1957). *Envy and Gratitude*. In Klein, *Envy and Gratitude and other Works, 1946–1963*. London: Hogarth Press, 1975.

Kockelmans, J.J. (1978). Daseinsanalysis and Freud's Unconscious. *Review of Existential Psychology and Psychiatry, 16*, 21–42.

Kohut, H. (1971). *The Analysis of the Self*. New York: International Universities Press.

—— (1977). *The Restoration of the Self*. New York: International Universities Press.

—— (1978). *The Search for the Self: Selected Writings of Heinz Kohut, 1950–1978*. 2 vols. Ed. P. Ornstein. New York: International Universities Press.

—— (1984). *How Does Analysis Cure?* Chicago: University of Chicago Press.

Kraus, Elizabeth M. (1998). *The Metaphysics of Experience*. New York: Fordham University Press.

Lacan, Jacques (1936–1949). The Mirror Stage as Formative of the Function of the I. In *Écrits: A Selection*. Trans. Alan Sheridan. New York: Norton, 1977.

—— (1948). Aggressivity in Psychoanalysis. In *Écrits: A Selection*. Trans. Alan Sheridan. New York: Norton, 1977.

—— (1953). The Function and Field of Speech and Language in Psychoanalysis. In *Écrits: A Selection*. Trans. Alan Sheridan. New York: Norton, 1977.

—— (1953–1954). The See-Saw of Desire. In *The Seminar of Jacques Lacan, Book I: Freud's Papers on Technique, 1953–1954*. Trans. John Forrester. Ed. Jacques-Alain Miller. Cambridge: Cambridge University Press, 1988.

—— (1954–1955a). The Dream of Irma's Injection (Conclusion). In *The Seminar of Jacques Lacan, Book II: The Ego in Freud's Theory and the Technique of Psychoanalysis, 1954–1955*. Trans. Sylvana Tomaselli. Ed. Jacques-Alain Miller. Cambridge: Cambridge University Press, 1988.

—— (1954–1955b). *A, m, a, S*. In *The Seminar of Jacques Lacan, Book II: The Ego in Freud's Theory and the Technique of Psychoanalysis, 1954–1955*. Trans. Sylvana Tomaselli. Ed. Jacques-Alain Miller. Cambridge: Cambridge University Press, 1988.

—— (1955–1956a). Introduction to the Question of Psychoses. In *The Seminar of Jacques Lacan, Book III: The Psychoses, 1955–1956*. Trans. Russell Grigg. Ed. Jacques-Alain Miller. New York: Norton, 1993.

—— (1955–1956b). The Other and Psychosis. In *The Seminar of Jacques Lacan, Book III: The Psychoses, 1955–1956*. Trans. Russell Grigg. Ed. Jacques-Alain Miller. New York: Norton, 1993.

—— (1955–1956c). On Nonsense and the Structure of God. In *The Seminar of Jacques Lacan, Book III: The Psychoses, 1955–1956*. Trans. Russell Grigg. Ed. Jacques-Alain Miller. New York: Norton, 1993.

—— (1955–1956d). The Hysteric's Question. In *The Seminar of Jacques Lacan, Book III: The Psychoses, 1955–1956*. Trans. Russell Grigg. Ed. Jacques-Alain Miller. New York: Norton, 1993.

—— (1957). The Agency of the Letter in the Unconscious or Reason Since Freud. In *Écrits: A Selection*. Trans. Alan Sheridan. New York: Norton, 1977.

—— (1957–1958a). On a Question Preliminary to Any Possible Treatment of Psychosis. In *Écrits: A Selection*. Trans. Alan Sheridan. New York: Norton, 1977.

—— (1957–1958b). *Le Séminaire 1957–1958, Livre V: Les Formations de l'Inconscient*. Paris: Seuil, 1998.

—— (1958). The Direction of the Treatment and the Principles of its Power. In *Écrits: A Selection*. Trans. Alan Sheridan. New York: Norton, 1977.

—— (1959–1960a). *Das Ding*. In *The Seminar of Jacques Lacan, Book VII: The Ethics of Psychoanalysis, 1959–1960*. Trans. Dennis Porter. Ed. Jacques-Alain Miller. New York: Norton, 1992.

—— (1959–1960b). The Death of God. In *The Seminar of Jacques Lacan, Book VII: The Ethics of Psychoanalysis, 1959–1960*. Trans. Dennis Porter. Ed. Jacques-Alain Miller. New York: Norton, 1992.

—— (1960). The Subversion of the Subject and the Dialectic of Desire in the Freudian Unconscious. In *Écrits: A Selection*. Trans. Alan Sheridan. New York: Norton, 1977.

—— (1964a). Excommunication. In *The Four Fundamental Concepts of Psycho-Analysis*. Trans. Alan Sheridan. Ed. Jacques-Alain Miller. New York: Norton, 1981.

—— (1964b). Presence of the Analyst. In *The Four Fundamental Concepts of Psycho-Analysis*. Trans. Alan Sheridan. Ed. Jacques-Alain Miller. New York: Norton, 1981.

—— (1964c). Sexuality in the Defiles of the Signifier. In *The Four Fundamental Concepts of Psycho-Analysis*. Trans. Alan Sheridan. Ed. Jacques-Alain Miller. New York: Norton, 1981.

—— (1964d). The Subject and the Other: Alienation. In *The Four Fundamental Concepts of Psycho-Analysis*. Trans. Alan Sheridan. Ed. Jacques-Alain Miller. New York: Norton, 1981.

—— (1964e). Of the Subject Who Is Supposed to Know, of the First Dyad, and of the Good. In *The Four Fundamental Concepts of Psycho-Analysis*. Trans. Alan Sheridan. Ed. Jacques-Alain Miller. New York: Norton, 1981.

—— (1966). *Écrits*. Paris: Seuil.

—— (1972–1973). On the Baroque. In *The Seminar of Jacques Lacan, Book XX: Encore, 1972–1973*. Trans. Bruce Fink. Ed. Jacques-Alain Miller. New York: Norton, 1998.

—— (1977). *Écrits: A Selection*. Trans. Alan Sheridan. New York: Norton.

Laing, R.D. (1959). *The Divided Self*. Harmondsworth: Penguin Books.

Lee, J.S. (1990). *Jacques Lacan*. Boston: Twayne Publishers.

Leibniz, G.W. (1981). *New Essays on Human Understanding*. Trans. and Ed. Peter Remnant and Jonathan Bennett. Cambridge: Cambridge University Press.

Lerner, P.M. (1985). The False Self Concept and Its Measurement. *The Ontario Psychologist, 17*(6), 3–6.

Levin, J.D. (1992). *Theories of the Self*. Washington, DC: Hemisphere Publishing Corporation.

McTaggart, J. (1964). *A Commentary on Hegel's Logic*. New York: Russell and Russell.

Mahler, M.S., F. Pine, and A. Bergman (1975). *The Psychological Birth of the Human Infant*. New York: Basic Books.

Marcelle, M. (1992). *Jacques Lacan: The French Context*. Trans. Anne Tomiche. New Brunswick, NJ: Rutgers University Press.

Masterson, J.F. (1981). *The Narcissistic and Borderline Disorders*. New York: Brunner/ Mazel.

May, R. (1983). *The Discovery of Being*. New York: Norton.

Meissner, W.W. (2000). The Self as Structural. *Psychoanalysis and Contemporary Thought, 23*(3), 373–416.

Merkur, D. (1996). The Numinous as a Category of Values. In Merkur (ed.), *The Sacred and Its Scholars* (pp. 104–123). Leiden, The Netherlands: E.J. Brill.

—— (1999). *Mystical Moments and Unitive Thinking*. Albany, NY: SUNY Press.

Miller, A. (1981). *The Drama of the Gifted Child*. New York: Basic Books.

Mills, Jon (1999). Unconscious Subjectivity. *Contemporary Psychoanalysis, 35*(2), 342–347.

—— (2002). *The Unconscious Abyss: Hegel's Anticipation of Psychoanalysis*. Albany, NY: SUNY Press.

—— (2002). Whitehead Idealized: A Naturalized Process Metaphysics. *Process Studies, 31*, 32–48.

—— (2003). A Phenomenology of Becoming: Reflections on Authenticity. In R. Frie (ed.), *Understanding Experience: Psychotherapy and Postmodernism* (pp. 116–136). London: Routledge.

—— (2005). A Critique of Relational Psychoanalysis. *Psychoanalytic Psychology, 22*(2), 155–188.

—— (2010). *Origins: On the Genesis of Psychic Reality*. Montreal: McGill-Queens University Press.

—— (2012). *Conundrums: A Critique of Contemporary Psychoanalysis*. New York: Routledge.

Mitchell, S.A. (1988). *Relational Concepts in Psychoanalysis: An Integration*. Cambridge, MA: Harvard University Press.

—— (1992). True Selves, False Selves, and the Ambiguity of Authenticity. In N.J. Skolnick and S.C. Warshaw (eds), *Relational Perspectives in Psychoanalysis* (pp. 1–20). Hillsdale, NJ: Analytic Press.

Muller, J.P. and W.J. Richardson (1982). *Lacan and Language*. New York: International Universities Press.

Naso, R.C. (2010). *Hypocrisy Unmasked: Dissociation, Shame, and the Ethics of Inauthenticity*. Lanham, MD: Aronson.

Otto, R. (1932). The Sensus Numinis as the Historical Basis of Religion. *Hibbert Journal, 30*, 283–297; 415–430.

Pinkard, Terry (1988). *Hegel's Dialectic*. Philadelphia, PA: Temple University Press.

Pizer, Stuart (2006). 'Neither Fish nor Flesh': Commentary on Jon Mills (2005). *Psychoanalytic Psychology, 23*(1), 193–196.

Plato. *Cratylus*. In *The Collected Dialogues of Plato*. Ed. E. Hamilton and H. Cairns. Princeton, NJ: Princeton University Press, 1961, pp. 421–474.

—— *Epinomis*. In *The Collected Dialogues of Plato*. Ed. E. Hamilton and H. Cairns. Princeton, NJ: Princeton University Press, 1961, pp. 1517–1533.

—— *Gorgias*. In *The Collected Dialogues of Plato*. Ed. E. Hamilton and H. Cairns. Princeton, NJ: Princeton University Press, 1961, pp. 229–307.

—— *Laws*. In *The Collected Dialogues of Plato*. Ed. E. Hamilton and H. Cairns. Princeton, NJ: Princeton University Press, pp. 1225–1516.

—— *Meno*. In *The Collected Dialogues of Plato*. Ed. E. Hamilton and H. Cairns. Princeton, NJ: Princeton University Press, 1961, pp. 353–384.

—— *Phaedo*. In *The Collected Dialogues of Plato*. Ed. E. Hamilton and H. Cairns. Princeton, NJ: Princeton University Press, 1961, pp. 40–98.

—— *Phaedrus*. In *The Collected Dialogues of Plato*. Ed. E. Hamilton and H. Cairns. Princeton, NJ: Princeton University Press, pp. 475–525.

—— *Philebus*. In *The Collected Dialogues of Plato*. Ed. E. Hamilton and H. Cairns. Princeton, NJ: Princeton University Press, pp. 1086–1150.

—— *Republic*. In *The Collected Dialogues of Plato*. Ed. E. Hamilton and H. Cairns. Princeton, NJ: Princeton University Press, 1961, pp. 575–844.

—— *Symposium*. In *The Collected Dialogues of Plato*. Ed. E. Hamilton and H. Cairns. Princeton, NJ: Princeton University Press, 1961, pp. 526–574.

Polanowski, Janusz A. (2008). *The 'Imago' of the Self Within Whitehead's Metaphysics*. Nashville, TN: Vanderbilt University Press.

Ragland, Ellie (1995). *Essays on the Pleasures of Death: From Freud to Lacan*. New York: Routledge.

Reisner, Steven (1992). Eros Reclaimed: Recovering Freud's Relational Theory. In N.J. Skolnick and S.C. Warshaw (eds), *Relational Perspectives in Psychoanalysis* (pp. 281–312). Hillsdale, NJ: Analytic Press.

Richardson, William J. (1993). Heidegger Among the Doctors. In John Sallis (ed.), *Reading Heidegger* (pp. 49–66). Bloomington, IN: Indiana University Press.

Ricoeur, P. (1965). *Fallible Man*. Trans. C. Kelbley. Chicago: Henry Regnery Company.

—— (1966). *Freedom and Nature: The Voluntary and Involuntary*. Trans. E. Kohak. Evanston, IL: Northwestern University Press.

Ross, David (1923). *Aristotle*. London: Routledge.

Roustang, F. (1990). *The Lacanian Delusion*. New York: Oxford University Press.

Rudolph, Kurt (1977). *Gnosis: The Nature and History of Gnosticism*. San Francisco: Harper and Row.

Sallis, John (ed.) (1993). *Reading Heidegger*. Bloomington: Indiana University Press.

—— (1987). *Spacings of Reason and Imagination: In Texts of Kant, Fichte, Hegel*. Chicago: University of Chicago Press.

—— (1986/1995). *Delimitations: Phenomenology and the End of Metaphysics*. 2nd edn. Bloomington: Indiana University Press.

Salman, S. (1997). The Creative Psyche: Jung's Major Contributions. In P. Young-Eisendrath and T. Dawson (eds), *The Cambridge Companion to Jung* (pp. 52–70). Cambridge: Cambridge University Press.

Samuels, A. (1997). Introduction: Jung and the Post-Jungians. In P. Young-Eisendrath and T. Dawson (eds), *The Cambridge Companion to Jung* (pp. 1–13). Cambridge: Cambridge University Press.

Sartre, J.P. (1943). *Being and Nothingness*. Trans. H.E. Barnes. New York: Washington Square Press.

—— (1963). *Search for a Method*. New York: Vintage/Random House.

Sarup, Madan (1992). *Jacques Lacan*. Toronto: University of Toronto Press.

Schacht, L. (1988). Winnicott's Position in Regard to the Self with Special Reference to Childhood. *International Review of Psycho-Analysis*, *15*(4), 515–529.

Schelling, F.W.J. (1800). *System des transzendentalen Idealismus*. Trans. Peter Heath as *System of Transcendental Idealism*. Charlottesville: University Press of Virginia, 1978.

—— *Die Weltalter* (second draft, 1813). Trans. Judith Norman. In Slavoj Žižek and F.W.J. Von Schelling (eds), *The Abyss of Freedom/Ages of the World*. Ann Arbor. University of Michigan Press, 1997.

—— (1856–1861). *Sämmliche Werke*. 14 vols. Ed. K.F.A. Schelling. Stuttgart and Augsburg: Cotta.

—— (1967). *Ages of the World*, A Fragment, from Writings Left in Manuscript. Trans. Frederick de Wolfe Bolman. New York: AMS Press.

Schneiderman, Stuart (1983). *Jacques Lacan: The Death of an Intellectual Hero*. Cambridge, MA: Harvard University Press.

Schopenhauer, A. (1818). *The World as Will and Representation: Vols 1–2*. Trans. E.F.J. Payne. New York: Dover, 1969.

Segal, Hanna. (1957). Notes on Symbol Formation. *International Journal of Psycho-Analysis, 38*, 391–397.

Sherburne, D. (1966). *A Key to Whitehead's Process and Reality*. Chicago: Chicago University Press.

—— (1969). Whitehead's Psychological Physiology. *Southern Journal of Philosophy, 7*(4), 399–410.

Solomon, Robert C. (1972). Hegel's Concept of *Geist*. In A. MacIntyre (ed.), *Hegel: A Collection of Critical Essays* (pp. 125–149). Garden City, NY: Anchor Doubleday.

—— (1983). *In the Spirit of Hegel*. New York: Oxford University Press.

Stern, Daniel (1985). *The Interpersonal World of the Infant*. New York: Basic Books.

Sulloway, Frank (1979). *Freud: Biologist of the Mind*. Cambridge, MA: Harvard University Press.

Taylor, J.H. (ed.) (2010). *Journey Through the Afterlife: Ancient Egyptian Book of the Dead*. Cambridge, MA: Harvard University Press.

Vanheule, S. (2011). *The Subject of Psychosis: A Lacanian Perspective*. London: Palgrave Macmillan.

von der Luft, Eric (1994). Comment. In Robert L. Perkins (ed.), *History and System: Hegel's Philosophy of History*. Albany, NY: SUNY Press.

von Hartmann, Eduard (1868). *Philosophy of the Unconscious*. Trans. W.C. Coupland. New York: Harcourt, Brace and Company, 1931.

Walsh, David (1994). The Historical Dialectic of Spirit: Jacob Boehme's Influence on Hegel. In Robert L. Perkins (ed.), *History and System: Hegel's Philosophy of History*. Albany, NY: SUNY Press.

Wartenberg, T.E. (1993). Hegel's Idealism: The Logic of Conceptuality. In F.C. Beider (ed.), *The Cambridge Companion to Hegel* (pp. 102–129). New York: Cambridge University Press.

Weber, Pearl Louise (1940). Significance of Whitehead's Philosophy for Psychology. *Personalist, 21*, 173–189.

Webster, R. (1995). *Why Freud Was Wrong*. New York: Basic Books.

Weeks, Andrew (1991). *Boehme: An Intellectual Biography of the Seventeenth-Century Philosopher and Mystic*. Albany, NY: SUNY Press.

Wehr, G. (1985). *Jung: A Biography*. Boston: Shambhala.

Wheelwright, Philip (ed.) (1966). *The PreSocratics*. Indianapolis, IN: ITT Bobbs-Merrill.

Whitehead, A.N. (1920). *The Concept of Nature*. Cambridge: Cambridge University Press.

—— (1926). *Religion in the Making*. New York: Macmillan.

—— (1925). *Science and the Modern World*. New York: Free Press.

—— (1927). *Symbolism: Its Meaning and Effect*. New York: Capricorn Books.

—— (1929). *Process and Reality*. Corrected Edition. Ed. D.R. Griffin and D.W. Sherburne. New York: Free Press, 1978.

—— (1929). *The Function of Reason*. Princeton, NJ: Princeton University Press.

—— (1933). *Adventures of Ideas*. Harmondsworth: Penguin Books, 1948.

—— (1938). *Modes of Thought*. New York: Free Press.

—— (1948). *Essays in Science and Philosophy*. New York: Philosophical Library.

—— (1961). Einstein's Theory: An Alternative Suggestion. In Whitehead (ed.), *The Interpretation of Science*. Indianapolis, IN: Bobbs-Merrill.

Whittemore, Robert C. (1961). The Metaphysics of Whitehead's Feelings. In Whittemore (ed.), *Tulane Studies in Philosophy, Vol. X: Studies in Whitehead's Philosophy*. The Hague, The Netherlands: Martinus Nijhoff.

Whyte, Lancelot Law (1960). *The Unconscious Before Freud*. London: Basic Books.

Winnicott, D.W. (1960). Ego Distortions in Terms of True and False Self. In Winnicott (ed.), *The Maturational Processes and the Facilitating Environment*. New York: International Universities Press, 1965.

Žižek, Slavoj (1992). *Enjoy Your Symptoms! Jacques Lacan In Hollywood and Out*. New York: Routledge.

INDEX

Note: 'N' after a page number indicates a note.